Waves IN DEEP STILL WATER

Listening for Mind

CANDACE CROSBY, PhD

The opinions expressed in this manuscript are solely the opinions of the author and do not represent the opinions or thoughts of the publisher. The author has represented and warranted full ownership and/or legal right to publish all the materials in this book.

Waves in Deep Still Water
Listening for Mind
All Rights Reserved.
Copyright © 2014 Candace Crosby, PhD
v3.0

Cover Photo © 2014 Dudley Dana. All rights reserved - used with permission.

This book may not be reproduced, transmitted, or stored in whole or in part by any means, including graphic, electronic, or mechanical without the express written consent of the publisher except in the case of brief quotations embodied in critical articles and reviews.

The Center for Creative and Healing Arts

ISBN: 978-0-578-14323-1

Library of Congress Control Number: 2014940311

PRINTED IN THE UNITED STATES OF AMERICA

Dedication

*Sue, Terry and Christi Forest who inspire me
with their dedication and love for one another*

*Bonnie Bainbridge Cohen who taught
me to love questions more than answers*

Dudley Dana who keeps me awake to the power of love

Confluence

I

The elevator doors opened and I walked onto the second floor intensive care unit of St. Patrick Hospital feeling trepidation and certainty. I took the empty left hand corridor down to the last room. I paused, blowing out a long exhale, before I stepped past the half-closed door and into the relationship that reshaped my life.

Sue Forest was the first person I saw when I entered the room. I knew her as my psychology professor from the University. I sat in her classroom for the last two semesters. Here she was a mother engaged in a fight for her 18 year-old daughter's life. Although I knew she must be fatigued after nearly two weeks at Christi's bedside, it wasn't visible. Instead her petite frame nearly pulsed. She was like a concentrated meteor temporarily suspended in its flight across the sky. She introduced me to her husband Terry. His quick hello was somber, yet I heard a playful reverberation underneath, giving me a glimpse into his usual character. Our eyes met briefly and simultaneously turned to the hospital bed.

Sue took a half step back as her arm swept toward the bed in the next introduction. "This is Christi." She turned to fully face her daughter. "Christi, this is Candace, my student who I told you was going to come." The words and gestures suggested a normalcy at odds with the crisis underway. Although it was only a few feet to step around the bed to greet her, time and distance were distorted; it felt like twenty feet yet no motion to stand bedside.

I placed my hand on Christi's right forearm to greet her in touch as well as voice. I knew she couldn't see me or speak. She was in the altered realm of coma that we know so little about. Her head was swathed in a turban of white bandages. Her left arm inert, connected by tubes to the pole hung with colorless bags dispensing essential fluids, nutrition and medications. The ventilator made a downward whoosh sound as it kept her breathing steady through an insertion in her trachea. I left my arm extended and waited for her body to answer me back.

II

The determination and will of Christi and her parents, Sue and Terry Forest, propelled me to write this story about navigating years of incremental recovery from a severe traumatic brain injury. Christi defied all predictions that she wouldn't live, nor be free from a ventilator and feeding tube, never emerge from a "vegetative" state. No one envisioned the possibility of the present when Christi, wearing the supportive apparatus of an un-weighting harness, haltingly and determinedly takes a dozen steps forward. She has changed beliefs about severe TBI recovery possibilities.

The Forests are heroes. I tell this epic journey as a witness because the heroes are too busy living the experience. The demanding discipline of the recovery process, still a full time job for Christi, Sue and Terry thirteen years later, keeps them from being able to stop and tell you of its wonders and its aggravations. This book is a map of their travels through mostly uncharted territory. It's not necessarily a course others will follow, but rather inspiration and camaraderie for other pioneers on healing frontiers.

This book is also my story. I joined Christi's treatment team two weeks after the accident and never left. Before I began working with her I would have told you I understood a lot about body-mind awareness. I had trained in somatic psychology for four years and intensively studied in the School for Body Mind Centering™ for another six. I thought I fully respected consciousness arising from the body's tissues. But Christi challenged me to understand mind even more deeply and profoundly.

Sue, Terry, Christi and I know that some of the events we're sharing will be difficult for some to believe. It's tempting to keep our intimate and precious stories private rather than risk being ridiculed or misunderstood. We don't want to be told that what we felt, saw, and experienced wasn't real. We understand there are reasons for skepticism. After all, it was often hard enough for us to believe our firsthand experiences, especially when after the fact we, or others around us, logically categorized them as "not possible." But we also know that if we keep these stories to ourselves, we deny others the opportunity to see in us a mirror of their own experiences. Or, for those without similar observations, the opportunity to learn about them.

At times it's difficult to find words for experiences inherently distant from the realm of vocabulary. Our Western culture has some descriptive words for kinesthetic occurrences, but much *felt* knowing is a sensed, resonant, truthful moment, one where we know with certainty, but don't necessarily have language to adequately express the experience. Many insights and actions revealed here take place on bridges arcing between sensation, perception and language, as well as between one person and another. Awareness emerges in pictures expressing a timeless, simultaneous whole. Words, on the other hand, begin to turn what we experience into linear time and make it subject to logical critique. Yet, we need words because they help us make things tangible. They are the way we compare one person's set of perceptions and beliefs to another's. In this book I strove to find words to describe what Christi and others are revealing. I trust that many of you will say to yourselves, "I know exactly what you mean. I just hadn't put it into words." And if you don't know what I mean, I hope you'll suspend judgment long enough to investigate these phenomena that offer us an opportunity to expand our scientific understandings of consciousness and healing.

In the pages ahead you'll discover I love science as much as I trust my intuitive knowing. I'll share with you current understandings from traditional allopathic, as well as complementary and alternative medicine and psychology, that are useful in understanding what we experienced with Christi or point out a direction for further exploration. I hope that Christi's journey, as well as my own, stimulates deepening understandings of humanity and how our minds work. And when I say mind I mean the whole self, not just the tissue we call brain and commonly mistake for who we are.

In the process of aiding the Forests, inquiring deeply into my own experiences, interviewing other families, and writing everything down, I have been changed. I know there is no division between helper and client, helper and family, writer and inspiration. Consciousness is not an individual possession; it's an interactive, shared, spontaneous and relational phenomena. It is a verb, not a noun. What Christi and Sue taught me became grist for understanding myself more deeply. And each thing I learned along the way I brought back to them. The journey I took is not fundamentally different than anyone else's. The "injuries" I found in myself, and that you, the reader, may discover, were not as catastrophic as Christi's, yet they left their mark on the shape and function of my body mind. My hope is that by sharing our inquiry and discoveries, pathways of healing also open for you the reader.

Falling In

May, 1999

> *"Do you know how long it takes to adjust your whole life to a major, unthinkable trauma? Less than one second. After that it's just details... We are born with an incredible will to live, and it sticks with us even as we adjust for chaos and disaster- those things we thought would never happen to us."*
>
> Annalysa Aldren
Spinal cord injury patient

Despite the gently flowing introduction between Christi and I, you could say I barged into the room. In fact, I was uncharacteristically aggressive about inserting myself into this hospital scene. I called Sue a few days after the accident, while they were still 150 miles from home in the Coeur d'Alene hospital, and offered to come do a form of therapeutic touch with Christi. Sue asked me to wait until they were transported back to Missoula. When I called again she was still reticent, "maybe when Christi is more recovered from the next surgery, when there's less equipment in the room."

But I persisted. "I don't need any special amount of room. It's better for me to come before the surgery so I can help her get ready for it." I insisted because I'd spent the previous three months researching rationale and developing protocols for a study on body-system-focused touch pre- and post-surgery. I knew the data supported its helpfulness. The project fell through because, although the doctor was willing to incorporate a complementary and alternative medicine approach into his surgeries, there was administrative reluctance. So here I was, prepared to do the work, yet unencumbered by the research project's time demands. Sue already knew me as a credible person even if she didn't know anything about the work I was offering to do. And being the kind of person who trusts her instincts, she leapt too and said yes for today's visit.

Like in all relationships, in this first meeting with Christi, and with Sue and Terry, we were setting the form of our working relationship, establishing our rules of engagement. Sometimes rules are overtly acknowledged, but most times they go unspoken. I was not here as a friend, although I would become a confidante of sorts and they became part of the network of people who care about my life. I was here to be a helper, a support for Christi's journey. On the day I met Christi I had been working as a psychotherapist for ten years and I habitually fell into the rules of that form. As when I meet someone in my office, we had a few minutes of chitchat, and then settled into an hour where I primarily listened. With verbal clients I ask questions here and there to look down different alleyways or reflect on how the discrete parts of the landscape we've been exploring seem to fit together. The form and roles of psychotherapist-client applied between Christi and me, but our primary language was, and for many years stayed, the sounds of body currents. The "language" Christi and I communicated through is one you know without knowing you know it. It's built on the universal principles we use when we're with an infant and tune in to her expressions. Developmental psychologists call this intuitive parenting.

Another way to think of the language Christi and I used is by imagining you're listening to a symphony. The feeling of the whole probably carries you along, all the instruments working together to produce a cohesive sound. If you want to, you can interrupt your perception of the whole and pay attention to a single instrument, maybe even hearing individual notes. You know that the composer is taking you on a journey in this symphony, perhaps telling you an emotional story. The musicians you're listening to are trained to both hear and play. In the performance you're hearing they are letting the notes arise from the creative silence within them so that the timelessness of the composer's voice is heard, and they are in union with all the other performers.

What I hear distinctly is the symphony of the body. A few years ago it was popular to name different types of intelligence, like social or kinesthetic.[i] I recognized immediately that one of my strongest forms of learning and perceiving is kinesthetic. I augmented my psychotherapist training with somatic studies at the School for Body Mind Centering™. Through years of training in touching and perceiving the body's movements and various physical components, like muscles, bones, and lymph[ii], I developed my capacity to "hear" what Christi was expressing in a way similar to what musicians learn in their years of training. Some of you reading this page may have learned this same skill and you will have your own experiences hearing and naming what I will describe in the story of my work with Christi. Others of you will resonate with the truth of the story even though you haven't consciously noticed the individual notes that I point out.

My introduction to Christi, fourteen days post accident, was the day before surgery to place a shunt in the left ventricle of her brain. Several minutes of silence passed after I first placed my hand on her arm. Then, beneath my hand I felt a sensation of rising, like a shadow emerging from a grey background. It was far away, a sound reaching me from across a chasm. Imagine standing on a trail above the valley a small creek has cut. You have called, "Are you there?" across to the trail you see on the opposite side. And now you hear the sound of reply although the words aren't decipherable. Perhaps the person you hear calling back is several hundred feet away, even standing behind a group of trees so that you can't see her form, yet you hear her sound. You don't doubt how real she is just because you don't hear her words distinctly or because you don't see her. Just the sound connects you, marking your places relative to one another.

In the first hour of meeting Christi my focus was to become acquainted. I familiarized her with my presence through the touch of my hand, and I opened the door to hear her through her body sounds and movements. In the only way she could, she was also touching me and teaching me about her vibration and tone. My intention was to convey acceptance and friendliness to Christi as I reached out to her in greeting. Probably though, I was a bit stilted and overly serious. Sometimes when my concentration is intently focused on listening to something unknown, as it was in this meeting, others read my manner as cool, reserved or analytical. Yet, before I left this first meeting, Christi broke the ice between us and turned upside down my non-conscious expectations.

I was serious with Christi because I was awed by the magnitude of her injuries even though I only had the most basic outline of information. I knew it was a miracle that she was even lying here in this hospital bed because the doctors in the first hospital doubted her survivability. She was in a deep coma. And I knew that she required surgery to regulate the fluid flow in her brain because without it there would be dangerous swelling that would create even more damage.

Much later I learned the details that brought us to this day. The accident happened on Christi's drive home from her freshman year at Willamette College. Like her peers, she spent the last week with many late nights, studying for finals and in a whirlwind of goodbyes and celebrations. She had a cold that she was looking forward to sleeping off once she got home to her own bed and her Mom. Her drive home was the first time she made the ten-hour trip alone. She checked in regularly by cell phone with her parents each time she stopped for snacks or gas. The last call to her Dad, just a half hour before the accident, was to tell him she was glad to be on the home stretch.

Sue missed the last call because she was still at work, listening to final reports from my class, "Early Intervention Services." On her way home she was disconcerted by a sudden episode of rapid breathing. She thought aloud, "Oh my, you must breathe deep." Taking a breath was all she could concentrate on. Then in an instant the sensation went away and her breathing was easier. Once she was home she started to tell Terry about the strange breathing episode and it happened again.

Then the doorbell rang. It was about the time Christi was due so Sue thought it was her, playfully arriving at the front door. Instead it was a police officer, confirming Sue's identity before he offered instruction to call the Coeur d'Alene hospital. His ashen face warned her that he knew more than he'd say. Once they had the hospital on the phone they were told to come quickly. Sickened, Sue knew the meaning of the breaths. The surgeon told them that Christi seemed to be fighting to hold on to see them again but he was uncertain she could make it long enough for them to get there. He agreed to keep them updated during their three-hour drive. Unfortunately, cell phone technology doesn't include coverage when the highway winds through mountains. Sue and Terry could only call in twice during their drive and heard the same assessment both times. Three more times Sue fell into episodes of rapid breathing, fervently intoning a mantra of "keep breathing" until it quieted. Later Sue learned that the EMTs and doctors revived Christi five times and she wondered if her double-time breaths matched those exact seconds. With each mile Sue and Terry felt like they were fighting time that was going too slowly and too quickly all at once. Even if they were to lose Christi they wanted the chance to say goodbye, to tell her how much she was loved, that she would always be in their hearts.

When Sue and Terry finally arrived at the hospital, expecting to be rushed into Christi's room, they were met instead by the medical team representative and the chaplain. They said Christi, as her parents once knew her, was already gone and now she was a technology-supported, barely-alive-shell. "It's best for you to authorize us to discontinue life support and give the gift of organ donation." Sue and Terry protested, "We want to see our daughter first." But the chaplain persisted. Acknowledging their distress he sought the decision first, not wanting them to have false hopes. Sue and Terry refused to be denied. "She's waiting for us and we need to see her."

Most of us can't imagine, and don't ever want to know, what a parent actually sees when walking into an intensive care room. There is too much and too little information. The monitors beep, tubes protrude from every part imaginable, and the bed frame marks a territory of exclusion. Sue and Terry searched for the daughter they knew but her outer shape was motionless. Shock made them want to fall down on their knees and cry out in wrenching grief. And it made them want to rush closer, push aside the images of devastation, to reach with heart and solar plexus and find her alive beneath a mound of loud silence.

Sue and Terry felt immense gratitude that they made it to her bedside in time. They each held one of her hands and using the cadence of prayer whispered, "We're here." They searched for connection. Sue found it first in the oddest detail- Christi's fake nails. In one of their last conversations Christi had told her that she planned to celebrate the end of finals with a relaxing manicure. "Well, Christi, at least you have all your fake nails. Not a single one is broken."

After many minutes they asked Christi for her choice. "You know how serious this is. If you want to go it's ok. We're glad you waited for us, but if you want to go we're ok. And if you want to stay, we're here, we'll help you."

If you've ever stood at someone's bedside and thought or asked aloud this question, or offered this kind of promise, you know you're not necessarily looking for the blink of an eye, or even a sound. Those are bonuses. You're waiting for a feeling, an answer in the pit of your stomach. Or for a spark of light or motion that you see plain as day even while your rational mind says this isn't real. Something shows itself in the spaces between things.

Both Sue and Terry were convinced they experienced "I want to stay" from Christi. Many years later Sue wrote about that day.

I wanted her involved in the decision. I remember holding her hand and saying, "Christi you have been very severely hurt. You have a brain injury that is severe and it will be a long hard road back. I want you to know how much I love you and what a wonderful daughter you are. I want very much for you to remain with us and know that I will do everything I can to help you. But know that while I will be sad and will miss you - I will understand if you decide that you need to go. I want you to make the decision and let me know what you want because this is about what you feel you can do, not what I want." I asked her to give me a sign to let me know if she wanted to continue. It was right at that moment that her breathing became steadier and she squeezed my hand hard twice. I asked her again and said I just wanted to confirm her answer and she squeezed my hand again two more times.

They informed the doctors they wanted treatment to go forward. If they needed to reconsider the decision they would do so when they brought her home to Missoula, when they weren't in shock and away from the support system of friends and family.

The doctors protested. They said Christi's injury, a diffuse brain shearing just above the brain stem, prevented any kind of thought or communication. They intimated that Christi's expression of choice was only a parent's wishful thinking. A day passed and the lead doctor tried again, pushing for organ donation. He said, "Christi will be in a vegetative state for the rest of her life, she wouldn't want that. She, and you, have the chance to help someone else in need." Sue wanted to scream at him, "How dare you presume to know what my daughter wants. You don't even see she's there."

The chaplain and social worker pulled them aside and counseled them to change their decision. They too believed Sue and Terry's decision was only unwillingness to let Christi go. But Sue and Terry stood firm. Sue recalled reading an article about a test that determines whether there is blood supply to the brain. She asked the doctor if he'd run it. He said there wasn't a need to; he knew Christi's brain was ruined. Sue wouldn't be deterred. "I want that test." Reluctantly he relented and ordered the test. The doctor was sheepish, yet oddly still defiant, when he returned with the answer, "There is blood flow." Sue nodded, knowing they had a chance of some kind of recovery.

Sue and Terry weren't prepared for what happened next. They were shunned. It was three more days before Christi was stable enough to be transported back to their home hospital. Although they had a hotel room they virtually lived at Christi's bedside. But for most of the staff they may as well have been invisible. The doctors walked past with no sign of acknowledgment. The majority of nurses were efficient yet without warmth. Sue felt they were being punished for their decision, for believing that Christi was still there. There were a few stolen moments when first a nurse, then one of the doctors, told them in quick asides that they thought they made the right decision. The unspoken message was that this could only be whispered in private because each must seem to remain in agreement with the more powerful team members. Still, Sue and Terry took comfort in these messages of support and from the actions of two special nurses. On Sunday morning Sue arrived and noticed instantly that the stale room smell was gone, replaced by wonderful scents. Seeing Sue's pleasantly surprised expression, Rita and Patty, weekend shift nurses, explained, "nobody had taken care of her, yet." They had bathed Christi and applied lotion everywhere. Sue remembers their simple act helped humanize Christi even more and "gave me fortitude." Sue and Terry were boosted as well by a meeting with four of Christi's friends from school. They were closest to Christi in her first year of independence and concurred that Christi would want the chance to recover.

Behind the scenes a few arguments about transport took place between the Couer d'Alene hospital and St. Patrick's Hospital in Missoula. If Christi's prognosis was as dismal as the doctors said, no one would pay for the transfer. Fortunately for the Forests the program director at St. Pat's overruled her staff and authorized transport. "We need to let this family come home even if we never get paid."

All of that determination and intuition was why I was standing beside Christi, listening with my hand, despite all odds against it. Radiating up into my open palm was the feeling of deep still water. Water as it appears in the middle of a lake. Midnight black, reflecting light back upward, at first seeming impenetrable. Although there was no outer movement from Christi or me, I began to sense softening on the surface of her body and a barely perceptible substance in the deep water below. Perhaps if this lake was fed by an underground spring this is how we'd know its presence. For a long stretch of time I stood silent, sensing Christi.

And then I was surprised. It was like being in a group and a person who's been completely quiet startles you with a quick-witted comment. That's what happened next. A nurse came in and checked the bags hanging from the IV pole. She told Christi and her parents that she would be taking vitals next, saying this as if it were a treat. "I'll be back in a few minutes, ok." A squirt of fluid darted through the space just beneath my hand. I "heard" the quip, "Yeah, like I have I choice." I nearly stepped back in surprise. Regrouping, I internally chuckled at the exclamation. It's a dark humor joke, making light of the worst circumstance.[iii] I've shared this kind of moment with psychotherapy clients before but had never known it in the non-verbal realm. I'd never before had the experience of hearing a sentence clear as speech come to me through my hand. My disbelieving intellect backpedaled. "What's a person in a coma doing throwing a one-liner as if to solidify our relationship!"

Still, I remained with my hand on her arm and re-collected myself into listening. Open-ended stillness returned for several more minutes. I re-engaged my professional session format. It was time to leave for the day. I nonverbally thought my intention to go so Christi would feel it through my hand. I said aloud, "I'll be back tomorrow." I pulled my hand away the first few inches in slow motion, and then resumed normal speed as I turned to Sue and Terry. I mumbled something about returning at the same time tomorrow and Sue thanked me for coming.

The elevator taking me to the underground parking garage was crowded but I was so full of the experience I just had I didn't register anyone else. My thoughts were completely silent, yet my head seemed dense, filled by white shadow, like fog rising on a spring morning. Surprisingly I also felt clear. I didn't ask myself what I was doing there or if I should go back. Everything seemed simple, elemental, and essential. When I reached my car I sat motionless for a full minute before starting to drive out. Once I drove out of the garage and into the sunshine I shook my head in curious wonderment and said aloud, "That was wild."

When I returned the next day Christi was lying peacefully. Sue and Terry were there. They seemed quiet, as if husbanding their resources for the surgery scheduled for later that afternoon. I placed my hand on Christi's forearm again in greeting. I spent a few minutes in undirected listening, sensing again still water. Today though I also had an agenda to help ready her body to cope with the surgery. After a few minutes I turned my perception to fluids swaying gently through my body. Silently I invited her body to match this motion. I knew this type of motion would help her body to metabolize the anesthesia and stress hormones of surgery.[iv] The still water feeling in Christi was replaced by the sensation of slight rocking and the image came of a raft on gentle water. To double check myself, I asked Sue if Christi liked being on the water, if floating would be a comforting image to her. Hearing an enthusiastic yes from Sue I kept this image in my mind's eye and also coached Christi out loud. I told her to imagine herself floating on a raft. "You can use this image to relax before the surgery and when you wake up afterwards. It'll help your body take care of the medicines they have to use." Through my hand I sensed her ease in the rocking, as if it really was a pleasure. I withdrew my hand and left Christi in this calmed state, and promised to return tomorrow. And when tomorrow came I was delighted to learn that the anesthesiologist was impressed that he didn't have to use as much medicine as he expected and that she returned to baseline quickly after the surgery.

I came to see Christi early every afternoon for a week. In one session I put my hands on her feet to listen to the rhythms of left and right. This is like listening to your stereo speakers to see if right and left are both turned on and working in unison. At first I sensed a tidal rhythm only in her left leg but eventually the right leg matched the left's force. As I left that day I passed another University professor coming to see Christi. Lucky coincidence because the next day she told me that during her visit everyone noticed that Christi seemed to be spontaneously moving her feet. The foot movements fifteen minutes after our session match what researchers have found about coma patients' time-delayed movements after stimulation.

At the end of the first week working together I had my hands on her feet again. I felt like Christi was straining to reach out but couldn't cross a deep chasm. The desire was powerful but her body couldn't act in a cohesive manner to bring this intention to gesture. I was aware that often when I touched Christi I perceived her on two levels. One was the rhythm of body fluids. The second was a quality state. It was distinct from the bodily tissues, as if the quality was simultaneously pushing her body and riding above it. The dominant quality I felt was Will. I sensed it as simultaneously colorless and formless, and as a dark, metallic grey ocean sponge. This is what I felt straining to reach across the chasm.

Although I had my hands on Christi I knew it wasn't me she wanted. I was a tool to use. Sue and Terry were here in the session as always. Partway into today's work they spontaneously, wordlessly, got up from their chairs. Each stepped closer, stood beside her bed, one on either side, as if they felt something too. I said aloud, "She is reaching so hard." They each took a hand, gazed intently at her face, and said, "I know you're there. I know you're trying hard. We'll wait for you." The four of us performed this dance of perception and communication as if we had worked together for years.

I left the session very aware of my responsibility in the ensemble. I was a bridge for movement and voice. My job was to support the connection that's there between parent and child. Any skill I had in hearing Christi needed to be in service of their relationships with one another. What was clarified for me today was that Sue and Terry intuit something too so it appears natural to them when I voice something on behalf of Christi.

For several days the primary work I did with Christi was listening to currents begin moving beneath my touch. I placed my hand on her and after a few moments the volume and density of motion would increase, coming towards my hand and the surface of her body. Typically after a few moments of this increase she seemed to reach some marker, an outer limit of capacity for activity, and I sensed swift retraction, a reflex like one would employ in pulling back from touching something hot. Christi seemed to require so much stillness that her own internal activity was frightening.

Christi's parents weren't the only ones in the room when I saw Christi for our daily sessions. Sometimes other close friends from high school were present. Oftentimes it was her maternal grandmother, Bea. I wanted everyone to feel empowered in their connection with Christi so when it seemed comfortable I invited them to hold her hand or touch her arm. I encouraged them to use quiet, simplified touch to avoid over-stimulating Christi.

The most awkward combination of visitors in Christi's room was her end-of-semester college romance and her long-time high school boyfriend. For a few days there was an uncomfortable silent negotiation of space between them. Tom, Christi's first true love, was practically a son to Sue and Terry. The ease between them was palpable. Equally evident was the misalignment between her recent college boyfriend and her parents. Sue was put off by his need for her to comfort him, as if the primary trauma was his. He seemed not to see how great their distress was as well. Fairly quickly he departed and there was the equivalent of a group exhale of relief.

Through the people that visited I learned fact and personality tidbits about Christi. One group of visitors had ties through high school track. They appealed to Christi by reminding her of her physical training strengths and used sports slogans of winning, toughing it out, etc. Another group was from her pre-college job at a local café. They mostly ribbed each other and her in an attempt to bring the frivolity of teen interaction into the somber situation. Typically they ended a visit with a "we want to see you back at work" meant to remind her that she belonged somewhere, and to ease their own discomfort at seeing someone like them whose life had suddenly been radically altered. Everyone, no matter how they were initially tied to Christi, signed a pair of sneakers. It was a ritual like signing someone's cast. Flowers and cards covered all of the available counter space. A CD player, sometimes on quietly in the background and other times on teenager full volume, played her favorite pop music and a recording of flute pieces she once played in recital. I didn't actively work with Christi while activities were high in the room because the subtleties of her expression were dimmed below a threshold I could sense. It was as if she were lying beneath a down comforter made up of the voices and energies of those around her and her emphasis of attention was on what she received without resources left to express outwardly.

What I saw through her friends was that Christi had exuded magnetism her whole life. It wasn't because she was the most vocal, the top star, or even the most socially gregarious. It was because she had the qualities "deep and true." She was the one in elementary school who befriended the child with severe handicaps and brought his wheelchair into the circle of popular kids. She was the one you saw in the corner of the high school cafeteria listening intently to a friend pouring out distress over a dilemma.

Sometimes in my journey with Christi, in the hospital as well as when I worked with her in the years ahead, I caught myself wishing I knew her before the accident. I wished I had my own memories of hearing her laugh or seeing her model her latest Nordstrom's shoe purchase. In her house a large high school graduation picture hung in the hallway. Sometimes I stared at it, wanting to know firsthand her dark gemstone eyes and slightly impish smile. The natural order of things in our culture is to know someone first from her outside activities, then from her inner self. But I didn't have that luxury with Christi. When I was envious of others' memories of her I reminded myself that I was privileged to learn about her the other way around, from unadulterated spirit to actions.

Christi held steady medically for the first full week she was back in Missoula. Her eyes intermittently opened halfway, unpredictably though, and she didn't immediately respond to requests to direct her gaze. Then the doctor warned that her temperature was fluctuating too much. During my next session everyone seemed on edge, waiting. When I put my hands on Christi's arm her parents sat numbly silent, diagonally behind us, away from the window and near the door. A medical specialist came in to talk to them, not even glancing at Christi and me. Without preamble he told Sue and Terry he thought Christi, "may have meningitis." At these words a higher intensity motion of fluid flitted by under my hand. The doctor had no awareness that Christi was hearing his words much less having a reaction. Sue and Terry asked a few questions. The doctor left with a worried "wait and see" and the intimation that meningitis would mean even more destruction for Christi's already assaulted brain tissue. Sue seemed to perceive Christi's worry and came to her side. Through her voice and touch she offered the special kind of mother comfort that calms. I wondered though if when Sue went home at night her serenity cracked and she felt the agony of her own fears.

Terry was the only one in the room with Christi when I arrived the next day. The room seemed extra quiet. The air tasted metallic, like tin. I looked down at Christi while inviting into my mind the question "Where to touch today?" As if the spot was marked by a momentary slash of light, I was instantly drawn to stand on her left side, placing my hands just over her spleen. Facing the bright west window counterbalanced the room's dark somber mood. There seemed to be an extra long silence inside Christi. Sometimes silence can be like absence. However this had a quality of expectancy, as if something were about to reveal itself. During the whole session I never perceived the fluid movements I had been sensing previously, but I did feel heat. The surface of her body felt cold but beneath that there was a raging heat. It was like touching a frigid glacier and the churning molten lava of the earth's core at the same time. After about five minutes I began sweating profusely. Droplets of sweat fell off my face, onto my arms. My hands felt locked into place so I couldn't wipe off the sweat that continued to bead up. For a moment I was self conscious about how I looked to Terry, but he didn't say anything. In fact I felt him in the room almost like the softness of a pillow supporting Christi and, by extension, me. Inexplicably the temperature lock broke and my hands were released. I left the room without saying much to Terry beyond mumbling, "That's enough for today." Because I had no rational idea what just happened I couldn't access language to make a comment.

The following day when I saw Sue my remark to her was tentative, exploratory. "Yesterday Christi felt so hot inside I was even sweating." Sue nodded in conspiratorial acknowledgment, "I had the same thing." Sue had been lying down next to Christi, holding her hand, aware of the medical team's concerns that they might need to put ice blankets on her. Suddenly Sue became excessively hot. The heat reached a crescendo and then disappeared. It was like the proverbial elephant in the room: neither Sue nor I said aloud that the experience of participating in the discharge of Christi's heat was far beyond either of our preconceptions. We focused instead on the good news that Christi's temperature dysregulation abated in the night and the threat of meningitis had passed.

Hospital life abides by its own laws of time and the healing progress. There is continuous hustle and bustle but often little discernible forward movement. Several days go by fused together as if they are one seamless rotation. I took advantage of the relative lull in activity to offer Sue and Terry more of an explanation of what I'd been doing with Christi. Because I was conscious of how overwhelming all the new medical trauma language was, I did this in a letter. They could read it at their own pace at home or whenever they felt like adding more information.

Terry and Sue,

Since I casually use words like "resonate" and Christi and I "worked on" without ever defining them I wanted to give you a description, as close as words can convey, of something that is essentially non-verbal language. I very much appreciate that you have trusted me in my work with her without knowing any of the specifics, but want you to know that I am glad to try to explain whenever you have questions.

When I say resonate I mean that whatever system (such as body fluids or nerves or bones) comes up in perception when I am touching Christi, I consciously feel in myself. My training with Bonnie Bainbridge Cohen (Body Mind Centering™) is very, very specific in this. We spend hours and hours learning and practicing in each system. Sometimes I am matching what Christi is doing. Sometimes I am complementing what she is doing by being in another system which supports where she is or introducing the idea of more options within the system. For instance, in this last week we worked one day on the transitional fluid in cells in her hands. As I held her hand and the perception of extra-cellular fluid was present I felt rigidity in the flow which had the effects of her muscles being more bound and nerve impulses being jerky. So I introduced the idea of more fluid movement in and out of cells (transitional fluid) by accentuating the focus of that activity in my own hand which she then perceived in her hand and began to match. After we did this for awhile I became more aware of brain function and how the area between the top of the brain stem and the basal ganglia supports movement and particularly responds to the qualities of transitional fluid. In the last few weeks the brainstem area has felt very active in Christi.

When I say working on, I mean this type of activity. BMC is a system of bodywork that is based on listening and introducing options, but not making the other person's system "do" anything. When I said yesterday that Christi and I were "working on" a diagonal line in her brain, it meant that I was listening with my hands to what activity was happening between two points. The act of being an active listener seems to allow an area to heal itself, as if it finished one story and creates a new level of homeostasis. This is very similar to really listening to someone tell you a problem. The act of speaking and being heard seems to bring a resolution or a relief. Sometimes there is not resolution, something stays knotted up, but the telling is still the beginning of an opening. In some of my work with Christi, for instance with her jaw activity, there is a lot of listening on my part to all the nuances of that behavior and just beginning to loosen the knot by supporting each aspect. In my perception what we have worked on so far is: how the jaw's movement is an automatic expression of activity level; when it is expressing an anxiety; how she uses it to set her position; and when it's a follow through of a speech impulse.

I have been keeping a log of what Christi and I work on each day. I recently started adding the comments you each give me about of how it is going. It has felt very important to me to record what Christi is teaching me and the progression of her recovery. I believe that this can someday be very important in helping others. Any time you would like to see the notes I will be glad to share them. Candace

Blessedly, waiting was offset by visitors. Christi had her nails done by her usual manicurist, just as she would have done in her first week home from college. Debra Shorrock, her flute teacher from sixth grade through high school, came to play songs she knew Christi loved. In an "it's a small world" twist, independently I knew Debra as a fellow practitioner in Body Mind Centering. In another month we secured Christi's assent for Debra to change roles, leaving behind their teacher-pupil relationship and Debra became part of the hands-on bodywork treatment team.

Most days when I worked with Christi it felt like we were friends sitting together on a park bench, not really talking, just hanging out. So I was surprised when I arrived much later than usual one afternoon and put my hand on her arm in greeting. Instantly it felt like a vacuum was created as she pulled away, leaving behind empty space. It was like I was standing outside someone's door. I waited. The word "mad" came into my mind. I asked silently if she was mad. The subtle reverberation told me, "close, but not exactly." I listened deeper with my hand to the still silent space. Although still empty it seemed whoever - whatever - pulled away was at least looking, as a toddler would do, peeking out from a hiding spot. I silently blurted, "Did you think I wasn't coming?" I sensed softening. I spoke out loud. "I'm sorry I'm late today, I had something else I had to do first. I should have told you."

I knew it was the right conversation from an increased pliability under my hand. But in the back of my mind I was listening to myself and saying, "I can't be having this exchange. How can someone who's in a coma know what time it is, much less have an expectation and express disappointment? This makes no sense to me." Even so I offered Christi a promise. "I'll tell you before I leave when to expect me the next day."

If I were doing traditional psychotherapy with Christi, I wouldn't be surprised if somewhere in the first three or four sessions there was a slight misattunement. After all, strong and trusting relationships aren't about being perfect. They're about being able to quickly perceive and repair little hurts. Nonverbally Christi and I had just repaired our first glitch.

I quieted my mind's disbelieving chatter and focused on the sensations I perceived under my hand. Christi seemed to be continuing to work on tolerating her own internal sensations. The magnitude of fluid presence in her arm had been increasing each day, like water filling up a holding reservoir. Still, when the fullness reached a certain threshold Christi's arm tensed or began to tremble, as if she were reacting in fear to the amplitude of her own presence. I rode this wave with her, inviting the increase in volume and then helped to calm the nervous system tremor when it went too far. I think of this like training muscles. When we start an exercise program our muscles fatigue quickly, but over time they are strengthened and can do a greater workload. Christi was working out her sensory- processing "muscles." I felt this work going on even while I heard a report from the weekend doctor that they were discouraged by the lack of progress they saw.

Christi was also training my sensory-processing muscles. First, she showed me, then tested me, in a "yes," "close," "no" system of signals. When I silently or verbally put into words what I thought she was communicating I typically "heard" back three variations. One was a spacious silence, a bit like standing in an open room; this meant I got the words right. Or I perceived an even pulse of fluid that was a tone correction, meaning I was close, try again. If I sensed back a crisp silence, one with a flat taste, I got it wrong.

At the end of every session I waited for a few seconds after I signaled my intention to leave until she let me go, like she demagnetized my hand where it touched her. I tried to always tell her when I expected to be back. I considered she may want this in part because she wanted to have some control in a situation where the hospital staff, even friends and family, came and went based on their timing, not hers.

We were entering the third week when Christi began to reveal to me very brief snippets of the sensation of the accident. Think about the way you develop intimacy with any friend. You tell them more and more about yourself to see how they're going to handle it. Will they be judgmental or supportive? If you expose a bit of raw emotion, will they ride through it with you or will they look away and change the subject, giving you a message of "I don't really want to know" or "this is too much for me?" Christi had been testing my reaction to determine how much she could lean on me. And I found out later, she also began this explicit testing of what her Mom could handle by conveying to her a global feeling of terror.

I had been working almost exclusively on Christi's right arm (no tubes), feet, and occasionally her abdomen. My attention, however, increasingly was drawn to her head. Christi frequently dropped her head to the left and down toward her chest which looked very uncomfortable. I suggested to Sue and Terry that my work shift from primarily stabilizing and supporting to a working phase. I didn't have a conscious agenda about what this meant. My intention was to deliberately meet the obstacles with an invitation to change. After their agreement I began working by placing my hands on either side of her skull. I listened to the fluid presence in her brain. I sensed the fluid dimension as a three part whole: I imagined balancing cellular, transitional, and extra-cellular fluids. Think about standing in a tidal pool. You can feel the wash of the tide, moving in and out against your legs, as well as the distinctness of the single pool you're standing in. Touching Christi in this way seemed to bring her to a more restful placement of her head on the pillow.

In addition to left and right, I also placed my hands on the base of her skull and her forehead. There seemed to be a stuck place at the top of the brainstem, like a plug made of thick felt. Pressure pushed up against it from below. If you've ever taken a yoga or stretching class you've undoubtedly bent over to touch your toes and then rolled back up to standing, sequencing one vertebrae at a time. If you think as you roll up of organs stacking up, kind of like a tower of squishy water balloons, it'll go something like this. First comes bladder and intestines filling the deep belly. Then the second mid-layer of stomach, spleen, pancreas and liver. Next, heart and lungs drape over them. Your trachea and esophagus give a lift into your head, and finally the brain rests on top of everything below.[v] In Christi I didn't feel this continuous flow of connection. It was as if there was a separation and the body parts were not talking to one another. At the top there was a twist in the stacking column that prevented the brain from relaxing into the support of everything else below. This was where I sensed the "felt plug." I didn't know the meaning of this state so I relied wholly on listening. I just breathed while being aware of my organs stacking up, invited Christi to feel mirrored and recognized, allowing resonance with me to invite connections within her system.

I worked with Christi in this brain-body realm for four days in a row. Near the end of each session I had visual and/or movement sensations of scenes of the accident that lasted a few seconds. I sensed myself rocked hard side to side, as she probably was when her car swerved and flipped. Much later I found out that witnesses to the accident said it looked like she slightly veered to the right and overcorrected, losing control. The jeep rolled five times before the impact sprung Christi's seat belt and she was partially ejected from the vehicle. Miraculously not a single bone was broken, just a small crack in L-5. I felt the sensation of the right hand gripping the steering wheel. Then sensations of whole body bracing, sensory overload, terror, slam. After the sessions Sue, who was at Christi's left side as we worked, reported that she was feeling fear and the impact of the seatbelt across her own torso. Neither of us explicitly told Christi what we perceived. In fact it was so outside our own conceptualizations we seemed barely able to tell each other. Perhaps too we were muted by secondary shock that made talking more difficult.

Because we were in the hospital we were sometimes interrupted, like when a nurse came in to take Christi's temperature and pulse or to adjust the bed. On the fourth day of our brain-body work a nurse shooed me from the room because she needed full access to Christi. Although we were not finished I had to leave abruptly. Christi's reaction was "no." A sharp, metallic taste and smell filled my nose and mouth. I leaned close and promised, "We'll work on whatever you want tomorrow." I didn't say this because I expected her to have an agenda. I said it because I was sensitive to her controlling her own timing.

When I arrived the next day I discovered that she did have an intention, although it took her several tries for me to get it. I came in with my usual hello of a touch on her forearm, ready for a slow entrance into her underwater world. Immediately she shifted her head to the left. I was surprised since this gesture had pretty much stopped over the last few days. Sue and I both reached in to adjust the cushions that supported Christi's head. As I reached for her arm again she turned her head harder to the left. Sue and I both assumed we didn't get the cushions right and tried again. As I placed my hand on her shoulder she turned her head left again. I saw that the initiation of this turn wasn't from her head but was a contraction of her left side that began at the waist and was completed by the turn of her head.

"Are you telling me a story?" Incredulousness made me blurt this out loud. As if everything that had already happened wasn't enough of a challenge to my preconceived notions, this was way beyond.

Despite the challenge to my logic I placed my hands on Christi's head, this time in support rather than to change the position. It was like I'd just touched a time travel machine, one that also made the boundaries between us even more porous. We were immediately at the accident scene where she had landed on the ground. I heard silence and then a rush of people. I felt panic internally and in the swirl of witnesses who came running. At the same time I was aware of the hospital room and my hands on the front and back of her head. I sensed a thin thread flowing between my fingertips connecting the pineal, mammillary and pituitary glands deep inside her brain. The descriptive phrase "hormonal chaos" arose in my mind. And then I was swept into her memory again and waves of shock and despair swamped me, nearly pushed me back. In a hundredth of a second I saw her decision to leave her life or stay and fight. Sound ran helter skelter in my head. Time, abiding by the rules of shock, was both indefinite and fast. Fluid tone, beneath my hands and in my own body, went still.

I had no practiced technique for this. I was a witness at her side, a presence beside her aloneness. I took a peek at Sue who stood on the opposite side of the bed, her left hand holding Christi's. Her face was serious and fierce, determined to hold her daughter's turmoil. Christi pulled her left arm into her stomach, a hard-wired impulse to cover the site of injury. Sue took deliberate breaths, for herself and for Christi. Christi pulled her Mom closer, moving her arm up towards her chest.

After several still moments I silently suggested to Christi, "It's enough for today, perhaps you can rest now." But she didn't release us yet. My hands were now on either side of her head. I felt something melt and the soft spray of a fountain passed through the center of her brain; the word thalamus came into my awareness, as if I were reading a word from the picture page of an anatomy textbook. The magnetic pull let go and I returned to my position at her side. Christi very slightly turned her head left to look with partially opened eyes at Mom. Sue's eyes reached back, like a mother would to her just born baby. Then Christi shifted in micro-movements right and looked at me. Since I was on her right side and that eye was nearly fully closed, I leaned way down, almost to her chest, to make seeing me easier. It felt like I was confirming my presence. With my eyes I acknowledged that I saw what she showed me.

I left the session in shock. I didn't expect Christi's sudden initiation of trauma processing and such graphic sharing. I didn't expect my own as-if-I-were-there perception. I wasn't sure I wanted the gift of sensing another so deeply. My usual coping skill for high intensity experience was to use rational understanding, as if naming it allowed me to securely place it into its logical spot. But in this case I had no framework. In my psychotherapy practice I'd sat with clients as they remembered traumatic incidents, but while I was impacted by their emotion and physical distress, I didn't share the scenes as I did with Christi. My unacknowledged preconceptions about coma as being without the capacity for thought, emotion and action collided with first person experience. Outside the hospital room Sue and I spoke briefly, tentatively, in half sentences to one another. "I felt the seatbelt." "It was the accident scene." This wasn't to share the details because we left those unexpressed. We simply needed to say aloud that we had each experienced ourselves present in Christi's trauma.

My silence about the details of witnessing Christi's accident real time wasn't just with Sue. Even in my daily journal I limited the words I wrote down. With my friends I shared headlines: "intense," "important," "powerful." Internally I was filled with the experience but I felt myself in some kind of sound barrier chamber that blocked creating a story line, even in my own head.

I went to our session the next day more prepared for the possibility of explicit detail. It wasn't that I wanted it, more like I was entranced, as one is with an accident scene you can't look away from. Sue seemed ready too because as we approached the bed together to resume our same positions I noticed she seemed fortified. When I placed my hand down in greeting, the sensation word that came to me was aggravation. I said this to Christi and there was receptivity. She picked up her revelations from the day before. This time we were arriving at the emergency room. I sensed blood in her right eye, and anxiety. With her left arm Christi pulled Sue's hand up toward her heart. My hands on Christi sensed vibration from brainstem to tailbone.

Sensations and images began to flow rapidly. I perceived myself three places at once: in this room with my hands on her, as witness in the ER room, and within Christi's first person experience of the events. I sensed a collar around her/my neck (I assume it's a stabilizing collar put on for transit). I saw energy shapes move like jerky dancing shadows in the space around her. A needle was going into her/me, just above the collarbone, on the left side. From the point of view of the current time hospital room I looked at her neck. No marks. I wondered where the sensation came from. Again I had no technique, simply breath and presence.

As we worked there were numerous sound interruptions that I'd never heard previously even though we'd been working in this hospital setting all along. It was as if they were part of a play being enacted. Code blue was called twice and a call for personnel once. Sue and I whispered assurances to Christi this wasn't for her. "You've already made it through. You're safe now." Finally Christi dropped into a deeper sleep. An odd thing to say, I know, about someone who's already in a coma. But she seemed to let go and fall sleep like anyone would who had just lived through an exhausting ordeal.

When we left the room Terry met us in the hallway. I asked he and Sue about the images of blood and the needle. I learned that Christi's contact lens was lodged and they couldn't remove it right away, which created bleeding in her eye. The needle was part of the surgical procedure in the emergency room. Immediate action had to be taken because Christi's mesentery artery, the main bloodline to the abdomen, was severed by the seatbelt impact. She lost three quarters of her blood. Amazingly, the trauma team repaired the artery with no damage to any of her internal organs.

It was essential that Sue participated in these sessions with Christi. They had a very strong intuitive link. The three of us needed one another because the severity of the trauma was too great for one person to hold. Have you ever had a friend stand by to back you up while you do something incredibly scary- like walk across a log over a churning river or give a public speech? You know you're doing it yourself but her presence seems to give you an anchor, even a little extra energy, so you can reach deeper into yourself and perform the difficult task. This is what was happening for the three of us. Christi used Sue and me to have the strength to begin acknowledging and integrating her experience. Sue and I used one another's presence to tolerate the explicitness of being active witnesses. Three months from these sessions Sue told me she knew no one would believe us that the trauma processing happened. Before experiencing it herself she wouldn't have believed it either. Yet now she knew first hand and valued it as an essential element in Christi's recovery process.

From the Overlook, 2008

Nine years after first meeting Christi I had a partial manuscript draft ready to share. I read the first chapter aloud to her. We were sitting together in her childhood bedroom, the place we often worked when she was first discharged from the hospital. I sat in the rocking chair I always used and she was in her wheelchair, parked in front of the window overlooking the backyard garden. We were so close our knees almost touched. She responded to my description of our work with an audible "ah." She contracted as I read the passage about her parents racing through the mountains to reach the hospital. A memory was triggered that I "heard/saw" as it passed across her like fast moving shadow. At the accident scene she wanted to make a sound, knew she was losing blood. I paused in the reading to let her flash of recognition disperse. As I continued and read the words about pulling her Mom closer she moved her right arm up over her heart and then released it down. And at the end she very slowly, trembling, moved her arm half way in and out. I paused in silence for a long minute. Then I said, "I see you never knew you shared so much explicit detail with your Mom and me." I realized her memory of the early years was like very early childhood, vaguely known without words and time sequence to it. Her response confirmed for me that I wanted to persist, wrestle with the inadequacy of language, to find the right words to give back to her.

As I drove away from her house I felt my passion to help move her story into the world. I still marveled at the mystery of how we came into one another's lives, knowing something greater than any of us individually had been at work. So many times Sue and I seemed on the verge of lost, stranded. We were like explorers standing at the North Pole, no compass to tell us which way to go, taking whatever next step we could see, certain we had to keep moving.

> "For the ill, the promise of a reconciliation between body and mind in the practice of medicine has more than a philosophical meaning. The hope is not just for the healing of the body but for an empathic understanding. To be seen. To be known. The sufferings of the body, as hard as they are to describe, make for epic experiences. Shaken, left without any way to articulate the nightmare, and therefore isolated not only by bodily trauma but by its incommunicability, I have felt an overriding desire for recognition."
>
> Susan Griffin,
> What Her Body Thought A Journey into the Shadows

The Forests

I have the luxury of a slower pace as I tell you this story. I introduce you to one character at a time so you don't get too confused with many names and personalities. In actuality there are five doctors, eleven nurses and rehab aides, five visiting family members, Christi's two best friends, two dozen close friends, and four new home health aides. With the benefit of hindsight I tell you how events played out as if they were in an orderly sequence. But in reality the next few weeks in the Forests' lives are a swirl as they put into action the reality of a drastically changed family. Order only comes when Sue and Terry do the equivalent of yelling, "freeze," so they have a 10 second window to grasp what's happening.

Christi's condition is re-diagnosed as spindle coma. This means she goes in and out of coma. She opens her eyes and responds to the environment and then goes back in deeply and appears unresponsive. After the sessions revealing the accident trauma memories, Christi recedes further. When I put my hands on her she feels like distant, frozen tundra. She seems locked between withdrawing inward and bracing herself against anything external. I imagine that she has two protective reflexes signaling at once - pulling her arms into her chest, and extending them outward to stop a fall. It's rather like the seizing up that happens if you give your computer two signals too close together. I try beckoning Christi with reasons to come out. I remind her of qualities like curiosity and engagement. Yet with less fluid tone moving beneath my hands it's more difficult to hear her. Her sleep looks more like exhausted collapse than restful recuperation.

Sue and Terry seem to be a bit discouraged by Christi's distance. Their eyes and shoulders show the fatigue of virtually living at her side in one hospital or another for over a month. When they perform a task they mobilize from somewhere deep down in order to override the inertia that entices, "go home and sleep a dreamless sleep for twelve hours."

Despite her current unresponsive appearance, Christi is medically stable, so discussions begin about what to do next. The medical team recommends placing Christi in a nursing home. Sue and Terry have visions of their lives becoming a long extension of hospital life. No matter how good the quality of care is in a residential facility they don't think it can compare with being in your own home. They also know they see things about Christi's presence with them that the medical staff discounts. Yet, on days like today, that presence is elusive. They are nagged by the medical team's discouragement and doubt. As I leave the session I walk down to the elevator with Terry who's listlessly on his way to the cafeteria for a late lunch. We ride the five floors down and up twice as he expresses his frustration at their helplessness. The only comfort I can offer is to listen.

Eventually the hospital team relents to the Forests' advocacy for home placement. They decide that Christi can go home with Sue and Terry if they prove their capabilities to monitor the medical equipment and clear the ventilator when needed. They ask Sue to commit to a continuous three-day stay in the hospital. The first night she complies, but then balks. For the past week she's already been doing all the tasks they want to see. "All this will accomplish is me being completely sleep deprived and exhausted by the time we bring her home. How can that possibly be best for her care?" She feels it's a set-up for failure: a failure the rehab doctor is already predicting, saying, "In three weeks the family will regret bringing her home."

However, they take solace and encouragement from Dr. Seagraves' support. As their family doctor, he knows them not just medically, but personally, because he's also their former neighbor. As a teenager Christi babysat his kids. Dr. Seagraves was the first person they called for advice from the Coeur d'Alene hospital. He concurred that it seemed too early to make the decision to discontinue life support and supported the family's decision to come back to St. Pat's. And since they've been back he's come by each day while on hospital rounds. He's seen the brain scan, knows "this is bad," and feels the sadness of the situation. His intimacy with the family allows him to override the bias of his medical training that predicts a dismal outcome. He advocates for the Forests, telling others, "When you know the family you know they need to have the chance." When he visits Christi's room he nods in approval at the decision to go home, saying he believes if anyone can succeed it'll be them. Thankfully, the nursing staff also speaks up and acknowledges they've already seen Sue and Terry's skillful care. Permission is given to drop the three-night requirement and bring Christi home on July 6th, just shy of eight weeks since the accident.

Coming home is a relief even though there's a lot to do. Christi's room is emptied and refilled with the specialized hospital bed and ventilator equipment. The walls, however, stay adorned with her favorite posters- Phantom of the Opera and a boy and girl walking hand and hand on the beach. Over her bed there's a poster of a round earth, the bottom half all oceans where whales and turtles swim. It's a talisman of companionship for wherever she sleeps in the intermittent coma. The balloons from her hospital room are hung on the pegs that once held clothes. Interviews are begun with caregiving aides who will be assisting Christi and relieving Sue and Terry of some of the full-time care. Even with help there will be no relief from extending their attention continuously to her room like the waving tentacles of an anemone, constantly scanning, checking for need.

When Sue remembers the return home many years later she still sighs with the relief she felt then. She recalls: "Now recovery and rehab will begin. We all slept that first night for the first time in months. The next morning the sunlight was coming in Christi's window and the dogs jumped up on her hospital bed. Even though we had the equipment for life support - the overwhelming sense was she was back in her room - just as she had left it when she was home for Spring break several months before. I remember calling family and saying we have her home."

Sue, the Director of the University of Montana's Early Intervention Specialist training, is now the recipient of services. As the professor, she was in charge of teaching students how to sensitively and respectfully work with families who have a child with a disability so that the myriad of services available to them are well coordinated and appropriate. Now she's on the receiving end. In one of her lectures last winter she told us families can be grouped generally into two categories: the privacy, primarily self-resourcing group; and the social, primarily external-resourcing group. I see the Forests' situation through that lens. They are a "within our own home" kind of family. They don't usually share personal, intimate information with those outside their close network of family and friends. In a time of crisis they're more likely to rely on one another than seek out community services. And if they do use those services they're likely to go to them rather than invite them in. The strong family unity of Sue, Terry and Christi allows them to pull together to get through the life-death crisis and make the decision for home care. But their familiar comfort zone is blown apart by Christi's high level of need. Privacy is rare. There's always at least one other person in their home, more often two or three, and numerous others drop in for hour-long treatment sessions.

Tom is the daily visitor that helps them feel a glimmer of normalcy. He's been a constant in their home since high school, even going on family vacations with them. Sue and Terry know he and Christi officially broke up during the winter, citing the distance between their colleges. Christi told Sue and Terry, however, that she and Tom were talking by phone as summer approached, preparing to see one another again "and see what happens." They had looked forward to hikes they'd take up Pattee Canyon, and visits to Dairy Queen where they'd sit under the elm trees just like they had so many summer days the year before. Maybe it would be a resurgence of romance, or at least the chance to take measure of how the first year of college had changed them.

Familiarity is what everyone wants now. Everyone believes it will help coax Christi back. It's like holding a seat for someone at a crowded show so they can easily slide into place no matter how late their arrival. Tom makes CDs of their favorite music for Christi. He introduces the songs like a nighttime DJ setting listeners up for the whole package. "Here's one from our first movie, *Jerry Maguire*." A pause and slight chuckle. They've talked of this first date innumerable times. It didn't go exactly smoothly. He adds, "even if you don't count it." Seeing Tom sit quietly, without expectation, next to Christi's wheelchair it's easy to see why they are best friends. Every once in awhile, he leans in close to Christi to say something softly. As I watch their heads bent together, just inches apart, his blond hair contrasting with her inch long dark spike, it's easy to imagine them close like this as they stretched after track practice or danced together at prom.

Despite the comfort of home Sue and Terry have hours, even whole days, when they're overwhelmed by figuring out, with minimal privacy, all the new systems for managing Christi's care. In one of the first weeks I arrive early for a session with Christi. A froth of activity is taking place outside the bedroom door as an aide readies the wheelchair and the housecleaner vacuums. Terry enters Christi's room and discovers she has had a bladder spasm and the bed and all her clothes are wet. When people jump in to help him he can't take one more minute of being crowded and his frustrated, "Just let me take care of her," has the effect of instantly silencing everyone and pushing them out of the room. The next day Terry greets me at the door with a big hug and apologizes, "It wasn't about you." I'm touched by his sensitivity and tell him, "It's fine, no offense taken." I know those of us in support roles need to be generous in our allowances to the family because the amount of strain they're under is immense. As it turned out, the problem wasn't just a spasm. It was a failure of Christi's catheter and the nurse had to put in a new one. That day wasn't the last time the catheter causes a problem.

Amidst the adjustment to a whole new household schedule Terry has to return to work at the engineering firm. Although his colleagues have understood, the reality of project deadlines and workload means he needs to get back to being part of that team. Fortunately, he has the latitude to come home for lunch each day, giving him and Sue time to connect and for him to help with some of the caregiving tasks. Sue has more time to decide what she'll do about work because she can delay her return to the University until fall semester. Sue feels the need to supervise caregivers and to learn from the physical, speech and occupational therapists the techniques they should employ to help Christi. It's also a two-person job to move Christi from bed to wheelchair. Since Christi doesn't have the ability to hold herself in a sitting position, shoulder straps, foot straps and a headband are all required. She also must wear a chest- to-hips plastic body brace for at least another month while the cracked vertebra heals.

The strength Sue uses to accomplish all she does has little to do with muscles and bones. It's a more ethereal strength, like liquid steel, that propels her petite four foot nine frame through one challenge after another. Her strength is equal parts determination, persistence and willingness to believe her perceptions rather than accepting the status quo.

It's easiest to imagine Sue if you've ever made Jiffy Pop the old fashioned way, in a pan shaken on the stove. There's a moment when the dome of steam has inflated the cover to make room for the exploding kernels. After the first cacophony settles, a steady rhythm takes over, almost precise in pop-pop sequence. Sue is a person with that assertive and steady rhythm. Her bursts don't jump out of the pan, but stay contained within the domed structure of body to accomplish her purpose.

Everyone has language mannerisms. Sue starts most conversations with a "yes, ..." It's a signal that she's ready to respond to whatever request, observation, or declaration you're going to make. This "yes" is how Sue has continually oriented herself to meet whatever challenge comes next in Christi's recovery process. Even her "no," reserved for objecting to limits, is really just a forceful "yes" for what she does want.

Sue's optimism and driving will, although strong, can't prevent sometimes getting caught by uncertainty and discouragement that turns her usual glistening eyes into flattened opaque disks. This happens a few weeks after Christi comes home when my session yields no quality of personal contact. My touch stops at diffuse and impenetrable fog bank. I seem as invisible to Christi as she is to me. Afterwards Sue walks me to the door, asking me about the session, scanning my face for some sign of hope. I tell her about the quiet and distance. The undertow of a wail pulls against Sue's words. "I've read that some coma patients like the dream state and don't want to wake up. What if that happens to Christi?"

The fact that I couldn't sense Christi's presence either validates Sue's perception of being locked out. After striving against the odds it is frightening to enter floating inertia. I stand speechless for a few moments. I want to offer Sue some salve but I have nothing. I believe Christi wouldn't have fought so hard only to become lost now, but how can I be sure. This recession even deeper into her self is like the evil part of a fairy tale where the princess is abducted and hidden beyond anyone's reach deep in the forest. My brain refuses to come up with words to express my perception. I don't sense Christi's deliberateness or will to be in another state. I wish I could offer soothing platitudes, bypass Sue's fear and my own uncertainty. The best I can offer before driving away is my commitment to keep showing up to listen, to beckon.

Although they've been home only two weeks Sue's intuition is that they need to return for medical help. She asks the doctors to check the shunt because she's read that a failure can cause increased sluggishness.* When the doctors bring her in for the CAT scan they find this is the case. Perhaps it's not a surprise since Christi never had the right sized shunt from the beginning. There's a procedural requirement that a patient must have two shunt failures before becoming eligible for a specially calibrated one. Christi, a petite young woman, only 101 pounds, is too big for a child-sized shunt. That was the first one that failed. And she's too small for the adult version, the one failing now.

So, it's back to the hospital for another surgery. Christi's regular neurologist is out of town so a young resident takes charge. The surgery seems to go well. Sue stays at Christi's bedside late into the evening while Terry goes home to sleep since he still must work the next day. Around 2 AM the resident comes in and tells Sue he doesn't like the looks of the scan done after the operation. He doesn't think Christi will revive after this surgery, even back to the partial coma state. He tells Sue he thinks they only have a matter of hours.

Sue spends the next six hours agonizing. She wonders what time to call Terry and wake him and when to call their family. Her thoughts ping-pong back and forth between

---

* a shunt channels fluid away from one area in the body which is not draining properly and empties it into another functioning area of the body. A shunt placed in the third ventricle in Christi's brain removes excess cerebrospinal fluid that is not being properly absorbed by other parts of the brain. If this were not done a condition of hydrocephalus (enlarged swelling) would occur.

planning for a funeral and the next steps in rehab. At 8 AM the resident comes in with a bounce in his step and gregarious, "Good morning, how are you this morning?"

Sue looks at him incredulously. She can't seem to speak because his demeanor is so bizarre. If he could read behind her frozen eyes he'd see the words, "How do you think I am after being here all night wondering if my daughter will stay alive?" After a long pause she's able to gather her voice and ask about his assessment from the night before.

"Oh that" he says, waving his hand dismissively. "I called one of my professors and he said don't worry about that anomaly." Sue's relief clashes against her desire to punch him. How could he leave her here all this time in anguish when he'd found out he was wrong? She wants to scoop Christi up from the bed and get her home again, away from this hospital that feels like a source of harm instead of healing. It's bad enough they're here going through a third surgery just because the cost containment protocol required Christi to "prove" she needed the custom shunt. The two extra surgeries have cost more than the cost savings and with significant additional risk.

Instead of staying mad, the Forests use one of their strongest coping skills and switch their focus to the good news. The doctors determine that Christi's lungs are clear enough that the trach can be removed. This is a milestone the original treatment team in Coeur d'Alene never thought was possible. Without the trach Christi will begin to be able to smell, taste and make sounds.

Once they get settled at home again, Sue reaches out via e-mail to the many well wishers who have been following their story. The group list, telephone-tree style, is over 45 people long. She writes:

July 20, 1999

I have decided to send a general e-mail to all of you who have sent your thoughts, prayers and wishes. First off, for all of you who provided meals while we were in the hospital- those meals were greatly appreciated and very needed. I cannot tell you how wonderful it was to come home and have food there. For those of you who have never experienced what we are going through, thank you. It is almost impossible to function as we did prior to this trauma. For those who have sent cards and letters and e-mails, thanks for your words and thoughts. I know for some of you it has been difficult to write down what you want to say. It's OK because I know that words are very hard to come by at this time. Just seeing your names and reading your cards is very cathartic for all of us. We decorated the hospital room with them, to make it a little less blah and of course we read them to Christi. I strongly believe (as a number of authors and individuals who have been through comas have indicated) that Christi is present and can hear or at least in a very special way sense that people care. We received the most decorated hospital room award...

It has been 10 weeks and Christi at times becomes very semi-comatose. That means that her eyes open about half way, she can at times respond to commands like "turn your head", "squeeze my hand", she tracks with both of her eyes and they do work together tracking, and she has regained the ability to almost hold her head up. But the hard part is that it happens intermittently and variably. She is semi-comatose about 10 to 20 minutes at a time about 5 or more times during the day/night, but there is no consistency to it. What will happen next is anybody's guess. The doctors assure us that at this point it may take time to get the right pressure setting on the shunt. Until then it is our family's decision to keep Christi at home where she can see friends and receive occupational therapy, nursing services, physical therapy and speech and language therapy. Her doctors come to visit her at the house. They are very supportive of our decision to recoup at home until she is ready for rehab.

I know some of you want to know when I will be returning to work. I cannot describe in words the desire I have to be doing my job/jobs, but I'm completely unable to focus on, or put any priority on, anything besides being there for Christi. In my heart I know that she hung on the night of May 13th to be with us and we decided that we will be there for her and help her to recover as best she can. Some of you may not know this but she was a very difficult child to conceive. Terry and I went through a lot to even have her, so it is not possible for me to turn her care over to someone else. I am just not there. Know that I have strong intuition that this will get better and that things will change, but she needs time. I am working hard at taking care of myself and making sure I eat and get some sleep. Yes, I do make some time to get away, but it is still hard to meet people and talk about what happened and try to always be optimistic. That is part of the reason for this message. I wanted you all to be equally informed, and not misinformed, and to know that we deeply appreciate all the thoughts, prayers, cards, calls, flowers, signs, food, etc.

Sue is now mother, rehab aide and case manager. At night she and Terry take turns at 10, 12, 2 and 4 checking on Christi and rolling her onto her side or back. Sue looks for communication signals by relying on her experience as an early intervention specialist and professor. As professor Sue told classes the story of a 5 year old everyone believed incapable of speech, movement or even having an intention. When they placed the little girl in a resting position so she wouldn't have to use valuable resources to struggle to sit up they saw that she turned her head toward her favorite food smell. This led them to develop a communication method based on turning towards a smell. More importantly, perhaps, it let everyone know she was "in there." Sue now had to bring this kind of patience and creativity to her interactions with Christi. It's sometimes difficult to wait patiently for Christi's responses because we don't know what's happening behind the opaque screen of her barely-open eyes. Is she busily pulling together the means to convey intention? Or has she fallen back into the coma realm, no longer remembering what her intention had been?

It seems that Christi is gradually shifting from her reliance on raw will to intention. Will is like the ocean pushing a wave up from deep currents. It comes as a power surge, propelled through whatever is resting on the surface. You feel it coming towards you before you see it break through, hurling ten feet onto the beach. Everything in its path is swept along. Intention is more like gliding on the surface, carried along by rhythmic swells of energy that melt back into the whole once they've catalyzed action. Intention places an object gently, yet decidedly, on the beach. As Christi negotiates the will-intention balance she sometimes seems to lose her way. She seems to struggle against being pulled under to places too far away to reach the shore.

I start dreaming about Christi. In each dream there's a sudden change. In one of my first dreams, Christi wakes up in her hospital bed, realizes she can talk, and jumps up to go shopping at the mall with her friends. In another dream she's with her parents, everyone waiting, as if in a video on pause. Then she speaks and they all race off in different directions with scarcely a goodbye, facing outward as they yell over their shoulders that they'll meet at home later. Each time I'm left standing on the deserted empty stage, trying to figure out what happened. It seems to me as if these dreams are like versions of what would have been. It's as if the momentum for the happily-just-home-from-college reality exists in a parallel universe and is trying to pull the action into its flow and out of the groove everyone fell into when the accident and brain injury happened.

In my waking hours I'm often wondering what's happening. It's not that Sue, Terry and Christi are leaving suddenly like they did in the dream. In fact, it's the opposite because they've become a central part of my daily life. When I first went to work with Christi I only had the intention of helping her ease into and out of surgery. I believed I knew how to accomplish that task. Instead, one session led to the next. I am in unfamiliar terrain where I can't see landmarks. It's been nearly two months and I see Christi almost every day. I don't have a plan or a map. I just keep showing up, ready to listen to whatever facet of body expression is revealed.

Once when I was in the grocery store perusing the row of artisan breads, I was startled by a glimpse of falling motion behind me. When I turned I saw an older, burly-framed man collapsed onto his back with his eyes open in a questioning look of disorientation. A few feet away other shoppers stood suspended, looking, yet motionless too. Since I was closest, I was the first to break the spell and kneel down beside him. He grabbed my hand in a tight grip that clenched our two hands together into a single fist. One person ran to call 911 and another handed me a wad of napkins to wipe the blood from his forehead. After a few minutes I thought, "why am I here with him? I have no idea what to do." I looked around for another more knowledgeable person to step in and take charge, but no one else came to his side. To leave him I would have had to forcibly break my hand away. It would be an act of desertion. So I met the force of his grip, holding on to him so he wouldn't be alone. I gently dabbed his forehead, not so much because of need but for the gesture of care. I had no personal relationship to this man but I felt the power of the universal qualities of human touch and need for connection. When the ambulance arrived and the EMTs approached he let go of my hand, releasing me so he could receive them.

Sometimes with Christi I feel the way I did that day in the grocery store. I think some other expert person should step in and do whatever it is that would help that I don't know how to do. Since we never knew one another and can't engage in any of the usual methods of relationship I wonder if she perceives the individual me. But I never doubt that she feels the universal qualities of human presence that come through my hands. I feel like she's "grabbed my hand," just like that man did in the grocery store, and I need to hold on until she lets go.

The changes taking place in Christi seem so subtle that sometimes it's hard to value them, especially when the medical treatment team is discouraged by her lack of consistent alertness and coordinated movements. There are days when I'm infected by that discouragement. I'm sometimes tempted to replace my perceptions with those of the medical team, as if healing falls into discrete black and white, right and wrong, categories instead of shifting shades of grey.

Sue begins to get phone calls or visits from people who promise their method of intervention will be the magic bullet that "pops" Christi out. One woman leaves a business card that lists "healer" as her occupation. I don't know her, but I feel envy. My envy isn't really for this person specifically. I just wish I knew how to do more to help Christi heal. And if anyone does know what to do, I want Christi to have that help. Christi is alive, a miracle in and of itself, yet the fantasy of a sudden awakening, Hollywood style, lingers as an unspoken hope for all of us. The extravagant offers of cure don't ring true for Sue - maybe because of method or timing, she doesn't know. She keeps going with her instincts to stick with the team she has.

Invariably when I catch the discouragement bug something happens in my connection with Christi that lets me know it's important to keep coming, to keep being part of the miracle of slow healing. I'm reminded over and over that my discouragement isn't about Christi and her progress. I create the feeling myself by judging myself inadequate. I want so much more for Christi than what I know how to give that I fear I'm letting her down.

In my journal I write, "How does the essence of oneself manifest in gesture and action?" I believe I've felt the essence, or core qualities, of Christi through my hands. What's needed are pathways to express these qualities in movements and words. In the lingo of self-esteem it's common to differentiate between "being" and "doing." Being is a quality that exists in and of itself, like intelligence or compassion. Doing is the quality in action, for instance, intelligence used to solve a math problem or compassion utilized to comfort a sick friend. I believe all Christi's "being" qualities are still within her, but the accident disrupted her brain's ability to coordinate the expression of them in "doing" form. As I wonder in my journal about Christi's essence manifesting, I also write a prayer for myself. Bainbridge-Cohen used to remind us in BMC training sessions that we practice "being" so that when we are "doing" it comes from the place of "being." This is my prayer:

> *May I let go of self-judgments of doing. Let my actions flow from being. Use without effort or thinking the kinds of pathways I hope Christi can rebuild.*

There's an old expression, "resting my weary bones." At times this seems to be what Christi is doing. She's resting all the way down into her bones. In BMC work we associate the literal body with aspects of consciousness. Bones are a powerful foundation of rest, life creation, and movement. They can crystallize blazing truth, as in "I know it in my bones." They're a place we hear the reverberations of our ancestors. At the core of our bones is the marrow that produces blood, a source of energy. We can rest in bones, like coming home to sleep in our favorite bed, relaxing as our body literally refuels itself. Debra, transition complete from flute teacher to bodywork team member, has begun doing afternoon BMC sessions with Christi. We both notice that when we increase our awareness of bone marrow, it quiets Christi's nerves that otherwise fizzle and sputter like high electricity wires. Bone marrow mind does however have a shadow side. Resting there can tempt a person to drift away into a peaceful realm of infinite time. The marrow can be like a siren's song, making us forget to enliven movement. I think Christi sometimes drifts in this peaceful state and forgets her outer connections. This frustrates Sue and those of us on the treatment team who are working hard to help Christi find the means of re-engagement. We all want to support Christi in her deep self remembrance and rejuvenation, yet also remind her that bones are the levers of movement into the space around us. Our ligaments and muscles - the mind of action - are woven into the surface of bone, facilitating the journey from inner home to outer expression.

Sometimes when I visit Christi I see she is resting, refueling, reweaving herself. On those days our work together is slow and quiet, like barely audible whispers. And on other days I feel the impulse to call her out to play. I want her body to feel again the sensation of silliness, not linear movements, but surprising curlicues. I want her to feel in contact with the space around her, to feel her own actions having an impact on the environment. I bring her toys to play with in her hands- a dense fluid squeeze ball, a koosh ball and a collapsible geodesic sphere. I look for ways to engage her curiosity in anything outside herself, beckoning the tiny droplet I sense inside to shape itself into a wave. It's more than Christi wants to or can follow. Her resources are needed inside, and for her own priorities.

Christi has her own internal sequence of healing needs. One Wednesday when I'm there she seems to be trying hard to "wake up enough" to work on something specific but cannot. It's like she's straining forward but can't take a step because the back of her shirt is caught on something. I tell her to rest up and "we can work on whatever you want tomorrow."

The next afternoon Sue wheels Christi's wheelchair into the living room. I bend towards Christi in greeting, saying hello by placing my hand on her arm, and positioning my face at eye level. All at once several different thoughts pop up in my mind. I wonder how her period was affected by her injuries. Then, even more randomly, sense the question if Sue and Terry are having sex. It seems not a curiosity about them but about people in general. There's a long silence. I hear no clues, and then there's a closing feeling, like a shutter coming down softly, like a punctuation mark.

I look to Sue and say it seems like Christi is trying to express something. Sue seems to feel this fullness too. She tells me that Christi is about to get her period. I wonder to myself if I sensed something about sex because this is a time Christi usually feels more sexual. On impulse I ask, "Is there a story you might not have told your Mom?" Christi contracts forcefully, like I've pushed into her abdomen, her arms and legs crossing over the cavity this creates.

Sue is behind Christi's wheelchair with her hands resting on the handles. She is like a narrator standing stage left while Christi and I face one another. This seems to provide voice and privacy for Christi. Sue says, "When we were in the hospital we had to know any medications Christi might have taken. Her roommate told us that before Christi left for the semester she had intercourse with her boyfriend and the condom broke. She took a morning after pill."

I bend closer to Christi. We somersault down a rabbit hole. When we land I ask, "Do you think the accident has something to do with the sex mistake?" Her jaw drops slightly, exhaling she releases the tension in her chest.

Sue continues the narration. "Christi's roommate thought the relationship was wrong -that having sex with someone you're not married to is against God's wishes. Christi told her roommate she didn't see it that way."

Although no one speaks I think all three of us hear Christi's conclusion at the same time. "Maybe the accident is God's punishment for being sexually active." This feels exactly like the "aha" moments I have experienced in countless psychotherapy sessions. Someone who's been peeling back layers of rational thought suddenly sees how an emotional moment crystallized itself into a belief made from self-blame, helplessness and confusion. The irrational masquerades as reason.

Sue comes around from behind Christi's wheelchair and takes her position as mother. We each assure Christi there's no relationship between the accident and having sex, that God wouldn't punish her that way. The contraction in her solar plexus releases. She may not whole-heartedly believe us but at least it's a start. A week later, after a good session working on stretching out her arm, the subject arises again. Christi wants to clarify again that her accident isn't God's punishment. I hold her hands and encourage her to imagine resting into God's support for her healing, like being held in a mother's lap. I feel more like a minister than psychotherapist or BMC practitioner. It seems to help, though, because Christi falls into a deep sleep.

Sue and I don't talk about how surprised we are that Christi is creating and expressing emotion-based ideas. We are both traditionally trained in psychology, a discipline that assumes the functioning brain is responsible for thoughts. We put the unexplainable aside into a quintessential "save-for-later box," a box that already contains our experiences of sharing vivid accident memories and passing the heat of Christi's body through our own.

I write in my daily journal, "It's so powerful working with unconscious so directly. But also difficult for me because she doesn't hold the witness position herself. I guess this is similar to therapy when a person goes further than their capacity. But then there is the chance to help them re-stabilize, to catch up. The form with Christi is so raw."

I reflect a lot on how Christi uses Sue and me to process experience, emotions and thoughts. "Container" is a word often used by psychotherapists. Imagine a friend has just confided in you a secret that he feels a lot of emotion about. He'll say something like he "hopes you can hold it" or that he needs "someone else to hold it." If it's something that has an element of shock to it you might observe that it seems almost too big for him to "hold" inside because he can't digest or assimilate it yet. By placing the story in someone else's hands he gets a perspective not available internally. This self-witness role will be evident in expressions like, "I heard myself saying…" or "now I can see…" This is the kind of sharing Christi is doing with Sue and me. What has happened is too big for her to digest. Anchored by our "seeing" a scene with her, she can metabolize a sensation, like the spinning of the car, without getting lost or overwhelmed in the sensory experience. Because Sue and I are "holding" the story Christi can begin to get objective perspective without being flooded by the complexity of thoughts and emotions. Each session that processes a bit of the accident or medical intervention relieves a bit of pressure from the flood of information that threatens to drown her. This allows Christi to begin stabilizing her regulatory systems. Revealing an emotion-based belief frees up the energy being utilized to keep it tamped down and allows a new construct to be built.

Christi can't give us her story in carefully controlled increments. It flows out unadulterated and chaotic instead of linearly. We are external regulators much like a parent is when she soothes an infant who is distressed. Between us, Sue and I create calm by pretending the trauma sharing is commonplace. We talk instead about the literal, observable things that mark Christi's progress. The trach button is removed. The dose of Dilantin, taken as a preventative for seizure, is reduced to once a day. As Christi becomes more alert I move with her more quickly and spontaneously, even brush long strokes up her arms, which she seems to integrate rather than becoming overwhelmed and scrambled.

―――――•♦•―――――

Candace

The relative slower pace of summer gives me opportunity to reflect more on the path my life took that allows me to work with Christi and Sue the way I do. Studying BMC was a serendipitous choice right from the beginning. At the time mainstream psychology still relegated mind-body interaction to a top down model. Even seemingly gentle guided imagery interventions carried the intention to manage behavior rather than obtain insight. I wanted more than that. I sensed depth I couldn't articulate or reach. I had augmented my traditional counseling psychology studies with intensive workshops with a Gestalt and neo-Reichian therapist. With her guidance we paid attention to how energy moved or was blocked in our bodies as an integral part to understanding ourselves psychologically. This teacher was the one who understood my craving and suggested I investigate BMC even though she herself only knew about it indirectly, yet thought it "very interesting." Within two weeks I had researched the school and signed up for a week long intensive in the winter of 1990.

I couldn't name it at the time but I was searching to know the language of the body directly. I wanted to know its life force, to understand something from a completely different point of view. What I discovered in my first intensive class was both invitation and pathway to perceive the origins of movement from the perspective of body, not thought. It felt like the difference between looking through a window into a room and being in the room itself. Just this preliminary taste, to know directly what was still like a foreign country, enticed me to sign on for a full four years of study.

One incident from 1992, during a summer semester of Body Mind Centering studies, keeps coming to mind as significant. An experience that was a homeopathic taste of a brain injury that helped train my perceptions to respond with acuity to Christi's injury.

July, 1992. Our curriculum at school was dense and by the time our break for the 4th of July came I was ready to let all the stirred up perceptual snippets non-consciously settle themselves. I went to visit family, a full house of siblings and children guaranteed distraction. In the middle of play with my four-year-old niece, giving her a "horsey-back" ride down the hallway, a searing headache erupted. For the first two days I managed it with Tylenol until it receded into a faint background shadow. When I returned to school I noticed that my left eyelid was drooped nearly closed. My eyes cringed when I walked into the brightness of outdoor light. My thinking was molasses slow, like my whole brain was waiting to wake up from a shot of Novocain. Years later when I looked at my class notes from the next month I saw they recorded facts without personal elaborations, as if I were only capable of parroting the instructor's words without deepening their meaning to me personally.

One of the primary focuses in the summer's curriculum was the fluid systems of blood, lymph and interstitial fluid. It would be hard to describe a "typical" class since methods varied in order to utilize as many direct learning modalities as possible. Sometimes we were lying on the floor, eyes closed, listening to an instructor guide us with structure and function imagery, using attention to perceive that system within. We experimented with moving as if expressing the "mind" of a particular system. It fascinated me to play with what differences I found, for instance in my different paced expression of arterial blood and venous blood. We examined textbook anatomical drawings and colored in the related pages from the *Anatomy Coloring Book*, not just to memorize facts, but to sync the information with nonconscious knowledge. I wrote home to one friend that I often felt school was a blend of meditation practice, anatomy class and expressive dance.

An odd thing started happening in class whenever someone referenced lymph as a system: I fell instantly asleep, even when I wasn't tired. I heard "lymph" and immediately positioned myself on the edge of the room and stretched out on the floor. It's not that I fell into sleep. I was yanked under into sleep, as if an underground plant reached a vine up and snatched me around the ankle, pulled me into the plant's Venus-fly-trap mouth and folded petals over my head.

After 10 days my eyelid was still half closed. I hadn't spoken to anyone directly about my symptoms even though anyone looking at my face saw evidence something was wrong. Oddly it didn't occur to me to talk about it, perhaps part of my overall numbness. Finally one of the assistant teachers brought it to Bonnie's attention. Concerned about my well-being, she set up a time after the day's classes to "listen in" with her hands. Late afternoon light slanted in on the opposite side of the warm room. I had chosen a spot in the shadows to lie down, as close as I could come to the feeling of a sheltered nest. I was on my back, eyes closed, while her hands cupped my skull.

My notes from that day, written by a friend and transcribed into my notebook, recorded Bonnie's focus on tissue fluid, on the in-out exchange of tidal pool and ocean. I could hear everything Bonnie said, but the exact words slipped over me like slow water over a rock and I couldn't capture any of them to hold. My body heard her encouragement and tried to shift. But I was stuck, suspended. I knew the truthfulness of what she was saying about my system's over-emphasis on a point of view from inside a cell. I didn't feel tension, as if I was holding myself back. But I did sense being marooned. My mind was a landlocked puddle. I had an image of a droplet of water condensed on a glass. The droplet had a natural cohesion keeping it suspended, albeit in a slightly trembling whole. Eventually the cohesion would break and the droplet would form a rivulet down the side of the glass. For now though a sticky cohesion blocked any impulse I had to create language or movement.

Bonnie murmured geography of the brain: cerebellum, pons, cortex, brainstem. Instead of squishy articulations between these continents a dry air pocket prevented communication. She sensed me pushing to find the connections and directed me downward. "Imagine bringing fluid from head to heart, from head to pelvis, then all the way out to skin." I knew there was a key somewhere that would help me float, to glide on the surface of water instead of pushing myself like a heavy gondola.

Bonnie's work with me, although insightful and validating, didn't yet bring the full shift I needed. However, she did provide me with two keys. The first was an association. "I'm remembering reading somewhere a description of Horner's syndrome," she said, pausing to listen to what floated up from her memory bank, "but that's all I remember." I filed this tidbit in my mind and focused on her second recommendation: I should work right away with a local gifted bodywork practitioner, experienced in cranial-sacral work. His work would help free the rhythmic flow of the cerebro-spinal-fluid system (CSF); provide buoyancy for my brain to sway again, softly like a paper lantern in the gentlest breeze.

Within two days I had an appointment and was under his listening hands. As his perception augmented my own, eyes closed, I sensed my body torque to the right. I logically knew that my legs and feet were parallel on the mat, but the energy sensation was of my left leg crossing over the right by about a foot. It's intent to set off a spiral motion was so strong that if I followed it I would pirouette rapidly clockwise. The light touch of his fingertips held the edge of the spiral in suspended time until the tension of it subsided and my energy shape and body shape were unified again.

In another session my point of view was from in the middle of my spinal cord, just below the base of my skull. I fell off a platform in a backward swan dive. Suspended upside down and backwards in space my body followed a pitch-black rollercoaster ride, wilder than any in real life. Sudden right angle direction changes were interspersed with equally surprising crescendos and drops. The word neuropil came to mind even while I sensed this part of my spinal column inherently unknowable. By definition it is mysterious. I know there was a story Mom told of me falling from the bureau high changing table into a clothes hamper when I was only a few weeks old. Logically I suspected I might be revealing the sensory component of this injury and subsequent adaptation, but I had no explicit memory to tie these sensations to the story. For now I was content to let the experience be a story unto itself.

I left my summer studies without understanding all the clues I was writing into my notebook. Sentences like, "Neuropil is a bridge between spirit and the physicalization of matter." And pages and pages of drawings of double lobed butterfly wings. I drew them as invitation to open the energy movement pattern in my brain that guided homolateral movement, our early crawl that looks like a lizard. Each drawing done with my left hand was misshapen with drooped wings on the right side. If this butterfly were a plane it would be banking hard right.

By fall I was in the eye doctor's office, still trying to figure out what was wrong with my half closed eyelid. I didn't know why every afternoon I had to stop whatever I was doing and sit down to rest for 10 minutes. Dull headaches kept coming back. He sent me for an MRI and a neurological consult. At my request to understand visually what he was saying the neurologist put my brain scan up on the light box and pointed out the problem. Repeated spots of white space he said were outside the normal range. He diagnosed Atypical Multiple Sclerosis and told me we'd just wait to see what happens with further symptoms.

But in the meantime, in desperation, I wrote my eye doctor a three-page letter of what the experience felt like inside my body. The revelations I made to him were not ones I'd normally share, but thinking there was something wrong inside my brain propelled me past typical reticence. My condition felt personal in a way no other injury had before. It had a "me-ness" not present in something observable like an injured elbow. I told him the location in my brain where I sensed a blank spot, a tiny white hotspot at an axis point ear level just behind my damaged eye. I told him how I sensed communication broken between my cerebellum and this point and whatever was beyond. Even as I wrote the letter I knew the details would sound ridiculous to him. Once before, when I had an eye infection in this same eye, I drew a picture of what it felt like to differentiate it from other eye problems. The nurse frowned at me and said, "You can't feel your eye, there aren't any nerves there." I wanted to say, ok, yes, but obviously I feel something or I wouldn't be able to tell you why it's different. But I said nothing. Now the stakes were too high for silence. To his credit the doctor said nothing about my letter's oddity, only that "You won't find an answer in Missoula. You can go to Portland, Seattle or Salt Lake. Your choice and I'll make the referral."

I ended up in Seattle at the most perfect match, a neuro-opthamologist specializing in Multiple Sclerosis. He was the author of a medical textbook chapter on Horner's Syndrome, which ultimately was his diagnosis of my condition. It was the association Bonnie named three months earlier. Upon closer inspection my MRI didn't show de-mylenization of nerves, only more than the average number of veins which showed up as empty spaces. In Horner's syndrome a bleed in the carotid artery damages the sympathetic nerve. This was why my left pupil couldn't respond to light changes or express my inner emotions. In the next six months my eyelid gradually returned to its normal position although the lack of mobility in my pupil remained.

I never had the opportunity to tell the doctors what story I pieced together for myself, one I came to understand in part because of what transpired in my psychotherapy office over the next four or five months. I could listen attentively to each client, but if I tried to construct a thinking response, one where there was a sense of an "I" putting together the puzzle pieces, the pain was so immediate it functioned like shock therapy. I learned to pause, to wait, to perceive a rising of components already made whole. As the white hot spot began to fill back in I perceived it as changed. Where once there was a straight railroad track there were now girders going in multiple directions. I believed a necessary change was manifest in a shift from two-dimensional linear thinking to three-dimensional thinking. After months of limiting my conversations with friends to the most superficial topics I saw that I'd let go of my attachment to an identity of serious thinker. I began to jokingly describe myself as loving superficiality, and truly, I did find greater pleasure in the most mundane. I picked up a gorgeous colored ball of chenille yarn and appreciated the sensual experience without a thought of what it could become.

In BMC the carotid gland, situated in the neck by where my injured carotid artery passed, embodies the mind of silence, the space between each syllable in the spoken word. It is about attention and presence. Temperamentally I had, and have, a predisposition to silence and stillness; it's one of my strengths. And yet it was a misused coping mechanism, especially when my sensory system got overwhelmed. Although traditional Western medicine compartmentalized it, my injury wasn't one with only mechanical meaning. Its location was a nexus where my personality habits, early development and physical structure were woven together. In my school notebook I recorded "heightened awareness/self knowledge allows system to change itself." And that's what I know happened to me, although through an initially unpleasant manner. By the next summer I wrote into my notes to "keep voice present even in the silence."

Now, nearly twenty years later, I still have questions I'd like to ask the doctor. How do veins affect thinking? Is there a way to see what the glia cells rebuilt in the trellis structure of my brain or capture the different firing pattern of neurons? I wonder if doctors ever wish they could hear the whole story, the one with the richness of tangents, the one that plays out over the course of years. Throughout my work with Christi I remembered this experience. I appreciated how impactful and energy consuming a tiny injury was in me and this increased my awe and patience with what healing massive injury must be like inside her.

Christi and Sue

Christi and I start working on a repetitive chewing motion she's making with her mouth, and the tightness in her jaw. A tense jaw isn't only a post-accident phenomenon. It's always been Christi's gesture of concentration and effort. In flute lessons Debra used to write on Christi's sheet music, "Release jaw. Open mouth."

Although Christi initially seemed hesitant about the change in relationship, Debra has quickly become an essential member of the team.* On one afternoon Debra and I do a session with Christi together. While I place my hands on Christi, Debra plays her flute. We find that when she plays a low vibration with no changes in pitch there is a settling in Christi. Debra watches this with her eyes as she

---

* Debra works with Christi for the next ten years, combining her knowledge and skills in BMC, massage, and Body Talk™.

plays and I feel it under my hand. It's as if sand that was suspended by a crashing wave sifts back down to the ocean floor. If Debra plays high notes or fast changes there's an increase in activity that quickly changes into contractions, especially in Christi's arms. Towards the end of the session Debra puts down her flute and holds Christi's feet while I hold her head, both of us just listening to the subtle rhythms gently rippling through her body. Resting quiet like this and accepting touch is far from Christi's pre-accident style. Debra says that Christi was "action girl" and that even lying down on the floor for ten minutes to relax her breathing was a stretch. Back then if Debra had touched her she would have become rigid. Christi preferred to be in her own defined space. Now need supersedes preference.

Christi wouldn't have described herself as psychologically oriented before the accident, but that too is something she now needs. In the hospital the primary attention was focused on the physical crises: temperature dysregulation, shunt malfunctions, the physiological shock of the accident, and initial medical interventions. In the early days at home she needed physical rest and time to adjust to all the new care systems. Once stabilized we began the work of integrating emotion and thought, of constructing meaning out of her experience. First, she questioned the reason for the accident. Now that Christi has at least temporarily answered that, she turns her attention to her new identity.

The night before our next session I dream about changes in my relationships, house, and career. I see flashes of these in motion. Each is dislodged from its location and floats like an oil droplet on water. I don't have to work very hard to figure out the dream in concrete terms. My husband, Dudley, and I have been talking about remodeling our house. I'm continuing with graduate school, but I'm unsettled. I'm reluctantly beginning to admit that I'm not fitting in very well in the department. I miss being regularly engaged with Body Mind Centering training but I know I have to leave it on a back burner while I juggle a demanding psychotherapy practice and academic study. Deep inside I know there's cohesion, but on the surface they feel like disparate fragments.

In the morning I'm compelled to draw an image I see of the brain with a diagonal line from forehead to base of the occipital bones. It's a connect-the-dots line between the forebrain and the cerebellum. I think about myself and also about Christi. I wonder if Christi is letting go of an old image to experience herself as new.

Hours later I sit behind her with her head resting gently into my open hands. In my mind an image appears of a spider web bridge being built: the tiniest fibers link together the parts of the brain responsible for internal perceptions of organs, vestibular orientation, and eyes. The awareness arises that Christi is letting go of who she was in order to make room for who she's becoming. After the session Sue and I stand at the doorway and I tell her this. She responds by telling me that she's been reading about this very thing in Amy Mindell's book about coma.[vi] I'm gratified to hear validation that someone else has perceived not-fully-awake patients beginning the process of re-defining themselves. Simultaneously I'm glad I haven't read the book yet. Since I've never read this before I know I'm tracking direct experience and not projecting ideas or interpretations onto Christi. My body listening skills allow me to follow along in uncharted territory. It's been like discovering hidden meadows and waterfalls instead of reading about them in advance and then looking for them. Still, now that Christi, Sue and I have a baseline, I'm ready to begin reading more to look for resonance in other people's experiences and stimulate new ideas for our work.

It's not surprising that a dream I have about my own change process relates to what I'm seeing with Christi. It's a myth that doctors, rehab therapists, or practitioners of any kind are operating on pure reason without the bias of their own preferences or life stages. This myth reflects our culture's faulty belief in compartmentalized life. In reality, each practitioner brings her life story into the medical appointment or treatment session each time. Touching someone, with words or hands, isn't a one-way process: that's the old linear model of science. Scientists now understand that we mutually influence one another. Each moment is a spontaneous creation born of states bumping into one another in a constantly unfolding dance. How hungry we are, what we believe from past interactions, the emotions we're feeling, and the circumstance we find ourselves in, all combine to shape both perceptions and actions. As a psychotherapist I was carefully trained to recognize when I'm projecting my own experience or emotion onto the client. This has helped my confidence that I'm not doing that with Christi. Yet, what isn't talked about as much in psychotherapy or medical training is how our own life story can parallel that of the person we're working with. The synchronicity isn't in the specifics but in the universality of themes. I think this is why a dream I have of my own change process, where I'm betwixt and between changes in work and life roles, helps my ability to be aware of Christi.

Over the next week the subject of change comes up in several of my sessions with Christi. In one I sense her grieving for the self she fears she lost. I see Christi first from a long distance away, bent over like she's crying. Then, as if a camera has zoomed in, I see how the tears track slowly down her face. There's no sound, as if a mute button has been set.

Each morning I write questions and observations in my journal that no textbook can answer for me. "Layers of grief... With Christi the core self is more exposed, can't be covered over with behaviors that look good to the outside world, or even look good to the ego-created image. How is ego rebuilt in a comatose person? Has there been a melting or shattering of concepts and now she is unsure how to be out? Being in suspended time, what is she rebuilding?"

One summer in BMC school we had a class where we went around the circle of 85 people and each person spoke aloud one question. No answers were given. We just asked our questions aloud and learned by hearing the perspective inherent in each inquiry. We learned to "hold the question," much like a koan, rather than grasping for answers. I think I'm doing this same exercise in my morning journal. I'm just asking aloud the questions Christi is helping me formulate and holding them in an open palm.

On the final day of the week I have my hands on Christi's head again. Right away I notice a difference in volume. As I listen to the sensations I perceive in a single arising, "This is the place where tissue is not just functional but enlivened...The place where commitment to a course of life happens." I feel like I'm not just connecting with physical structure, like the walls of a building, but to Christi's individual life force merging with structure and becoming one and the same. For a moment I've been transported into a gigantic room. I instantly associate it with one of my favorite pictures of the fetus' developing brain, where neurons climb up the ladder of glial cells. They travel like the shoots of a vine eagerly sprinting to take their place in a spot of sunshine. The room I see in my mind's eye is cavernous, crisscrossing ladders of glial cells everywhere.[vii] From Christi's silent voice I hear a request, "Stand in this place to meet me- I am deciding how, if, I will fill the room." I wonder if "how" is a literal question and if she can re-knit the neurons meant to fill the space of her brain.

Perhaps the "if" part of the decision isn't as automatic as I assume because the next week Christi is silent under my touch. She seems more depressed, entrapped within a body that she can't move. Sue perceives something about the catheter so I ask Christi and get an anxious response, like "does this part of my body work," but not pain. Still, there's a sense of irritation. If you imagine throat to pelvic floor as a single tube there's a sensation that each end is plugged, like too much silt has built up and the river of energy can't flow.

My response to her retreat is to discount what I have to offer her. I feel like the service I provide her is so small in the presence of the magnitude of her suffering. I notice that when I discount the value of my offering, I'm tempted to turn away. It gives me an excuse to run. I provoke myself to flee with taunts. "I haven't done any good." "Christi doesn't like me anymore." During the hospital stay everyone, Christi included, was geared up for crisis, which has a powerful momentum. Now that Christi is home, rebuilding in a slow methodical manner, a more sustained energy is required. Without the passionate focus of crisis, the reality of suffering and frustration is more visible. I make myself slow down and sit quietly beside Christi. I ask myself if I have been respectful enough of the slowness of change. Maybe I'm siding with the impatience most of us feel when we're eager for change. Before the accident Christi was impatient in this way, but then invariably would settle into the hard work required. I implore myself to sit more quietly with the tug of war between infinitesimally slow rebuilding and the urge to quicken.

Sue and Terry have also been feeling Christi's retreat. The quality of the withdrawal is one familiar to Sue. It's as if Christi is a teenager again and has stormed off to her room, closing herself in until she sorts something out on her own. Part of Sue's exquisite attunement to Christi is knowing which of her roles needs to come to the front. In today's session it is Mom. This changes my role as well, into psychotherapist. The three of us sit together in a mini-circle, our knees almost touching. Christi is in her wheelchair, head back and eyes closed, but we can tell she's listening because we perceive a quality of substance. If we could touch the quality it would be the density of a squeeze ball.

Sue explains to Christi that she and Terry have talked. They are committed to helping her recover, "but we have to go forward even if you're going to be stalled." A burst of energy blooms in Christi's cheeks. If she had more control over her eye movements I imagine they would look intently and inquisitively at her Mom. Sue notes this and continues, "We need you to be the one who sets goals and commits to doing the work. We can't do that for you."

Because of Christi's retreat Sue and Terry have been talking with Dr. Seagraves about trying antidepressants. Dr. Seagraves, who drops by at least once a week when he's on his way home from work, has noticed the family's decline from optimism to weary concern. Sue doesn't mention this option to Christi because she doesn't want her to hear it as something wrong with her. Instead Sue and Terry prefer to try this talk first and wait at least a few more days before making the final decision.

I tease Christi that her parents are giving her the "tough love" speech. The three of us pause, as if the words have been laid down on a table between us and we're considering them. Then Christi becomes more deeply quiet, like she has taken this information into the center of an open flower and the petals are folding in to cover it over, like spring flowers do at night.

Throughout this story I have reported to you times when Christi is more there or less there. Although it may sound slightly odd, it's probably also familiar. We all have times when we're talking to a friend and it feels like they're nodding and looking at us, but "not really there" or conversely, "really there." Medical personnel also use this terminology, but it's not detailed in their charts. Dr. Seagraves comments that he notices times when Christi seems more or less present, but he can't define it, saying, "It's just a sense." Having this sense and using it to develop rapport with patients is part of what makes medicine an art as well as a science.

Reading subtleties of body language without being aware we're doing so is built into us as social beings. One of my favorite science experiments illustrates this. It was done in the Papoušek lab in Germany.[viii] Parents were given four line drawings of an infant and asked what action they would take based on the picture. They could choose playing, feeding, soothing, or putting the baby to sleep. The majority of parents picked the right action for each image with little hesitation. Then they were asked what made them decide. Usually they responded, "The expression on the baby's face." What they didn't know was that each drawing, each facial expression, was identical. The only thing different was the shape and position of the baby's hands.

If you were writing this story you might have different ways you describe what you feel or see when someone's really with you. You'd find your own unique ways to say what it's like for you. Just like the parents in the Papousek lab, our non-conscious attunement allows us to respond appropriately in a situation even if our descriptions of how and why are incorrect. The kind of in-sync communication experiences I'm telling you about with Christi are within all our capacities. It's just that as a culture we don't have adequate language for them. And, lacking words, we aren't encouraged to become more conscious of attunement information and therefore become more skillful with it.

If you begin to pay attention to nonverbal communication you'll notice that when your friend has high urgency or need you are more attuned. This is one reason Sue and I can "hear" Christi so well, at least intermittently. Christi needs us to hear her because she can't use traditional means. Sue is falling back on the kind of intimate "conversation" she had when Christi was an infant and she knew if food or sleep was required. She's relying on the attunement she used even when Christi was away at college and she followed her impulse to call on just the day Christi was discouraged by a class or had a spat with a friend.

Sue's heart-to-heart talk about goals seems to be the boost Christi needs. On that same afternoon she participates more in her physical therapy session. The therapists report her "being there" when her legs and arms are stretched. Then, at 2 AM when Sue goes into Christi's room to roll her onto her side, she finds Christi awake. Sue senses an invitation to come closer so she lies down next to Christi. After a few moments of companionable rest she perceives the question from Christi, "What goals are possible?" Pause. Sue hears question and lament. "Will I be able to drive? Go to school? Have sex? Sing?"

The seriousness with which Sue readies to answer the string of "will I..." is broken with the last question. She gets the joke and chuckles. "Well, I wouldn't want to rule anything out, but that might be asking a lot." Christi's musical ability was limited to playing an instrument, not carrying a tune. Then serious, Sue continues, "I can promise you we'll work toward any goal you want. No one knows what's possible or what the limits are. It's up to you to decide what you're willing to work towards."

The next day Christi seems more eager for her various therapy sessions. Everyone on the treatment team, without knowing this exchange took place between Sue and Christi, starts talking about goals that can be achieved by Christi's birthday. The speech therapist will keep working on swallowing to help Christi towards a goal of eating frozen yogurt. Debra and I keep working on modulating incoming sensory stimuli so Christi can participate in her party without becoming overwhelmed and cope by retreating deeper inward. Mary, the physical therapist, will work on Christi's sitting posture in the wheelchair. We all will emphasize balancing her arms in her lap instead of contracting them, freeing that bound energy for party stamina.

Mary's relationship with Christi is like that of a high school coach. She teases Christi to motivate her to meet a challenge. Mary always balances on the divide between celebrating what's just been accomplished and what comes next. She's like the track coach who yells an enthusiastic, "way to go," while reaching in to raise the high jump bar another half inch.

Christi's 19th birthday arrives just three months after the accident. It's a sunny August day so everyone gathers on the screened-in porch. I can pick out her old friends from work because they sport short spiky hairstyles from shaving their heads as an act of solidarity with Christi. A three-foot Happy Birthday banner in red and blue hangs over the windows that look into the garden. Christi sits in a place of honor beneath it. Today she's dressed in matching top and shorts, a shade of yellow bright enough to distract from the tape over her trach hole and the plastic body frame helping to hold her upright. Christi's met her goal of relaxing her right arm completely so it rests in her lap. Her left hand curls inward, hovering just over her heart. Her fingers are slightly uncurled, showing iridescent blue polish on her nails, a few shades darker than the eyeshadow she wears. A dozen friends have come. They fill the room with laughter and stories from their first year in college.

Sue and Terry are all smiles, the kind that crinkles the corners of their eyes. It's fun to be in celebration with friends instead of bonding through the intensity of hospitalization. The party that "would have been" is happening, albeit with modifications. Christi doesn't have the ability to smile yet so her face stays porcelain-doll-smooth, but I can see concentrated attention in the rims of her eyes, almost as if the bones are reaching out to connect. She can't swallow whole foods, but she's become accustomed to little bits on the end of a Q-tip. This is how she enjoys the flavor of her ice cream cake and the pizza.

Later that night Christi pulls the gastro tube out of the insertion into her stomach and Dr. Seagraves must come to the house to replace it. It's almost as if she's expressing her wish for independence. Dr. Seagraves and her parents don't admonish her for pulling it out. They commiserate with her discomfort and desire for freedom. His house call finishes with a piece of birthday cake, an unspoken acknowledgment that the direction they've chosen is leading where they'd hoped. They are celebrating the miracle that Christi is alive and breathing on her own.

A few nights later there's a second party with three friends from college and her best friend from high school, Holly. It's a sleepover party so they stay up late telling Christi stories of what they'll do together when she comes back to college. These are wishes strewn like seeds in a meadow, an invitation of what might grow there.

Working towards Christi's goals for her party has enlivened everyone with more optimism. Since Christi is increasing the length of time she is awake and aware of her environment, Sue and Terry start discussing the pros and cons of beginning structured inpatient rehab either in Missoula or at a regional specialty center in Denver. They bring the idea up to Christi, describing it as like what she would be doing if she were going back to college. In response Christi makes an exaggerated exhale noise and rotates her right hand palm up, a gesture her parents translate as an enthusiastic yes.

At the end of the month Sue writes to their network with news from the last month:

Aug. 30th

...*As of last week we have increased the amount of therapy to up to 6 hours a day five days a week. So, needless to say, our house is very busy. We anticipate that within the next few weeks she will be ready for the more intensive rehabilitation program. We have decided that she and I will go to Denver to the Craig Institute for rehabilitation. It is anticipated that we will be there for two to three months. She will be in the intensive inpatient program and I will be able to live in an apartment that is on the same campus. Terry will come to visit us every once in awhile. This was a tough decision but we decided that we wanted to give Christi every opportunity we could because she fought so hard to survive. At this point we are still not certain what she has lost or will have to regain as a result of the accident. Time will tell. We have gotten her contacts which made a tremendous difference in her ability to see. We had been putting on her glasses, but it appeared that it caused her more problems.*

Needless to say I will not be teaching this semester. I have postponed my classes until Spring semester.

I again want to thank everyone for the cards, calls, prayers etc. They have helped us through this very long and difficult time. It is my hope to write about this experience. I will be putting the final touches on all of my projects before I leave. Thank-you and I will keep in touch.

Sincerely Sue Forest

The next few weeks are a mixture of status quo and anticipation. In her sessions, Debra focuses on the qualities within muscle fibers. She notes a limitation on proprioceptive feedback, like a record that's skipping instead of sequencing into the next line of the song. Whatever will allow Christi to perceive where her body's parts are, and how they're moving, hasn't come back on line. In keeping with the principle that we move first and then record the movement patterns in the nervous system, the caregivers religiously help Christi adhere to a daily routine of stretches. The movements also keep her muscles limber and strong for when she will move on her own.

Sue asks Christi to begin to work on a signal for yes and no. "Perhaps," Sue nudges, "since Christi is ambidextrous she can use each thumb." But Christi is mulishly resistant. It seems her plan is to talk and she isn't interested in the interim step of gesture.

It's possible that Christi's lack of enthusiasm for developing signals is because she's waiting to see what Craig will offer her for communication. When her friends come to visit she stays alert and engaged. She tries to keep her eyes open, even if only half way. In my sessions with her, however, she is passive. She seems willing to receive, but not to exert effort. There isn't much of the intimacy we had when there was a lot of "talking." I wonder what she'll remember of, or from, me when she wakes up fully. My inner dialogue is, "I'm too old for Christi. I belong to her mother's generation." I recognize this as my idiosyncratic defense against being hurt by the distance I feel from her after so much intimacy. If a photograph could show the shape of our energies the viewer would see me leaning intently toward her, but Christi leaving the frame, toward what is happening next. With limited resources for attention she can't do both.

Despite my perception of distance we keep working. The nonconscious water state through which we converse is becoming less distinct under my touch as she nears coming completely out of coma. I begin making more sounds as I move her arm. They are spontaneous nonsensical or vowel sounds that resonate with the organs and glands of the deep belly. I turn words I want to say into sound shapes. We leave the deep fluid dialogue of the ocean floor and practice sound and movement currents in the shapes of waves.

Christi needs a swallowing evaluation and Sue intuits that Christi's nervous about it for three reasons. First, the idea of swallowing anything on demand provokes anxiety because she can only coordinate her mouth and throat when she's totally relaxed. Second, the very idea of performance evaluation brings tension. This isn't new. In flute lessons Debra worked endlessly with Christi on relaxing before a recital so that she could play as well in performance as she did in practice. And finally, Christi doesn't have much ease with the speech therapist doing the evaluation. They've met several times but are awkward together, like dance partners who can't get the flow of leading and following so their toes keep bumping.

Sue, Christi and I work together to rehearse what Sue and Christi will do as a team to help Christi stay relaxed. Since we have been working together for three months we have a specific language of touch and words we use. Our technique is similar to how an athlete might use visualization before a race. I begin by describing the nervousness she'll likely experience as a slightly floating feeling, as if she were up in the air, humming like electrical wires. Then we conjure images and sensations of preparation and ease such as: floating on a raft like she did before and after surgeries; the compact, pliable, water balloon sensation of organs in the pelvis; and inner ears registering gravity. Sue stands beside Christi's wheelchair, using deep breaths to solidify her awareness of ease and relaxed support, knowing that if she fully supports herself she'll be able to extend that calm to Christi. Christi, feeling the comforting touchstone of Sue's presence, can focus all her energy on using her mind to invite the fluid motions that will allow her muscles to perform to their capability. For both of them the goal is to yield into action instead of tripping over her performance anxiety.

When the swallowing evaluation finally happens the result is cautiously optimistic. But for Christi and Sue there's celebration because they got the result they most wanted. Christi stayed mostly relaxed and alert. And they get even more good news. A date is set to go to Craig in just five days.

> "We think we think with our brain. But in doing its job of creating consciousness, the brain actually relies on a vast network of systems and is connected to everything — eyes, ears, skin, limbs, nerves. The key word is 'processing.' We actually think with our whole body. The brain, however, takes what is shipped to it, crunches the data, and sends back instructions. It converts, it generates results. Or, when damaged, does not."
>
> Floyd Skloot, "Gray Area: Thinking with a Damaged Brain,"
> *In the Shadow of Memory*

Christi and Sue

For the second year in a row the Forests start September by packing. Last year it was with excited anticipation for college. This year it's for rehab. The timing is perfect because as Christi's friends come over to say good-bye before they return to school, they are spared their awkward guilt at leaving her behind. Sue is buoyantly optimistic because Christi is setting off on her own adventure as well. Sue believes that Christi is relieved to escape the undertow of discouragement, and that she understands that rehab is a sign of the progress she's made.

Unlike college, rehab includes Sue. Sue has a small apartment adjacent to Craig Hospital that gives her private living space in Denver. Sue and Terry juggle caregiving routines with scurrying about town on seemingly endless errands to get everything ready. Sue wants to leave the house well stocked for Terry who will stay home, carrying the steady beat of work. Sue can't quite imagine what her role will be at rehab so she's packing work supplies in case her afternoons or evenings allow time to prepare next semester's classes. Medical files need to be transferred down to Craig. Instead of a single phone call, the task requires numerous phone calls and paperwork that consume hours out of Sue's day. She checks and double-checks everything.

In our last session before Christi and Sue leave for Denver I feel excited anticipation, like I'm seeing a niece off to a semester in college or a trip to a foreign country. When it's time to say goodbye Christi tries to express something out loud to me but I can't understand the meaning. After all the "talking" we've done over these past three months I'm disappointed and apologetic that I don't know what she says. That night, though, I dream that she asks me out loud if I want to dance.

A private transport company for which Terry once did engineering work hears about their need to get to Denver and graciously offers to fly the Forests down on the company plane. Sue and Terry are happy for the offer, although when they arrive at the airport, they're dismayed. The plane's crew isn't prepared for a wheelchair bound patient needing significant assistance. And the seat arrangements don't accommodate a wheelchair either. After a few disjointed steps everyone puts their creativity into gear and they figure out adaptations. They take off thinking they've mastered their obstacles for the day; not knowing it's just the beginning.

The plan is that the flight crew will stay on the ground in Denver long enough to allow Terry to get Sue and Christi situated at Craig. Then Terry will return to the plane to fly home to Missoula. Each step goes awry. Once on the ground they can't locate the handicap van service contracted to take them to Craig. It takes an hour and several radio and phone calls to make the connection. On the ride to Craig they recollect their optimism, assuming they'll speedily breeze through admissions and get settled. However, they arrive at Craig in the middle of a staff shift change. No one appears to have any records indicating their arrival is expected.

At first Sue and Terry sit patiently, assuring one another resolution is imminent. Then they begin pacing, anxiously and helplessly, watching the clock. Christi's eyes are tightly closed. Fatigue and sensory over-stimulation combine to send her into a descent further and further down a deep burrow inside herself, closing her off from the uncertainty around her. Terry's tension is the worst because he also feels responsibility to the plane's crew waiting at the airport. It's not their way to get angry and bully their way into a resolution, so they wait in silence. Privately though, Sue and Terry are each disturbed, their confidence shaken. After all the hours on the phone making arrangements and transmitting medical records to make sure everything is ready, it seems impossible that no one knows who they are or why they're here. Finally, Terry can't keep the plane waiting any longer. Reluctantly he leaves Sue and Christi sitting in the waiting room.

They wait two more hours for a room to be found for the night. By the time Sue gets to bed she's exhausted past the ability to sleep and lies awake. Her mind replays the day's frustrations, each loop slowly dissolving dammed up tension, until the faint trail of optimistic faith in the decision to come to Craig begins to appear again and sleep comes. In the morning Sue is promptly greeted by their assigned staff who are prepared, however belatedly, to welcome them.

The first order of business is to meet Christi's new team of speech, occupational and physical therapists for intake evaluations. Christi's new team doesn't meet her at her best. The jarring travel schedule and new surroundings throw her delicate internal balance off. Her muscle tone is tighter and her ability to maintain attention is decreased, a regression to where she was at the end of July. At home Christi and Sue relied on caregivers they knew who had grown comfortable with the subtleties of communication. But here at Craig the combination of the regression and yet-to-be relationships prevents Christi from showing her full capabilities. The medical team focuses their concern on the Dilantin she takes to prevent seizures, assuming it is making her too drowsy. Since she hasn't had seizures they immediately begin to incrementally decrease the dosage.

In Missoula Christi was working up to five hours a day in combined complementary and allopathic therapies. At Craig, however, the system requires a formal process of assessment and treatment planning. They begin with only a few hours each day. They will gradually add on extras, like time in the pool. This means Christi initially has very long periods of resting in her room. In an effort to keep their spirits up Sue fills excess time with her own supplementary "therapy." For instance, she buys three bottles of differently scented body cream. "Do you want pear, vanilla, or rose," she asks, leaning in and slowly passing each bottle beneath Christi's nose as she says the name. Then she repeats herself, "pear, vanilla, rose," watching for the barely perceptible shift of Christi's head toward the bottle of choice. This routine is repeated morning and evening. Sometimes Christi makes the choice obvious by wrinkling her nose "no" for the ones she doesn't want.

Prior to the accident, Sue and Christi, both independent and energetic by nature, rarely spent their free time idly. Sue reasons that healthy stimulation is as good as bed rest. They begin exploring the hospital grounds and the surrounding area. Since Craig is a dedicated rehab hospital everything is designed for four-season accessibility. Sue wheels Christi down long corridors to find the pool and gym. They stop to watch a loud game of wheelchair basketball. They crisscross the skywalks between Craig and Swedish Hospital. It's beautiful early fall weather, most days hitting the 70s, so they go out into the gardens that frame both sides of their building. Surrounding the hospital are wheelchair friendly neighborhoods and businesses. Following whatever whim strikes, they go in and out of stores, meandering up and down aisles, Sue providing running commentary. Sometimes they find a new trinket to bring back to Christi's room for decoration. Eventually they find their way to Starbucks where they sit at an outside table, Christi's wheelchair pulled in diagonally to Sue, while Sue slowly sips her favorite cappuccino. It's comfortable to be in a location where someone in a wheelchair isn't such a novelty that they're subjected to sideways staring from other customers. These outings also give Sue the added benefit of exercise, especially the big push uphill from the stores back to the hospital.

Another reason they leave Christi's room is Angelina,[ix] Christi's roommate. Angelina is cause for a lot of sadness for Christi and Sue. She is a young girl, just out of fifth grade. As she was running into the street after an errant kickball she was hit by a truck. Angelina's parents were told not to expect her to ever regain intelligence or control over her emotions. They "should consider the child they once knew dead." No one helped them imagine a way to incorporate the new Angelina into their lives. They limit their visits to once a month, easing into the transition to long-term nursing home care. Angelina is independently mobile. She can crawl and climb out of her bed. To prevent injury the staff builds a large octagonal "playpen" out of mats so Angelina can move around during the long stretches of time she spends alone. Maybe once, maybe six times a day, Angelina wails. No one knows for sure whether it's loneliness, frustration, physical pain or unmet need. A few of the nurses can skillfully calm her and refocus her on something to play with. The aides who can't make a connection speak to Angelina in scolding voices, leaving her to wail until she succumbs to fatigue. Sometimes at Angelina's sounds of unrequited distress Christi opens her eyes wide. Sue believes she is imploring her to find an answer. Sue goes to Angelina and speaks in soft tones, her eyes searching out Angelina's as if to say over and over, "I see you in there."

On the same day I decide to call Sue I come home from University classes to find she has left me a message. "We had rough news about Christi yesterday. If you have time tonight can you call?" Her voice is almost a monotone, as if its evenness is keeping her steady.

When we talk Sue speaks slowly, measuring words. The gist is that Christi continues to have a hard time adjusting to the treatment setting. It's a very medical model. The speech therapist has a good personal connection with her, but the PT and OT, while technically good are not interpersonally sensitive to Christi's nuances and she performs poorly for them. Because Christi's brain injury was diffuse the doctor says it is uncertain how much damage was done, but it's highly possible she may never walk or talk again. They expect she'll be awake and they can find some communication mode. Because recovery is an imperfect science the doctor leaves the door open a crack with the caveat that he could be wrong. No one really knows the limits or possibilities for an individual patient. Later when Christi and Sue are alone Sue perceives Christi's intention as, "I'm going to prove him wrong." Sue is pulled taut between her sense of Christi's determination and the medical prognosis.

Sue and Terry hope that once Christi settles more, the treatment team will start to see the kinds of progress they saw over the summer in Missoula. Sue tells me that she and Terry believe that the Body Mind Centering work Debra and I did with Christi helped her build a foundation that supported all the other treatments. She asks how to get that in Denver, thinking that they'll add it in on their own time. In the hospital's parent support group they are told that 80% of families will choose to use some form of complementary and alternative medicine, yet the assumption is that this will occur at some other point since no such treatments are offered within the facility. On behalf of Sue and Terry I start calling around to see if there's a local BMC practitioner who will visit them. I long to go see her myself.

Meanwhile, Terry goes down for a weekend and reports their progress to everyone waiting at home for news.

> *Christi and Sue are working very hard at the Craig hospital. Their days start at 6 AM and go until 9:30 or 10 each day. On my recent trip to see Christi and Sue I found out just how hard it is to be "all things" to Christi every minute of the day. I was exhausted after only 3 days. Christi is looking good. Her hair is growing fast and must be almost 2 inches long now. Her eyes have a sparkle in them when she hears or recognizes someone. She is also trying to make more sounds and is eating up to a half cup of food per day. Sue is working with Christi both during the therapies and in between them. The amount of therapies has increased and Christi now gets to get into the pool 2 or 3 times per week. The medicine changes are being done slowly to be cautious. Christi does not seem to be quite as far along as she was here in Missoula. It is probably due to the changing environment and the medicine changes. She works so hard and does not seem to get too discouraged when things don't go as she wants. It is very clear to Sue that Christi understands most of the commands but at this time just can't do them. We are finding out that time is very slow. The doctors and therapists are working hard to allow Christi to progress and push her to go a little more each session. It is clear that the time the rehabilitation will take is years not months as we had hoped. We continue to be optimistic that Christi will continue to progress and*

many great things are ahead of her in the future. Your continued support of Christi and our family is very much appreciated. Terry, Sue and Christi Ana

Terry's e-mail conveys the shift that's occurring within the family- - a vision of years, not months, that they will be on the rehabilitation track. What he doesn't share is the heartbreaking conversation he has with the doctor as he leaves for the airport. Terry, who excels in the role of logistical problem solver, tells the doctor they're considering ordering a wheelchair accessible van. The doctor replies in a knife sharp tone, "Little hope exists for Christi to ever hold her head up, much less do anything productive. You'd be ridiculous to not get a van since you'll need it the rest of your lives." He moves away quickly, before Terry can muster a response.

Terry is shaken by the doctor's condemnation and calls Sue before he boards the plane. Going home to an empty house with the dismal exchange reverberating in his mind feels nearly unbearable after how far they've come. Their talk is short, but to the point. They know they need to find a balance point amidst the unpredictability of recovery, their hopes, and the medical pessimism. But the doctor's blanket dismissal strikes hard, reminiscent of the attitude in Coeur d'Alene. Hearing one another's voices solidifies Sue and Terry as a team again. They feel able to tackle whatever obstacles arise. They plan for Sue to talk to the doctor, but before she has the opportunity to follow up, he removes himself from their case. Another staff member confides in Sue that the doctor has a daughter Christi's age and being with the family is, "frankly, too traumatic" for him.

As Sue sits beside Christi's bed in the late evenings, watching her sleep, the poison of the doctor's pessimism arises as a shadow she fights to keep from falling under. On one of these nights a tech on the late night shift, one she hasn't met before, comes in to make the night check. He's a young man, in his late twenties, gentle in his approach to Christi, looking into her face as he lifts her arm to take her pulse. As he tends to her he glances sideways at Sue and shares that he himself had a severe head injury in his early twenties. His parents were so important to him, he says. One of them was always there to advocate for his continuing treatment. Then looking directly into Sue's eyes he says, "It is so important that you remain with her. It will give her strength. Even when you don't think it will matter - it does matter - she may not be able to tell you or show you right now but you will know."

This conversation is heartening to Sue. It replenishes her hope. She goes back to her own apartment and sleeps deeply. For the first time since coming to Craig she wakes rested. She wants to thank the young man for his words of encouragement so asks one of the day staff for his name. She's met with a questioning stare. "We don't have anyone by that description working here." Sue never sees the young man again. Many years later she still recalls his face and tender manner clearly. "He was an angel I needed. He let me know that as moms we are necessary and that healing happens when we are involved and there for our children."

Sue and I talk on the phone several times a week. I can't find any BMC practitioners based in Colorado to work with Christi. I can hear Sue's fatigue growing. She sounds like a tape player being drained of power, the voice speed beginning to drag. Despite her determination to adhere to optimism, it's hard without outward signs that Christi is engaging more fully in the treatments. I offer to come see them myself and, after a brief hesitation, Sue gratefully accepts. We plan for the next weekend, just before even more intensive therapy services are scheduled to start, hoping the familiarity of someone from Missoula helps.

I arrive in Denver Friday evening, place my hand on Christi in greeting, and barely take it off until I leave on Sunday night. I step into Sue and Christi's routines as if we haven't had a break from one another. We hang out in her room and meander around the hospital. Everything is decorated for Halloween. On the elevator there are posters hung up inviting everyone to the party next weekend, part of the strategy I suppose of reclaiming life. Unreasonably agitated I turn away from the posters. I think it's a failure of imagination on my part, or a previously unseen prejudice about disability, but I can't imagine the silliness or ghoulishness of dressing up in costume, playing with the masquerade of identity, within the somber business of rehab.

Beneath my hand Christi seems to be in neutral, suspended between high tide and low, a dense texture more like sludge than substance. I don't have to go way down to find her, but there's also no quality of drive like I often felt at home. Sue has been intuiting Christi's emotional state as defeat. Although I hear no exact words across the quiet expanse, the meaning appears to me like a single cloud on the horizon, "Help me remember the states, the pathways. I'm stuck."

Throughout the weekend we travel through a series of tiny swells of action or response. Each rise and fall is like a meditation bell ringing out the call for attention to "now, just this one instant" without obvious connection to past or future. If we're on an ocean voyage we're definitely far out to sea without any landmarks visible. Although there's little sense of where we're going and no tangible sense of forward progress, it also feels like steady riding, as if some unseen knowledgeable skipper has set the coordinates. In Christi, even more than Sue, there's a quality of surrender to the reality of a healing process that takes time.

Because it's the weekend Christi doesn't have any treatment sessions scheduled. And because Sue has established herself as such a competent caregiver needing little assistance from staff, we go through the usual routines of daily life nearly completely on our own. We wheel Christi down to Starbucks and she eats bites of a Frappuccino while Sue and I drink lattes, all three of us soaking up the warmth of the sun. We eat dinners from the cafeteria or take-out from the local Vietnamese restaurant. Christi sits with us, a tiny taste of pureed food in her mouth, while a liquid bag of nutrients drips a meal into the gastro tube. She "eats" this way so that her body will continue to register the clock of mealtimes, the taste of a food in her mouth, and the association of swallowing with nutrition.

At dinner on the second night Sue recounts how last week she was wishing she could talk to the hospital's psychologist about the rightness of pursuing treatment when he appeared and extended an invitation to talk. Sue told him about the Coeur d'Alene medical team's pressure to surrender Christi and allow her organs to be taken to save someone else. She told him about the conviction she and Terry felt that Christi made a choice to stay. Once she spoke the words out loud she felt her keen longing for validation. He offered just the understanding needed. When he's called into a bedside decision process he too tries to "get a feel" from patients about their wishes, knowing the feeling can come without sound or gesture. He reminded Sue that there are many on her treatment team who do understand the mystery of spirit taking place behind or within the medical story. The psychologist's understanding words served as a sleeping pill for another good night's sleep.

After our dinner hour we sneak into the exercise room to use one of the elevated mats. One of the nurses who befriended Christi and Sue mentions, casually looking away as she does so, that they won't be looking into that room after eight o'clock. Even if we'd been legal, we wouldn't have wanted anyone to see our clumsiness that night.

Sue is used to moving Christi from her wheelchair to a high bed, but not to something that requires a drop down to knee height. And I'm completely unfamiliar with the task. Sue stands at Christi's feet, draping her over her shoulder and lifting forward and up into a momentary stand position. I hold Christi's head and we pivot toward the mat. Unfortunately we're so focused on getting her up and not letting her fall that we don't notice that we've positioned ourselves between her and the mat. We end up lowering ourselves down with Christi balanced on top of us. Sue scoots out first and moves Christi's hips away from the edge and then I squeeze out, lowering Christi's head down to the mat. Once we're all safe we're free to start laughing about how ridiculous the scene is. Christi opens her eyes wide by lifting her eyebrows in high arches and looks at us with the expression of a teen appalled by middle-aged silliness. Amazingly she doesn't tense up at all. Maybe she's laughing at us inside and that keeps her loose.

We spend three quarters of an hour doing the stretches Christi practiced at home. We remind her through our touch to use the fluids of her body to pump the action of muscles. Our prompts are squishing massages, like putting our hands in wet moss and squeezing the water out through our fingers. We move her arms out to the side and up and away from the mat, each time stretching her a little bit further. We guide her legs into knee flexion. Finally, we practice a gentle roll side to side, shifting the organs like rolling water balloons. By the end it's as if Christi has nestled into a comfortable chair in the corner of her bedroom, relaxed because she's home, with the kind of quiet attention usually reserved for reading a book. Then Sue begins talking to her about goals, reminding her of the intentions they set before coming to Craig. Christi's face becomes more expressive. Her eyes move up and down quickly, as if she's searching a scrambled puzzle without finding any clues for a solution and so moving even more urgently. Her face appears angry. She makes a fist and exhales forcefully. Sue and I say in unison "ahhh." It's the kind of acknowledgment you make to a friend who has been holding something back and finally blurts it out. In the silence that follows, determination begins seeping back into Christi's core.

While I'm visiting, Sue takes the opportunity for some R&R. She does errands without focusing on time, knowing I'm attending to Christi. She goes out to brunch with her brother, who drives up from his home an hour to the south, and lingers over the meal. Meanwhile Christi and I spend long hours out in the gardens. I push her along curlicue paths, humming nonsensical songs with a repetitious beat. We stop beside a bench and I rest my hand on her arm, listening as I would to the sounds of a creek. I feel her energy arc in wide sweeps beyond her body, defining the space around her in lines like rake marks on the sand of a Zen garden. I attend her wordless story, silently resting into the center of my own deep places until I feel her relax, quiet again within the boundary of her skin. Later I position us alongside the fountain, within a square of late afternoon sun, and I place my hands on her skull to hear those sounds too. I feel pulses with no discernible pattern, sometimes a single beat, sometimes a rapid percussive tapping. Eventually a soft movement comes, the slow continuous movements of water in a pond.

Although I hear the chorus of body systems, Christi and I have no real "conversations" during the visit. Once though, she surprises me with an emotional outburst. Her face ever so slightly scrunches and the sound of a sob escapes her mouth. I can't hear if there's a story that goes with it or if it's a discharge of a previous cry. It travels up from her belly through her throat and face. And like a wave that crashes against the rocks, the particles of energy burst apart, flying up into the air. The space around her becomes infused with a deep sorrow. I wonder if she's just opened a pathway from inner experience to outer expression that can be built on for more expression.

On the last evening of my visit we spend nearly an hour in the shower room.* We gingerly transfer Christi to a special wheelchair made of plastic, Swiss cheese drain holes all around, and soak her head-to-toe. Even the shower is rehab for Christi as she learns to calm her initial startle response when the water slides across the surface of her skin. Like with the lotions, Sue pauses and encourages Christi to smell the soap and then the shampoo. The best part is the ending. We pull large absorbent towels from the heated closet and pat her down. Then we wrap a second warm set around her, a cocoon keeping her protected while we head back to her room. Christi hasn't relaxed completely but the warmth softens at least the surface layers of tension. I look at Sue guiding Christi's wheelchair, her face tender and efficient, and worry about her becoming completely exhausted. I know she ran at a super pace in her life before the accident so perhaps it's in her temperament. But I wish they had a spa on site for parents, so they too could be wrapped in heated towels and drift off to sleep.

---

* The shower routine was a point of early disagreement between Sue and the treatment staff. Sue requested Christi's showers to always be with a female attendant. The staff said that Christi isn't perceptive enough to know the difference, but Sue insisted, saying Christi wouldn't be comfortable with a young man nearly her own age, and "yes, she does know who's there."

By the time I fly home to Missoula the next day Christi has begun day one of the full rehab schedule. I hear later that night that it was finally the kind of day they were looking for. Christi initiated rolling to her side, just as we had practiced on the mat on Saturday night. Then she kicked and moved her arms in the swimming pool. And, upon request, without delay, she blew out a short stream of air for the speech therapist. Sue's voice is buoyant when she calls me. They're on their way again.

In Western culture we minimize the importance of body sounds. If they don't translate into motion or words we're content to leave them in the realm of "unconscious." Like the night sounds of an old house – the creak of walls or hiss of furnace – we usually have them tuned out, but if by chance they catch our attention we quickly label them of little significance – just sounds. However, when we approach consciousness as a multi-faceted whole, whether within our attention or not, the sounds of the body become their own language independent of whether or not we can decipher them.

In the past twenty years scientists have been giving us new information about how the brain receives the language of body and turns it into action. Particularly fascinating is the work of Benjamin Libet, a physiology researcher who has studied consciousness extensively. Through a series of elegantly designed experiments he found that when we "decide" to make a voluntary movement, like lifting a finger, we're already 400 milliseconds behind what our unconscious has set in motion based on sensory information received from our bodies. We receive body cues that effectively signal finger awareness, and then we "decide" to move our finger. Awareness, what we often think of as our consciousness, doesn't come until the cortical activation of the signals reaches a duration of .5 seconds. After a lifetime of study Libet concludes that "cognitive, imaginative, and decision making processes all can proceed unconsciously, often more creatively than in conscious functions…(They are) related to conscious mental functions but lack the added phenomena of awareness."[x]

So when I say I listen to the chorus of Christi's body systems I mean it like being aware of the sounds of the old house or the bubbling up of sensations that haven't formed themselves into action or awareness. When I become frustrated by not understanding what they mean I remind myself to stay mindful, patient, lest I fall into the clinical error of making up my own stories, falsely believing them to be Christi's. The normal sounds of the walls of the house settling onto the foundation could in my imagination become monsters in the basement. Or I could try to push Christi into prematurely deciphering an explanation. Instead, I intentionally trust that it's enough to hear her undercurrent of non-conscious rumblings, and when the volume of cortical activation increases to the level of awareness, I trust that I'll hear the words or story that Christi needs me to know even though she can't express them in verbal language.

The next few weeks are scattered with days that bounce between the reignited enthusiasm and discouragement. On days when Christi is slow to respond in therapy Sue feels caught between Christi's lethargy and the therapists' subtle frowns and tries to be cheerleader for both Christi and the therapists. No one takes the role of keeping Sue's spirits up even though she too needs the support. Even when family members visit on weekends, Sue focuses on making sure they stay optimistic. She can see the unspoken worry in their eyes when they see that Christi isn't "popping out." Sue begins to redefine the goals for the stay at Craig to changing medications and learning therapy techniques, and starts imagining the organization of outpatient treatments. And then, for no discernible reason there's a shift, and good days recharge everyone. The treatment team adds electrical stimulation to the muscles of Christi's neck and she responds positively. She meets with the neurologist and can move her arm a little when requested to do so. Christi continues to be able to sequence the roll onto her side and appears to love getting in the pool. On these days it's momentum rather than uphill effort that carries them forward.

One evening while Sue is massaging body lotion onto Christi's belly Christi suddenly arches and grips her abdomen. Sue has a momentary flash of the seat belt cutting into Christi, more vivid than the accident memories we witnessed several months earlier. Sue factually has known that the seat belt severed Christi's mesentery artery. This injury was what caused the loss of nearly three quarters of her blood. With this flash, however, Sue senses the terror this engendered. It's no longer an event viewed from a safe mental distance. The momentary flash passes quickly. As horrific as it is for Sue to know her daughter's anguish she reminds herself that being here now is providing an exceptional opportunity. Christi was alone in the accident, but in reliving it she has her mother's hand holding hers. And Sue can actively help dissipate the trauma, much like she did when Christi's temperature needed regulation, by letting it flow through her system as if she were a grounding wire. In the most helpless of all parenting situations, she has the opportunity to act.

Sue tells me about this flashback because she doesn't know how to talk to the treatment staff about it. Even though they acknowledge that integrative body-mind approaches can be valuable, no one has mentioned trauma memory. Sue is reluctant to bring it up. She doesn't want to harm her credibility with them since she and Christi are dependent on their assistance.

There are many different theories about where and how our body tissues "hold on" to traumatic incidents. From Sue's description, however, I pick the theory that focuses on the role of nerves. The idea is that a sensory nerve carrying a signal essentially hits a circuit breaker, at the level of the spine or brain, and the unreleased charge freezes up the nerve, blocking its ability to transmit other sensory information.[xi] One way to work with this is to very lightly place the fingertips of one hand next to the spine and place the fingertips of the other hand on the front side of the body directly opposite. It's as if you're imagining your fingertips inviting a current - in the back and out the front - to complete itself. I explain this simple technique to Sue. I know she can't do any harm with it and I don't want to leave her unsupported since her intuition and sensitivity mean that she's vulnerable to experiencing more flashbacks. Fortunately, the idea to work with nerves fits because a few days later Sue calls to say that she tried it when Christi again tensed her abdomen as if she'd been startled. Sue felt the suspended freeze quality and waited until there was a letting go, kind of like a tiny ice jam dislodging. Christi moaned and then the area around her spleen softened. The next day Christi rolled side to side seven times.

Time drags and flies. Christi's therapy sessions take up about 6 hours each day. Sue believes that the continuity of a single treatment team and a constant setting with predictable routines is helpful to her and Christi. The staff members accept Sue's presence in each session and are willing to answer her questions. The speech therapist in particular seems to really get both Sue and Christi and actively encourages Christi to believe that one day she will use her voice. She tells Christi to forget about the pressure to make words and instead invites her to spontaneously make sounds. Concurrent with the sounds more emotion shows on Christi's face. Her parents see the shape of a smile playing at her lips and once hear the start of a laugh. Sue even believes she sees a pink tone arise in Christi's face, a near moment of flirtation, when a handsome tech comes to help transfer Christi to her chair.

The Craig rehab philosophy includes integration back into the everyday world, so weekend field trips are arranged. The first one Christi and Sue join takes them to the Natural History Museum and Imax Theatre. After so many hours within the white walls of an institution, the stimulation of other sights and sounds refreshes their perspective. Sue begins to look forward to the weekends and the upcoming trips planned for the mall and the aquarium.

Before they get to the next weekend, though, a medical crisis interrupts. At 3 AM on Thursday morning the night nurse calls Sue to ask her to return to the unit. Christi is crying, moaning, and making sounds like screams. Someone even claims to hear a beseeching "Mom" slip out. A dose of pain meds doesn't seem to make any difference so Christi is sent to the adjacent hospital for a series of tests and an IV drip of pain meds. Her cries diminish from every seven minutes to every half hour. All day they wait but no answer can be found. Sue strains to read any signal she can from Christi's tension, several times asking her aloud, "Where do you hurt?" In response Christi stiffens even more, her stretched out right arm sweeping across her belly until her flexed wrist stops over her groin. Sue wonders about the bladder or the catheter. She even muses out loud about this to one or more nurses, but everyone's focus is on the intensity of pain and the major organs. By 10 pm Sue and Christi are both exhausted. Sue finds an older nurse who seems gentle and kind, and asks her to check Christi's catheter. Sue hasn't seen any urine flow for 2 hours and in her frustration is on the verge of pulling out the catheter herself. When the nurse removes the catheter Christi immediately relaxes and falls fast asleep.

The next day the story is pieced together. By midmorning on Thursday, during the most intense pain, Christi passed a kidney stone. In doing so she likely strained so hard her catheter slipped down and was in the wrong spot, causing a new and different pain. The doctor looked again at the CT scans and saw the signs of slippage overlooked the previous afternoon when everyone's focus was on her liver, lungs, spleen and appendix.

By Friday afternoon Christi is fully recovered from her day of pain. The Saturday field trip to Park Meadows Mall is back on. Sue and Christi have always enjoyed shopping together, for clothes, holiday decorations, and Christi's favorite- shoes. This day is no exception. Sue's own tension begins melting away as she finds this old connection still alive. From her place at Christi's side, holding up a new top for the sign of yes or no, she wants to cheer at the brightness that flashes in Christi's eyes.

Packages pile up in the pocket behind the wheelchair backrest and sacks hang off of the handles, swinging slightly as they move down the wide walkways in front of stores. Who knows what onlookers see, looking across at Christi and Sue. Perhaps they see them stop in front of Abercrombie's, Sue leaning in to say something in Christi's ear, a chuckle visible in the bob of Sue's body. It's not likely they see the slightest widening of cheekbones in Christi's reply. Sue is teasing Christi about her favorite tech being an "Abercrombie boy." It's even more unlikely that any onlookers would suppose this is a playful exchange. Even in this mall where wheelchairs are commonplace, it's more likely that most other shoppers would feel pity at the sight of a young woman strapped into her chair. They would instead imagine emptiness and miss the fullness Christi and Sue relish.

One of the stops pleasing them most is at a specialty cologne store. For nearly an hour they sniff multiple bottles before making decisions for a unique concoction crafted for each of them. They take a long lunch hour sitting beside an indoor waterfall. They feel connected to the rhythm of life away from the focus on injury and rehab. Sue talks aloud to Christi about the arrival in a few days of Terry, Grandma Bea, and Tom for a Thanksgiving visit.

Looking back, I wonder if the sweep of Christi's arm to her groin was just a random tension movement or was indeed an attempt to signal the location of pain in urethra and bladder. Did a nurse only hear the sound of a moan and mistake the "mmm" for "Mom?" Or did Christi's pain and intense desire to communicate cause something extraordinary to occur? Consider the story Dr. Haig tells in the 2007 Time special edition on mind body health. Dr. Haig recounts his work with a patient with a documented condition of a tumor that has ravished his brain to the point of no willful function. Yet in the patient's final hours of life he talks to his wife and children, saying a goodbye the nurses on duty witness. Dr. Haig writes:

> *What woke my patient that Friday was simply his mind, forcing its way through a broken brain, a father's final act to comfort his family. The mind is a uniquely*

personal domain of thought, dreams and countless other things, like the will, faith and hope. These fine things are as real as rocks and water, but, like the mind, weightless and invisible, maybe even timeless. Material science shies away from these things, calling them epiphenomena, programs running on a computer, tunes on a piano. This understanding can't be ignored; not too much seems to get done on earth without a physical brain. But I know this understanding is not complete, either.[xii]

Perhaps to understand Christi fully, including flashbacks of the accident and moments of purposeful gestures, we need to use Deepak Chopra's definition of mind. "A body that can 'think' is far different from the one medicine now treats. For one thing, it knows what is happening to it, not just through the brain, but everywhere there is a receptor for messenger molecules, which means every cell." [xiii]

Most of us have a cultural prejudice that describes "mind" as a top down line with our brains at the beginning of the line directing a downward sequence to our bodies. Or we see mind in the brain above the line and our bodies below the line. Even if we allow that below the line is a foundation it's still seen as a "lesser than" position. Mind or consciousness as a circle comes closest to the orientation used throughout this book. It's a porous circle, like a mesh strainer, allowing an ease between the comings and goings of what's inside and outside. The sense this image promotes is that one aspect of mind leads into another in a continuous movement. The concepts of chi and prana that come from the established modalities of yoga, Ayurveda, and Traditional Chinese Medicine fit within this perspective. Our bodies provide information to our brains and our brains provide information to our bodies, without hierarchy.

A conversation between Bill Moyers and Margaret Kemeny, a renowned psychoneuro-immunology researcher, published in Moyers' PBS Healing Mind and Body series, addresses the problem of heirarchy.[xiv]

> *Kemeny: From my own viewpoint, the mind and the body are two manifestations of the same process. Even to say they are 'interconnected' is improper, because they are two parts of one whole.*
>
> *Moyers: Finding a language for this is part of the problem, isn't it?*
>
> *Kemeny: I think the language is one factor that has prevented us from being able to even conceptualize mind/body processes. Just the fact that we use one kind of intangible language to describe the mind and another kind of material language to describe the body- languages that don't even have a way of connecting- prevents us from seeing that these two kinds of phenomena are actually two manifestations of the same process, neither one more important than the other, and neither causing the other. If we can figure out ways to talk that allow us to think about the mind and body as one and the same, we'd be better off.*

Mind itself is a whole, only our words fail to adequately capture it. Imagine again you're looking at a circle. All aspects of mind are contained within it. Think again of

Deepak Chopra's invitation to understand thinking as something taking place within every cell of the body. Every one of these "thinking" cells is within our imaginary circle. The expression of mind is like an image we see when looking into a kaleidoscope, a flow of changing shape and color influenced by the light from outside. Multiple elements- bones, nerves, the air we breathe, the people we're with - come together at any single instant to create a momentary expression of mind. And, all the colors of the kaleidoscope are already mind, mind in motion, before they settle into a unified pattern.

Although the holiday week is a short one for therapy treatments, Christi's progress in head control and attention sustainability inspires the staff to add the challenge of maintaining upright posture. They introduce Christi to a standing frame. A special seat pushes her upward, configuring her form into a vertical line supported by armrests and a pelvic sling. This gives her body the chance to bear weight again and increases sensation in her feet so that they remain an active part of her body systems' balancing efforts. It's an invitation to grow into her full height, to focus on what's out in front of her, much as one would when coming to standing after sitting engrossed in thought for a long time.

The arrival of her father and grandmother also invites Christi into what's out in front of her. Sue perceives eagerness in Christi to show others what she has accomplished. The Dilantin is finally completely removed from her system and she's able to stay alert for longer periods each day. On the day Tom arrives she stays awake all day. Sue thinks it impresses Christi that Tom drives twelve hours to see her and she wants to match the effort. After a traumatic shift in a family, such as a death or life changing condition such as Christi's, there is a whole series of firsts, each holiday or birthday becoming the first in the new configuration. When Christi's birthday arrived the family was in between the medical trauma and reaching for normalcy. Now the whole family is hitting a more comfortable stride in accommodating the new normal so Thanksgiving seems a more festive occasion. The Craig staff encourages the attitude of celebration and continuity between past and future.

For five hours on the afternoon of Thanksgiving the Forest family has use of the family cottage on the Craig campus. The cottage, tastefully decorated with holiday décor, has a full kitchen, dining area, living room and outdoor patio, all accessible of course. Sue's brother, sister-in-law, and nephew join them, bringing along a prepared meal from the health food store nearby, filling the room instantly with rich smells of a feast. All week they've been receiving cards and e-mails from other distant family members, friends, and work colleagues. The place, the family present, and reminders of all those who have been holding them in their thoughts all swirl together in the hearts of Sue and Terry as they look across the table at Christi, grateful most of all that she is still with them.

There's lots of time for play with everyone since the holiday segues so neatly into a long weekend. With so many hands to help, they devise a way to transfer Christi in and out of the jeep so they can venture out on family outings, the highlight being the aquarium. Terry and Sue take the opportunity to leave Tom or Grandma Bea with Christi and go out to dinner or coffee or just walk on the hospital grounds. After so much time each doing their separate part of recovery support and talking on the phone, they relish the time for companionship no matter what the activity.

When Tom sits with Christi he tells her about his classes, his new volunteer job as a DJ on the college radio station, and the news he's had from their high school friends. At first he feels awkward being with her, talking too fast and then too slow. He's not certain how to act when Christi grimaces or curls her arms inward to her chest. When Christi tires and her head drops forward, he worries he'll do something wrong in helping lift her head back up. He's afraid he'll cause harm. Until confronted with the reality of slow progress he didn't realize how much he'd been imagining something different. He'd been visualizing the pre-accident Christi when he read Sue's e-mails that Christi was making sounds and beginning to show expression. He thought the magic of a Hollywood ending was already happening. He doesn't say this to Sue and Terry. He doesn't want them to be disappointed in him or shake their obvious pleasure in the progress she's making.

After a few days, though, sitting with Christi becomes comfortable again. He again senses her strength and fortitude rather than being impeded by her frailty. He stops trying to reach her and unselfconsciously relaxes back into the deep place of his inner rhythm that matched Christi so well and made them such compatible friends. When he stops trying so hard he finds the subtleties of Christi's expressions drift toward him and he believes he knows her again. When Tom sends Christi her next DJ'd cd we hear how painful not being able to talk to her is. He says, "there are more than 1400 miles between us now, yet I can still stand by your side. I'd gladly trade a 2 minute phone conversation from the other side of the world for this monologue from only 2 feet away." The CD holds songs with themes of hope, determination, will power, and passion. In between songs he tells her he dreams of her, how in each dream she progresses a little bit more and he can talk, laugh and walk with her. "It's such a great feeling to stroll through those dreams with you by my side. I can't wait until such dreamscapes become real landscapes, when you and I can stroll once again through the park, swing on the swings, or grab a DQ on a hot summer's day."

After a few days of rest and reconnection, Sue and Terry enthusiastically begin planning together the house remodel that will make it easier for Christi to live at home. Terry has already been envisioning this project. It gives him a concrete task that will contribute to Christi's success and ease in their living environment. In taking the long-term recovery vision to heart they plan an independent living space for Christi in their previously minimally finished basement. It will include room for her therapies and a family area for them to hang out together. They meet with the hospital staff and agree that the date of departure will be December 20th. They will be home before Christmas. The day before Terry flies home, they take a long walk and shop for Christmas decorations.

Back in her room they are a family again, decorating for the holiday. A brilliant red fiber-optic Christmas tree, glow-in-the-dark snowflakes, icicle lights, and garlands are placed to give Christi something inviting to look at no matter which way she faces. For sound there's a stand up crocodile that swings its hips and sings "Crocodile Rock"- not really Christmas related other than a funny gift typically put under the tree, but in this case silliness they can't pass up.

The rehab team shifts into planning for discharge. This includes clearing up all the outstanding medical details. A consult is held with the urologist to see why Christi keeps rejecting catheters, and a very tiny hole in the trachea is repaired. The therapists add to the videotapes of their work with Christi so the team back in Missoula will be able to see the progression and continue from the place they left off. The tapes show Christi straining to accomplish what is still beyond her reach. She exudes concentrated will, yet the requested movement doesn't come. The therapists express their recognition of her visible desire. We all know the feeling of something "on the tip of my tongue" that doesn't coalesce into awareness or action. It's this edge of "almost" that everyone feels. They wish they could magically reach inside and help Christi connect whatever will link intention and action. As I look at the tapes I realize how many micro-movements I take for granted in coughing or turning my head upon request. Those simple moves require posture control, auditory processing, continuous breathing, and simultaneous attention to inner sensations and the presence of others in the room. At this stage of recovery Christi can do only one element at a time. For instance, she needs to close her eyes, limiting external stimuli, to achieve a single movement, like lifting her head back to neutral after a cough has thrown her forward.

Candace

I ready myself for Christi's arrival home. I'm not sure what I'm preparing for since my work with her has little agenda beyond showing up and believing that my BMC and psychotherapy skills will enable me to be of assistance. All fall I've continued listening to deep rumblings of my own change process, as if I can hear lava churning, turning itself over, waiting to be undammed. I used to tell people that my job as a psychotherapist was the best, most adventurous of any. Yet now, despite my care and respect for the profession and clients, I have fallen out of love. I was in love on a Tuesday and woke up on a Wednesday to find it had vanished. It felt that sudden. There were signs through the summer that I can see in retrospect.

One afternoon before I went to see Christi I saw a client who was wavering on the precipice of suicide. A precipice she had approached repeatedly over the last six months as the truth of her abusive childhood exploded in her awareness. Experiencing the raw truth of her pain, anger and confusion overwhelmed her. She longed for peace she imagined could only come with death. Internally I felt myself exerting my own will and intention, holding tight and steady to keep her from going over. And then an hour later I was beside Christi, beckoning her to come back with the same amount of intensity. The fragility of life stared me in the face. From both Christi and my client I sensed a deep fiber, impossibly thin yet the strength of steel, that I believed would keep them on the trajectory of life. Perhaps connecting so explicitly with this core in them energized my own life force, enlivening it to grow stronger, to make demands on my life course.

By the time of Christi's return the only clear understanding I decipher from the murmurs of my nonconscious is that I need to leave the safety of the therapy office. When I'm sitting in sessions with clients I realize that although I still believe in the importance of the work going on, the walls of the room have begun to feel too confined. I feel literally hemmed in, as if my office shrunk and I need to shed its skin.

I need to venture out into a bigger world, and there are no clues, no trail of breadcrumbs that I'm going to be able to follow. I've made many drastic changes in my lifetime, but this one feels different, because instead of going towards something predetermined, a new school, a new city or career, this change demands that I follow the push that's coming from inside. The grief I feel about knowing I'll leave my profession is sweet and miserable. Anxiety, eagerness and patience swirl around, my conscious mind formulating them into crystals of logic in an attempt to believe I'm in control of the change process. Meanwhile, the inside purpose seems unfazed, throwing just one stepping stone at a time in front of me, demanding a new kind of trust. Perhaps this is where the phrase "blind faith" gets its name.

FALLING IN

Frequently I'm contemplating a photo my husband Dudley took of Yellowstone Lake in early May, just before the ice went out. I find gazing at it peaceful and comforting. Even though it's a color photo it looks black and white because the grey of lake and sky mirror one another. A few wide cracks are visible on the lake surface, the dark streaks hinting at what lies below. The rest looks like mush. Ice crystals have become detached from their neighbors, whatever gave them solid form now gone. The cohesion of the lake's ice surface is only temporary.

A Distant Camp

Year 2000

> "He goes to his sense memory. He goes deep inside himself into a place where all his individual sense memories are stored, and that place then connects him with the universe... Even when there are no lines being said, you know something's going on in that mind, in that soul... It could be said that this place, unto itself, gives off a sense of its own existence, and it comes through, maybe even unknown to the personality itself. Because a mind is operating. Because a heart is beating in that chest."
>
> Sidney Poitier, The Measure of a Man

Christi and Sue

For Sue and Christi the transition from institution to home begins during the last two weeks at Craig. Sue moves out of her apartment and her station at Christi's bedside and the two of them move to the wing with transitional apartment rooms. Here they have their own microwave and fridge, so Sue can create meals on a time schedule that works for them. They are no longer bound by the rehab unit's institutional clock. A large TV provides shared entertainment. And adjacent beds let Sue begin adapting to the sleep routine she'll keep for the next several years: a few hours sleep, waking to turn Christi, then back to sleep for another couple of hours. On their last two nights there Sue dreams that Christi is talking and moving. The vision of these landmarks stays strong even though they'll leave the treatment center without having achieved them.

They arrive back in Missoula in time to enjoy a quiet restful Christmas. Terry, relieved to have "his girls" home, releases the tension he wasn't even aware of carrying. Now he can observe things directly instead of having to strain to make meaning over the phone. The dire change in their circumstances doesn't alter the comfort of sharing simple daily routines like coming home from work for lunch and reading the comics page aloud at breakfast. A few days before Christmas they go shopping for a tree and pull out the decorations that proclaim their holiday history, weaving connections between past, present and future.

Sue and Terry use the week between Christmas and New Year's for catching up with friends and taking naps. Especially after nearly three months away there's nothing like a nap on their own bed with one of the dogs curled up at their feet. All too quickly the week passes and, like millions of Americans, the Forests mumble, "vacation is over" with a combination of reluctance and eagerness. In-home rehab picks up. Debra and I resume sessions with Christi, one or both of us there every day of the week except Sunday. Patricia Skergan visits weekly to perform chiropractic adjustments. A new team of rehabilitation specialists forms around the nucleus of physical therapist Mary O'Connell who agrees to continue the work she began with Christi before Craig. Mary acts as if "of course" Christi is fully there, half teasing and half goading her to shoot for high goals even while patiently focusing on the details required to re-learn how to roll over. Mary, along with her occupational therapy and speech therapy colleagues at the private clinic, Sapphire, agrees to contract for 5 days per week. Three of those days are for in-home services and two days take place in their center so they can use the pool and their array of equipment. Sue plans to return to work 2 days per week so an RN is hired to monitor the tubes for feeding and urination on the days Sue is at work. A graduate from Sue's early intervention program also joins the team on evenings and weekends, her familiarity providing Sue with greater ease.

The fun activity of early January is a visit from Tom. He stays with the family for five days, updating Christi on how his classes ended, the next semester's schedule, and mutual friends he saw during the holiday break. His presence continues to provide Sue and Terry a glimpse into "normal" college rhythms. The day before he leaves I interview him about his experience of the journey with Christi. Before we go off to talk, Christi, Tom, Sue and I are sitting together. I ask Christi if there's anything she wants me to ask Tom. Her face furrows in seeming consternation and she turns her head away from Tom and Sue. From the hollow expanse I hear only a single word, "time."

In the privacy of the study I ask Tom a scattering of questions - how he reads Christi, the impact of seeing her work so hard to recover, being with the Forests, what changes he notes. A half dozen times he seems near tears even though his words are vague generalizations delivered in a flat tone. I read his cues as hesitant so when emotion disrupts his composure I steer us back to neutral topics, respectful that crying seems further than he wants to go with me, a stranger despite our connection through Christi. Finally though I begin to feel it's disrespectful to keep avoiding whatever is surfacing. I ask, "Is there anything you want to say to Christi?" He tightens his abdomen and barely releases it even with an exaggerated exhale. Phrases topple over one another. "It's hard. We were broken up when the accident happened. Now I've become part of the family, almost like Terry's son because we've spent so much time together. I don't want to break up with the family, they've been so good to me, they're like my own family. But when I'm introduced as Christi's boyfriend it's like pressure. I want to talk to Christi about it but I don't know if that's ok to do. We always could talk about everything, but now…" Tangled in uncertainty, he grinds to a halt.

As Tom spills out the dilemma, fumbling for words, I realize that Christi already knows. She's not asking him to wait. "Time" means that she knows her recovery will take a long time and that it's time to break up. I don't know if she has a vision for holding onto the friendship because in her single word there wasn't the momentum of a plan, only letting go.

I encourage Tom to talk directly to Christi, reinforcing that she can understand what he's saying. He needs to go back to school with permission to move forward with his life, to grieve what's lost. I tell him too that Sue and Terry will understand that high school sweethearts change even without traumatic injury. He seems relieved to have the truth on the table, heard by someone who knows the people and the convoluted story. Driving away from the house I feel sadness. Yet I also feel gratitude that our interview gave Tom an outlet and support for his feelings. I say aloud a hope, a prayer I float back toward the house, that they find the time for conversation.

After Tom's departure everyone intensifies their focus on establishing a routine. It's like starting a new semester at school when classes, study hours and extracurricular activities are set anew. Walking into the Forest house the tenor of earnestness is palpable, like a shift foreman has yelled, "Ok everyone, no more fooling around, this is work time."

In everyday life most of us take for granted all the little moments that make up a day. Taking a shower, drying and styling our hair, shaving or putting on makeup, all happen while conscious thoughts drift ahead or behind, anticipating what lies before us or rehashing a dream or a conversation. This is not true for Christi. Sue and the caregivers use every routine interaction, like bathing and dressing, as a learning period for rebuilding social understanding, vocalization, and motor skills. Everyone's full focus needs to be on this single moment. Christi's day of slow, time-consuming rehab begins as soon as she's awake. A caregiver helps her move while narrating each step - rolling Christi onto her side in the bed, shifting her weight to come up to sitting, pausing for a slight moment to give her time to register vertical posture and stabilize her torso, leaning Christi forward to rest her upper body onto the waiting shoulder, lifting to standing. Christi seems to try to help, as if in her inner body she's leaning forward to shift her weight even though she can't yet direct her muscles to perform the actions of sitting or standing. Sue and the caregivers use Christi's contribution without consciously noticing. It's the same synchrony parents use when they lean over the crib to scoop up their baby. They look into the infant's eyes, say time to get up, and then in the slight pause an alliance of direction arises that allows the parent to smoothly lift the child. They are like dance partners moving as one.[xv] This same kind of alliance is used to guide Christi's legs in two inch pivoting steps, turning her back toward the waiting wheelchair. Then Christi is dropping down, falling into gravity and the chair more than reaching for it. She doesn't often land with the best posture so there's more adjusting, scooching one hip or the other back into alignment, helping her shoulders settle against the backrest, guiding her head into the supportive curve of the headrest.

For showering and grooming, the washcloth or hairbrush is placed in Christi's hand. The beneficial by-product of high tone tension allows her to keep a tight grip. Helping to brush her own hair or wash herself in the shower is an extension of the therapy of learning to move her arm. Christi's status quo arm position is stiff with contraction, her forearm bent in to nearly touch her bicep, her wrist folded down, the little finger side of her hand pushing solidly into her chest. It reminds me of the instinctual curl of in utero life, arms curled over our hearts, defining our center point. Slowly, expanding a half inch at a time, Christi's aides help her move her arm up and out, regaining a range of motion that softens the elbow and lifts her arm overhead. Once Christi's arm is limbered up with stretches the aide and she work together to brush her hair.

Parents of a child with a disability hear a lot about tone: low and high tone. Usually the therapists are talking about the state of tension the muscles are in when the person is in neutral. Most therapists working with Christi talk about her high tone, thinking about her hyper-extended legs and curled-in arms. A shortcut to understanding what's happening in the muscles is to think about the two functions of muscles: range of motion and strength. Long fibers in the muscles slide out and in to provide range of motion. Strength is provided by microscopic "hooks" that bind the fibers crosswise to one another. For Christi, the muscle tone in her legs and arms is overly reliant on the strength function, making her more rigid. It's as if the will required to "hold on tight" to life hasn't yet relaxed.

Christi's tone is not uniformly high even though that's what's most often noted. The muscles in her torso are weaker, lower toned. And when we consider the tone of the organs - remember the idea of water balloons stacking up - it's as if the outside edges of the "balloons", each organ, have softened, allowing the "balloons" to sag against one another in an uneven, precarious stack.[xvi] The low tone in her organs and torso is most visible when Christi is sitting in her wheelchair.

When Sue and the aides assist Christi to move from lying down to sitting or grooming activities, they also carefully use each action to remind Christi to even out the muscle tone in her body. Using their hands to communicate, and sometimes words, they re-invite the glide of muscle fibers and more stable stacking of organs.

Christi is not just a passive recipient of therapeutic goals set by the rehab team. In one of our mid-January sessions I begin to perceive a pushing-out energy, as if she wants to interrupt a conversation with her own comment. I ask her what goal she wants to set. After several days the answer comes. No feeding tube. To accomplish this she will need to drink enough fluids to supply sufficient hydration and nutrition. Since she's only drinking a few sips a day, mostly as therapy for her mouth and to enjoy tastes, it will take effort to consume the necessary amount. As Sue sits on the mat beside her we make a plan for Sue to add four drinking times to the daily schedule. Christi seems to listen with intensified focus, as if down deep she sees a mountain she intends to climb.

Although when I'm communicating with Christi I usually hear in myself a word or phrase, her next idea comes into my mind as an image. It is a chart detailing the steps necessary for her goals. I share this hesitantly with Sue, less sure of myself because it came as an image and because it's a format I never use personally despite theoretically knowing it's a good idea. Sue laughs. "A chart is so Christi." Terry hangs a whiteboard on the wall of her room at eye level to the therapy mat. It has a place for the number of times per day to drink and the amount per drink. By the last week of January Christi drinks her first latte and consumes almost a third of her daily needs through spoonfuls of pureed meals. I imagine her desire to eat is enhanced by the aromas that fill the house each day. Sue has always been an adventurous cook, liking to experiment with generous pinches of spices. Cooking isn't just a necessity for Sue. It expresses and replenishes her creative spirit. The smells are so enticing I begin teasing Sue that she should turn her love of cooking into a cookbook for other families.

The Sapphire rehab team begins noting signs of progress. Christi can hold her head up for 60 seconds. She is beginning to decrease spontaneous, automatic early infancy reflexes. She can isolate individual movements of her arms and head. Several times a day, totaling 2 hours, she is lifted upright into the standing frame she began using at Craig. The therapists see that cognition exists, including strong memory, but the motor delay in processing the words of others and in following directions prevents them from knowing its depth. They begin searching for a reliable yes-no method for communication and introduce a communication board with letters and images.

Given how well everything is progressing Sue decides to add one of Christi's previous favorite relaxations - a bath. Terry constructs a bathtub on wheels that fits into the remodeled accessible shower area. Sue lights candles, puts soft music on the CD player, and fills the tub with warm water, Epsom salts and lavender. Christi is easily transitioned into the tub and lies in a relaxed position with her eyes closed. Then all of a sudden she startles, opens her eyes wide and begins to curl into a fetal position. A shrieking sound escapes her mouth. Sue's vision fills with a flood of red and she sees Christi back at the accident scene. She is in a pool of blood and people hover over her. The cacophony is overwhelming. Sue keeps her own shock, horror, and desire to turn away, at bay. She coolly and evenly invites Christi to re-orient to the present and the safety of being in her own home. Sue reminds her to breathe and models with her own breath until Christi begins to match her.

For the next week Sue reports that accident flashbacks continue at night. Christi is restless in her sleep, sometimes crying out in anguish. She seems exhausted by the uninvited interruption and falls asleep repeatedly during the day, no longer seeming to care about the challenge of therapy. Christi seems depressed and out of reach. The enthusiasm from her Sapphire therapy team fades and they start to become discouraged. Despite Sue's own need for sleep and recuperation from witnessing these traumatic episodes she doesn't let down a beat, unwilling to let the lethargy of Christi and the treatment team snowball in the wrong direction.

None of the flashbacks occur while I'm working with Christi, but I do acknowledge them and the sadness they bring. Unlike the flashbacks of summer and fall which arose and then fully dispersed, these re-experienced bits of trauma seem to be followed by a reflective period where Christi takes the point of view of "I", as in "what do I think about the fact that this happened?" Sometimes I sit on the edge of her therapy mat, lapsing into long drifts of silence with her, as if we are suspended, enfolded in an empty cloud. Intermittently, wholly formed perceptions arise in my mind which I speak out loud, trusting they fit even though she is utterly still in reply. Sometimes I even nod my head, the I-heard-what-you-said signal of the psychotherapy office, supporting the silence of inner processing. I look into the distant space, witness to the invisible. I offer sympathetic reflection. "It's hard. Sometimes the soul picks a journey difficult for the personality."

Candace

In late February I sit with Christi on the morning I'm leaving for a somatic therapy symposium in San Francisco to present the paper I've written about her survival story. Christi's face expresses a mixture of emotion, sadness still, but now with an edge, like displeasure or pain. I hear no words from Christi but at the end of the session Sue joins us and speaks the word that captures it, "shitty." This seems to unlock whatever was frozen and the phrase, "I didn't ask for this journey" emanates from Christi. My compassion and sorrow arise in equal measure, one making my heart sink and the other offering soothing. I tell Christi that later she'll be able to make choices about what she'll do with this experience. I don't say what I also know, that it has already begun growing into a life of its own, a story affecting each of us and combining to be bigger than all of us. Going to San Francisco is the beginning of sending the story beyond our individual experiences.

On the plane I note in my journal that writing and presenting the paper sends me "further into the direction of my own destiny- whatever that is." The seeds of this trip were sown last summer. The founders of six different somatic education training programs: Lomi, Continuum, Sensory Awareness, Feldenkrais, the California Institute of Integral Studies, and Body Mind Centering, were invited to send a representative to a symposium. We would each present written case studies articulating the approach our school takes in working with a client. Each school has its own unique emphasis, such as focus on fluid or muscle systems of the body or using breath or attention for grounding and accessing awareness of physical embodiment. They all share the basic principle that the physical self is an integral part of generating, shaping and expressing consciousness. They believe that we embody our truest self when we melt internal boundaries caused by blockage or numbness.

The School for Body Mind Centering put out a call to practitioners and teachers to send in papers for committee review and selection of a single representative. Full of the mystery of my work with Christi and eager to share it with my peers in BMC, as much to receive their validation as to further my own understanding of what had transpired, I took up the challenge of putting my experience into words. After a couple of months of waiting, and my own emotional rollercoaster, I learned in November that I would represent the school. I felt honored and some trepidation, still slightly insecure because I knew I was reaching beyond my own conceptual understanding of Christi's recovery process.

As I sit on the plane, the trepidation is still with me. Although being aware that traditional psychology will likely reject the authenticity of my experience, I'm also eager to be with other somatic therapists who will kinesthetically, and therefore mentally, get it. I want to tell them that I am changed, "a hopelessly verbal therapist working nine months in silence." I want them to be touched by the mystery of this story. I want them to feel Christi's will and courage to stay alive, to relearn everything, to be exposed beyond where she personally ever wanted to be. I also want to talk to my peers about practical matters of being part of a treatment team. I want to know how they balance their treatment approach with the allopathic medicine approach. I wonder how they negotiate fees or if they volunteer when insurance doesn't cover their service. Debra and I both work with Christi as volunteers. Although we're free from having to justify our services to an insurance company, our treatment impact is left out of the medical records. Therefore, we, and the services we provide, are invisible.

One other factor contributes to my trepidation. I am really sick. I have the worst sore throat and cough in my adult memory. I can barely take anything beyond a shallow breath or I trigger a coughing bout. I've resorted to antibiotics and gulp huge swigs of cough syrup to buy myself windows of calm and four hour blocks of sleep. Unfortunately, the cough syrup hangover leaves me feeling like I'm interacting with everything and everyone through a heavy fog bank.

On the morning of the symposium I arrive first, uncharacteristically early, in my eagerness to meet the group of teachers and practitioners. Each presenter will have a half hour to put forth his/her paper and take questions. Then we'll wrap up with a roundtable discussion of commonalities. During arrivals I realize that I'm the only one without previous connections to the other participants. The others have three or more other acquaintances and naturally fall into cliques of familiarity. My nervousness about presenting and the codeine rebound combine to make me awkward and stilted as I try to fit in.

When it's my turn to speak the fog in my head is so thick I can't even gauge the volume of my voice. I have no memory of what I said, only the feeling of standing at the hard edge of the podium, looking out at the faces. I came to the symposium eager for head nods of "I know exactly what you mean." What I find instead are nods with an accent mark on "interesting, curious, out of the ordinary." One teacher says, "I don't perceive the specificity of the things you're talking about even though I believe they're real." One or two nods are co-opting, "yes, yes, hurry up so I can tell you why that's already covered by the approach of my school" even though I know I'm offering a different approach to body systems. The cough syrup residue slows me down so much that I can hear each person's comments but can't enter back into the conversation quickly enough. Words fill the room but I can't feel the connections of heart. That's not to say they aren't there, I just can't perceive them. Like water that sits on top of compacted desert, unable to be absorbed, the encouragement I hear to elaborate further on what I've written, to continue finding my own voice, sits in a puddle threatening to wash away before it can nurture me. Even a month later, when Bonnie calls and leaves a message to congratulate me and thank me for representing the school – telling me the symposium organizer "was very moved," that I "spoke with authority, clarity, intelligence and great sensitivity," my "work a credit" to her - I write the words down so they won't vanish. They sit on a page in my journal, a reservoir I hope to someday tap.

As each of the other presenters speaks I am captivated, moved by hearing about the magic of connecting with clients through their personal gifts. But in between speakers an ugly shadow voice of my own chatters in the background. I want more time for me. This greed is unquenchable. The shadow imagines happiness if the whole conference is dedicated to my paper about Christi. Another part winces, "Are you kidding, that much attention would be intolerable." In between sessions I walk to buy coffee with one of the other presenters. I ask a single follow up question and he talks non-stop the rest of the break about his work. The content of what he says doesn't engage me, but I tilt in attention anyway because I hear longing and eagerness in his voice that tells me he too is starved for receptive and understanding attention. I feel compassion for all of us that we're too isolated on our islands within the dominant culture that splits mind and body.

After the symposium ends on Sunday afternoon I walk around our meeting location, a commercial area of town mostly deserted on the weekend. As if a meditation practice I'm drinking air into my compromised lungs while waiting for my airport shuttle. Finding no interesting distractions I sit in an empty park square, expecting the quiet space will revive my rather lifeless physical state and help me sort through my thoughts and feelings. Instead of revival, the grey sky, grey buildings and winter air merge and seep a chill into my heart. I feel more and more desolate. How can I be in a city of this many people yet be completely alone? Where are the people? Where is the life? At home in Montana I can be alone in the furthest reaches of wilderness and not feel lonely, but here in the city I feel cut off, encapsulated in the grey. For no rational reason I begin believing I have been a failure, that I've let Christi down. I haven't reached anyone. The gulf between internal experience and outer expression is too big to cross.

Once home I retreat for days. I don't know what difference it made that I was at the symposium, to others or to me. Rationally I understand the Somatics field is filled with differing perspectives all trying to find their unique way into, and out of, the prism of physical embodiment. It's not just me who struggled to put kinesthetic experience into language. All of us at the symposium are writing to help the field name itself and find its place. Each of us is on the fringe of standard medical and psychological approaches. Our mutual desire for acceptance binds us to one another yet also accentuates differences as we strive to be understood and integrated into mainstream thought.

I tell a friend about my surprise at not being immediately kinesthetically understood at the symposium and she replies, "I don't know why you expected anything else. BMC is on the fringe of all the schools already on the fringe." I'm wordless because I can't reconcile her words with my own experience of myself. I believe myself to be average, simple, non-imaginative, decidedly not fringe. I am the most literal of people, concrete about the mind of cells and bones. Yet, my concrete perception is adjacent to the most abstract: I am worlds apart from, yet right next to, the anatomists who believe all thought, self, and soul exist in brain neurons.

The feeling of being small and alone within the huge silent city eats away at my confidence to wake everyone up with Christi's story. I begin to understand that my shadow self who wanted all the attention at the symposium was desperate for help. The voice of the one who knows the story is bigger than my understanding. I often feel lost and too small for the task at hand. What was missing from my connection with the other participants wasn't heart or understanding. Missing was what I didn't even know I was looking for -- the experienced hand to help me, to pick me up and to open doors for me.

Once I went on a one-week solo backpack trip into the Bob Marshall Wilderness. On the third day I came to a creek crossing that abruptly stopped me. It shouldn't have been there according to my map. Stunned to realize I was lost, I found a rock a little way up the trail and sat for a long time with the map in my lap, unable to perceive where I had gone wrong. I'd periodically look back across the stream and wish for a cowboy on a horse to appear, oasis like, and rescue me. No matter that this was unlikely given that I hadn't seen a soul for two days. The surety that led me to strike out on the solo adventure had vanished. Inside my body I felt only silent dry space, wide like the prairie grasses surrounding the rock I sat on. I sat still for a long time on the rock until a feeling of moisture, subtle like morning dew, began to creep back in, nourishment that led my eyes to see my place on the map. I stopped wanting the cowboy's rescue, hoisted my pack and walked back into the adventure. This is finally what happens after the San Francisco foray. I pick up my work with Christi where I left off.

Christi and Sue

Usually each team member works with Christi independently. The Sapphire team meets together weekly and once every couple of months we all meet together. Mostly, however, communication happens through Sue because she is both case manager and rehab aide. It is up to Sue to perceive the common threads among the diverse approaches and to make the decisions about where to prioritize when there are differences in suggestions and limitations of time.

Sometimes we more directly work out our differences with a joint session. For instance, one time Mary and I meet together to look at the problematic issue of foot position because it is causing Christi difficulty in the standing frame. It is Mary's view that if the gross movement is in place, in this case standing, then the act of weight bearing will cause the foot to send the appropriate signals for balance to the brain. She wants to introduce the use of an arch support and ankle brace. My perspective from Body Mind Centering is that flexibility in the foot, and eliciting a push motion from the foot upward through the body, is a necessary precursor to stable standing. In BMC's view early developmental sequences can be re-elicited to support the most efficient balanced movements. In traditional physical therapy the gross movement comes first and fine-tuning comes later. Before our meeting I also consult with a Shiatsu practitioner and she names the imbalance problem as yang meridians overprotecting and yin meridians not bringing the earth energy upward. This too has a ring of truth that recognizes the relationship of Christi's foot position to the trauma experience. The challenge for us in working together is to find a way to capture the synergy of our approaches. Instead of becoming protective about our own "right" answer we need to keep merging our pieces of the puzzle. Otherwise, we put Christi and Sue in a "pick one, exclude the other", position. The tension between seemingly opposite approaches has been, and is, one of the on-going problems in marrying traditional and alternative medicine approaches. And for parents in Sue's position, where every form of help is welcomed and needed, it's not an esoteric quandary, but one where immediate action is required.

Mary and I resolve our difference by agreeing that standing needs to take place because it is helpful to Christi's bones as well as promoting movement. Therefore an ankle brace and arch support are added. We address my concern that more needs to happen in support of waking up the foot by increasing stretching exercises and looking for other ways to elicit push impulses. We put time into Christi's schedule for her to lie on her stomach on a body cushion because it's time on our bellies that, as infants, supports us to develop a push away from gravity, a push that sequences arms through torso, raising us up to discover what's around us. A push from the foot, travelling upward through the torso, begins our crawling forward mobility. Mary, Sue and I agree to keep emphasizing opening up Christi's hands so she can eventually use them to push herself upright. A few days later the Shiatsu practitioner and I conduct a joint session with Christi to help open the flow of chi. The practitioner places her hands top and bottom on Christi's right foot until the energy seems to build up past Christi's comfort point.

The mass of energy is trapped with no direction opening for release. Christi begins making aching sounds and from my position at her upper body I facilitate movements of her right arm and lightly touch her beneath her collarbone on the kidney meridian. She exhales with seeming relief as the congestion breaks open and a pulse of energy rises up her body, squirting like liquid up a straw.

In March Christi and I begin working again on the rhythms in her brain. I sit behind her and hold her skull, listening with my hands, like someone putting an ear to a door to hear what's going on inside a room. Sometimes I perceive a torque, alternately feeling the direction of a cap being twisted a quarter turn closed and then the opposite, unwinding. Each untwist seems to widen the horizontal space in the middle of her brain. With the release I perceive flashes of anger that the accident happened that's different from the sorrow and despair I felt a month ago. I tell Christi that in my years as a therapist I've often sat with clients as they shook their fist in anger at God for letting them get hurt. Their anger cleared out debris that had been blocking the way forward. An energy stream pulses down her right arm. Then she seems to let go. The appearance of torque dissolves into a neutral resting place lower in the brain.

The unblocking of emotion also occurs in Christi's speech sessions. As she and the speech therapist practice mouth movements, breath sounds, and tongue mobility, a flashback occurs and a fearful cry erupts. Sue steps in and re-orients Christi to current time and place, reminding her she is safe in her own house, refocusing her on the sensation of breath. It seems as though waking up each body part comes with the price of unfreezing bits of trauma. It's a mystery. Is the emotion held like a holographic image in the tissues themselves, in the cells of the vocal cords, or in the nervous system's read of muscles, or in the connections reweaving themselves in Christi's brain? Maybe the memory is in all of them. It seems odd that there is no communication between Sue and the speech therapist about the flashbacks that happen in speech sessions. The therapist accepts them as a blip in the action, but says nothing reassuring to Sue or Christi about them. They have no idea how they're integrated into her worldview or treatment plan. Because the categories of treatment are so sharply defined they don't mention to the speech therapist that directly after a session of letting her cries go, Christi has a strong bowel movement and her period begins.

In my next session Christi seems troubled. Twice she sweeps her arm outward to push my hand aside when I place it on her belly. It's like someone saying, "don't touch me, I want to be alone." After I pause for a moment, I take her hand, acknowledge her depression and ask how I can help. Immediately her arm softens and she lets me gently hold her hand. We sit quietly like that for many minutes. Eventually Sue joins us. Sue says she doesn't want Christi to hurt. She doesn't know what to do to take away the pain.

Later that evening I talk with Sue. She tells me she's extra discouraged because of a phone call she had last week from Mary on behalf of the Sapphire team. "We're not seeing the kind of progress we'd like to justify this many hours of therapy a week ... insurance might not want to cover such intensive treatment" and then her voice trails off. Sue is taken aback and fumbles for a reply, her mind racing. She wants to ask, "what does this mean," or "what are you proposing," yet she doesn't. "I know changes have been slow, but we are seeing differences, and there have been other things going on ..." Sue's voice ends in another unfinished sentence. No changes need to be made right now, Sue and Mary agree, but a warning flag has been raised.

There's no language or science that helps the team talk openly about Christi's flashbacks. Anyone would have a disorganized or down day after reliving trauma memory. We should expect that to be even more so for Christi because of her compromised processing system. All of us have varying moods that affect performance. Shouldn't we expect moods from Christi? Insurance payments for physical therapy are based on a steady upward progression. In psychotherapy there's an assumption that progress will include plenty of dips and especially long troughs in the early processing of major trauma. The kind of body mind healing Christi is engaged in, one that blends these two models, doesn't fit into ordinary insurance or rehab guidelines.

―――◆―――

Candace

During spring break week I leave my work with Christi to go to Florida to be with my ailing father and exhausted-from-caretaking mother. Dad has Parkinson's disease, a neurological disorder that affects movement. It came twelve years ago. First it manifested as greater difficulty concentrating and multi-tasking at work, so he took early retirement. My parents moved to Florida and slowed their life down, focusing on the simple pleasures of golf, reading poolside, and cooking. Then his arm shakes worsened. He adjusted his putting game and rarely wielded the kitchen knife. Eventually the shakes and balance challenge forced him to give up playing his beloved game of golf. He's always been a proud man, a good storyteller, the center of attention at parties. Presentation matters to him.

We all covered for him as long as we could, especially my mother, who filled in the gaps in his skills. She began laying out his clothes so he wouldn't have to make a decision. At pool parties she positioned them so that no one would notice he could no longer stand and maneuver his plate and conversation at the same time. His friends laughed with him when he lost track in billiards and expertly sunk the wrong ball. Then everyone's denial came crashing down. Dad was saying a prayer at the wedding reception of his lifetime friend's daughter and the words wouldn't come out. My mother threaded her hand through his and helped him finish. That is when, without overt acknowledgment, the family started to support his world becoming smaller. We didn't say much when he started watching Sunday church on television instead of going to the service in person. We all claimed eating at home was more fun and didn't admit it was so he wouldn't be humiliated at a restaurant when he tried to take a bite of his food and missed his mouth. We adjusted to calling it a good conversation when he said a few sentences when really the father we knew eloquently held forth on multiple topics. We stayed home to buy ourselves a more intimate quality of life.

In January he fell and cracked his hip. My sister Laurel and I went down for a few horrible days when they had him at a short-term rehab unit. His meds were so messed up he was continuously hallucinating. He'd talk with us and simultaneously reach into an imaginary tackle box and tie a lure onto the end of fishing line. Sometimes he would turn to imaginary people he saw over his right shoulder and tell them about us. Laurel was most nonplussed about it, saying "we only want to visit with you right now, Dad." I was more frustrated. I insisted on meeting with the staff psychologist after a jerking spasm almost toppled his wheelchair over backwards. My confidence in the facility wasn't helped when I learned that, even after working with him for a week, not one of the staff had brought his weird behavior or unsafe wheelchair set-up to anyone's attention.

So I'm relieved Dudley and I are able to make a spring break trip so I can see him again. He's doing much better now that he's at home and they've righted his meds. But my mother has to watch him vigilantly because he's not very stable on his feet. Our visit offers her a chance for respite. Dudley takes her shopping while I hang out with my Dad. We don't really talk since that's an effort for him. I self-consciously try to figure out how to be available to him without hovering so I don't rob him of autonomy. It's hard. I step into the kitchen to get something and he abruptly decides to get up, and falls. I'm only 10 feet away but can't reach him in time. Thankfully he's not hurt. As I help him back into the chair he hurriedly says, "Let's not tell your mother about this." He doesn't want her to worry more than she already does. I understand his movement problem. Impulses to move ignite motion before the rest of his body is organized. He can't inhibit his intention to get up long enough to get his feet positioned under him to stand up safely. Or, to get over the inertia of Parkinson's, he has to amplify the initiation signal and this propels his body into a motor action that's too large. I think about initiation a lot these days because of acutely listening so deeply to perceive it in Christi.

When it's my turn for a break I walk far down the beach, letting my thoughts ramble. I yield to the sound of waves and the pull of tide, allowing them to recalibrate me back into a body rhythm that perceives the big picture. I reflect on the journey I'm on with both Christi and my Dad. I imagine that Christi's mind is like a clematis vine growing shoots, climbing toward the top of the trellis, while my father's mind is like tendrils that are detaching themselves and letting go. Shoots of the vine that once bore flowers fall back toward the ground. I'm sad for his loss and ours and helpless to do anything.

As I walk the beach I'm sad too for my own seemingly tangled life. I don't know which shoots of the vine to nurture and which to let go of. I don't know what trellis is holding my life direction. Thank goodness I have Dudley for steadiness while I try to figure it out. I'm continuing to question my work as a therapist, but I can't find a way to actively let it go without having an idea of what will replace it. Graduate school hasn't panned out the way I'd hoped.

I've had lots of research ideas, but with Sue only part-time and my primary advisor on sabbatical, there's no one to work with me on getting them off the ground. I think of myself as an enthusiastic student because my curiosity and intrinsic motivation are so great. I entered school believing I'd merge science with my kinesthetic Body Mind Centering knowledge. But the way classes are taught has more to do with right answers and memorizing facts than with embodied knowledge. I am constantly taking long walks to translate the facts I learn into kinesthetic understanding. In BMC School many of the students said, "words are my second language, movement is my mother tongue." Even though I'm at home with words I need them to connect to physical knowing. In graduate school they're too separated. Yet, I won't let go of school so I'm stuck with the tangle it has me in.

In my dream world I am thwarted. In dream after dream I keep trying to get to the right airport or ticket counter but I never succeed. On the way to the airport detours arise and inexplicably I'm riding on slow buses and taking side trips through city shopping areas. I lose my bags or end up on the wrong plane. I'm certain there's a right flight for me but I can't get there.

I don't leave our vacation any clearer than when we arrived. Just like my Dad under Parkinson's grip, and Christi reconstructing intention-movement connections, I can't develop a "motor plan" for action. I am going to have to just keep doing what I'm doing and wait for a stronger signal to emerge.

Christi and Sue

Just before I left for spring break Christi's flashbacks receded. She seemed to shift to anticipating Holly's visit. Holly is her best friend from high school. They were inseparable as teens and kept in touch via e-mail and phone calls during Christi's year away at college and Holly's entry into the military. For months Sue has been holding the phone to Christi's ear while Holly speaks to her. Listening, Christi seems to hold herself very upright, an energetic increase from her normal posture. Although her eyes remain half closed, the slight furrow in her brow gives the impression that she is more intensely focused.

For a week Holly falls into the rhythm of Christi's life. She brings their favorite milkshakes from Dairy Queen. She reminisces aloud about their high school antics, like the time they moved all the orange cones from a road construction site, a silly laugh now, though then it was a daring prank. Holly learns how to listen for the subtle signs of a cough emerging and how to best position Christi to clear her throat. This gains them independence. They leave the caregivers behind and go for a ride up to their old hang-out in Pattee Canyon. On the last day of the visit Holly brings Christi a picture quilt her Mom made. The squares are filled with photos of them laughing uproariously at something, in swimsuits at Flathead Lake, and momentarily still in their high school graduation gowns while a flurry of action goes on behind. Terry hangs the quilt at the foot of Christi's therapy mat, inviting her to remember friendship and the continuity between past, present and future.

When I see Christi the week after Holly's visit her mood is mixed. While Sue fills me in with stories about the satisfying moments, there's a tone of relief from Christi. It's like smooth, solid ground that testifies to the strength of the connection. And then there's a darkening, an evaporation of the solid quality, and the feeling of sadness, loneliness and distance arises. Sue interprets. "She's afraid Holly is leaving her behind." I feel her frustrated dissatisfaction with one-way communication. Christi can't tell Holly her experience, can't draw her in to show her what she's been through the last year. A few days later when I'm sitting silently with Christi I hear the phrase arise, "I'm a vegetable." I know those words were said aloud in front of her at the hospital, a prognostication of who she would be, but no one in her current circle would speak them. The meaning I hear is "why bother." It seems like she cannot imagine a new identity in the face of such daunting rebuilding tasks.

At the end of the next day's session Sue joins us and the talk drifts toward the need for more independence for each of them. A new young caregiver, someone in Christi's peer group, is hired and she'll manage the majority of the daily milieu-therapy activities of grooming, stretching, etc. She'll also be the one who reads e-mails from friends so there's a buffer between friends and parents. The idea is for Sue to still be at the house, but working upstairs. The hope is that Sue can begin reclaiming her professional and Mom identities instead of primarily being in the rehab aide role.

The conversation is a signal that moving toward the future is part of the daily equation.

Christi seems to gain strength and momentum again. She responds to the speech therapist's prodding to use the spell board. When asked to select an afternoon activity her eyes flutter to indicate letters. Slowly she selects w-a-l-k. Mary starts the process of procuring a recumbent stationary bike to challenge Christi to strengthen her legs. And Sue leaves the house in short increments. For example, she meets a colleague at a coffee shop to plan next semester's University courses, just like she would have in the pre-accident days. Sue seems eager to share with students how this experience has deepened her understanding and compassion for children with disabilities and their families. She sends an e-mail to her colleagues saying, "one thing I have learned from this experience is to never assume that just because a person can't talk or respond in the way that we are used to that they don't think, feel, hear, or know. Christi has taught me the many nuances of being alive and learning how to communicate in alternative ways."

Late April and early May bring two significant travels away from home for the Forests. The first surrenders a link to the past. Terry, Sue and Christi return to Willamette to pick up all of Christi's belongings that remain in storage. These are the items Christi meant to use when she returned for her sophomore year. It's time also to say goodbye to her friends there. Last summer everyone parted looking forward to seeing each other at school again. As the year has gone on, contacts with these friends have become sparse. Terry and Sue don't know what possibilities are in Christi's future, but they're clear there will be no short term blossoming that puts her back in her class at Willamette. Picking up Christi's belongings ends the dream that started eighteen months earlier. Although Terry and Sue say that Christi seems to be more comfortable being out in public there's also a deep sorrow that friends are passing her. Once they're on campus she literally sees them racing away from her to get to classes. Loading Christi's things in the car feels like they are closing down an expedition outpost, an attempt at settlement that's proven unsustainable. They're retracting, consolidating themselves back into a nuclear family. When they drive away from campus all three have tears in their eyes.

The next week when I see Christi I notice that her face looks different. Even though I'm not sure what I mean, I record in my journal that "I see a strength in the composure of her face—almost like an underlying organization of facial muscles... This probably has a meaning that is not yet apparent." Her breath also sounds smoother, more coordinated and less effortful. During our session she seems to be waving through feelings. These are not deep, encompassing dips. It's more like being in choppy water that jars your boat as you move from one wave to the next. Even the anger that rises isn't held tight like it was previously, but is active, creating its own ripples of movement. I sense she's simultaneously processing leaving Willamette and anticipating with curiosity and some anxiety her second trip, one that is both diagnostic and future-reaching.

Although Christi's top personal goal is to speak, the next step that Sue intuitively follows is another priority. They will work with an eye doctor in Colorado. He is renowned for helping traumatic brain injury patients use specific eye exercises to regain eye movement control and visual processing. The Sapphire therapists have suspected many times that Christi is seeing double and that it is increasing her frustration in trying to focus. They also wonder if she is having light-sensitivity headaches. One of the caregivers makes the trip to Denver with Sue and Christi so they can be a team in maneuvering her in and out of the van and through modified bathing and feeding routines. A full day of evaluation by Dr. Thomas reveals good news because there is no damage to any of the muscle and nerve fibers of her eyes. Christi is getting visual input in both eyes and both eyes send messages to her brain's optical processing center. However, she'll need to do extensive visual training because she *is* seeing double, is very far sighted and is seeing objects as continuously moving or spinning. Sue is validated for an eye care choice she made back in the coma days. Although she couldn't remember the specifics, she remembered reading an article about moistening a patient's eyes to prevent damage that can occur when light reaches unfocused eyes. The medical staff had told Sue that they hadn't heard of it, but since there was no reason not to put in eye drops, they had no objection to Sue making it part of her bedside ministries. Now Dr. Thomas praises Sue's consistent efforts, which continue in the present, of using eye moistening drops. He says it's likely why Christi doesn't have the permanent bands across the visual field common in coma patients.

Besides providing the technical training of teaching visual exercises, Dr. Thomas also offers Sue a patient, hopeful view of recovery. He believes that strengthening Christi's eyes will positively impact motor planning and other sensory processing. His analogy is that Christi was hit with the impact of a large freight train. Her tenacity and modern medicine combined to help her be the 1% survivor. However, our sense of time and hers are not the same. A day in our life is a week in hers. Sue adds up the year of weeks since the accident and renames it as an astounding miracle of recovery in 52 days. Sue returns from Denver re-energized even though the daily regimen is lengthened with another row of exercises added to the whiteboard.

———◆———

Candace

While Sue and Christi go off to Denver I give myself the gift of a day at a meditation retreat with Eugene Cash. Eugene is a Vipassana meditation teacher in the Bay area who has formed ties with a group in Montana. I think the day of simple awareness practice will be excellent counterpoint to my externally focused academic demands.

After the first two alternating sessions of sitting and walking meditation, an inquiry question arises for me. "How do I go out in the world in the most natural way possible?" I assume this question is loosely tied to how confused I am about occupation. If my therapy practice is feeling too confined, what do I want to move into? My perception also is drawn to pain in my lower forearm.

Arm focus doesn't surprise me. Not only have I worked on Christi's arm intensively over all these months, but just the day before leaving I worked with her wrist and fingers. The session left me with a lot of open-ended questions and musings. The work started with a conversation between me and Mary, once again exposing a difference in our approaches. Mary believes Christi's bent wrist and fisted hand is just "hand mechanics." To me, Christi's hand position is a frozen, unresolved reflex. Mary and I talk apples and oranges together. I want to get inside the motivation, the organic intention, to assist Christi in resolving it. For me, the experiential state is like pulling into oneself hard. It's not just a retraction of energy. It also spirals it inward. I wonder what specific reflex has been evoked. Helping Christi open her hand isn't mechanical to me. It's part and parcel of helping her mind feel and express safety and open outward. It is a willingness to extend out into space through her fingers and to break the narrow confines of her kinesphere*. If her mind doesn't shift along with her hand Christi will be like the children I've worked with who crawl with closed fists. Their movement stays gravity bound, downward instead of outward. Because it's possible that Mary's attention to form might get Christi's hand opened sooner, I don't want to be a voice of resistance. Yet, I also want her open hand to be supported by mind.

Another reason I'm not surprised by my wrist pain is because it's the site of an old injury and my own stilted movement. When I was six I broke my wrist twice in a row, meaning I spent almost six months in either a cast or a brace. As a kid I habitually moved in a very contained manner. I

---

* kinesphere is basically the space around yourself you can touch without reaching. Once you go beyond this imaginary bubble you are "breaking" your kinesphere.

remember being a young teen and going shopping with my Dad. As we entered the store he looked over at me and, irritated, said, "move your arms like a normal person." I wasn't aware until that moment that I wasn't being normal. I looked around me to see how I was supposed to move my arms and tried to copy the gentle swinging I saw. This was most definitely form, not mind.

At the retreat I imagine that my broken arm memory and the sensation of pain are bookends on a shelf. I place my focus on the space between them to see what I can discover. I perceive a sensation in my wrist like jumping prickles. It feels like Fourth of July sparklers arising from both bones and nerves. There doesn't seem to be any relationship between the two. Each is so engrossed in its own sputtering that it doesn't register the other. I don't try to change anything. I observe without interference and trust my body's organic process.

When I'm doing walking meditations my perspective widens to feel all of my body. I particularly become aware of an upward flow from my pelvis to beneath my armpits in support of my arms. The full connection through each side of my body feels like it's reactivating a developmental precursor to swinging my arms. Eugene counsels me during our interview to consider focusing on a full out-breath. That seems slightly scary because it breaks my physical habit of making sure I keep a reserve. But as I continue walking and expanding my breath I also notice a flow of energy down my arm. It ends at my wrist as if it were stopped behind a dam. As I continue observing, however, a trickle starts to flow through, into the backside of my palm, and finally out my fingers. Now when I'm walking my arms gently sway in coordination with my steps. The sparking sensation vanishes. A thought emerges that bone and nerves have organized themselves and feel part of a resonant whole.

Driving home from the workshop I wonder about the relationship between kinesphere and ego. What does it really mean to be inside oneself or going beyond oneself? Given my introverted temperament I'll probably always spend more time in inner reflection than outer engagement. On this meditation day I experienced dissolving imbedded habits so that my movements are more organically natural. I briefly experienced thinking as an organic process instead of something filtered through a constructed point of view. As I drive home I'm aware of myself as identity in motion, as a reconfiguration process instead of a defined shape. None of these are thoughts I can consciously hold and examine. They flit through and go into my non-conscious compost heap.

———◆———

Christi and Sue

In late May Sue has a meeting with the Sapphire treatment team. The therapists can point to gains they see in Christi, but their summation is still "not enough progress." This is a horrible "catch 22" for Sue. Without demonstrations of more pronounced gain therapies can't continue. And without the therapies Sue knows the likelihood of gain is diminished. The team agrees to re-evaluate in another month.

I don't attend the team meeting, but the effects of it come into the session I have with Christi the next day. I begin as usual by sitting beside her on the exercise mat. There is a slight movement of her right arm sideways toward me. If I continued the line of energy it would end in taking my hand. Partway into the session, my hands front and back on her torso, there's a sudden dropping sensation. It's like what I feel in the pit of my stomach when an elevator begins to descend. I start singing her a song about a very long mythical journey. I'm inviting her to continue coming out. I observe my choice to communicate in song with an inner raised eyebrow, acknowledging how alien this is to me, yet continue with it because a sing-song voice seems right. Eventually sound drifts away and we are in silence together.

Sue joins us and says aloud, "changes might come in the team," and conveying more certainty than she feels, "sometimes the guides change along the way so you always have someone who has the skill to help you go the next step." It's hard to end the session because I don't feel the usual sense of closure. The magnetic alignment between us isn't released. I interpret this to mean Christi wants to tell me something, but I can't hear what and commitments elsewhere mean I can't wait. That night Sue calls to tell me that an hour later in speech therapy Christi used the spell board to say, "help me get better," and everyone's eyes filled with tears.

Despite Christi's efforts at reaching out for help, Sue and Terry talk privately about their fears that the Sapphire team won't continue. Maybe Sapphire won't act directly to remove themselves. Maybe the doctor overseeing the rehab plan will make a judgment call about the lack of progress that removes the funding. They worry that Christi will perceive it as her own failure and believe less in her ability to continue to progress. Sue and Terry logically know that rehab hours are predicated on achieving objective measures in a time-limited format. They've heard the doomsday prognostications that the only progress a patient will make is in the first year and know that for many patients that's when therapy ends. But they've been assuming that the subtle shifts they see weekly in Christi are signs of encouragement to everyone. Emotionally they feel betrayed. In-home therapy makes the relationships more personal than a clinical setting where the practitioner is clearly employed by the institution.

In my brief contacts with others on the treatment team I hear the "and/both" comments — both a recognition of progress and a discouraged outlook based on training and work with other clients. No one has experience with a patient with Christi's degree of injury *and* a family dedicated to round-the-clock rehab. There begins to be a subtle pushing back against Sue, as if others demand to see a crack in her armor of optimism. They want to know she accepts Christi as she is even if there's no forward progress. It's a "catch 22." A stubborn showdown takes place in silence. Taut coldness is embedded in interchanges for the next two months containing the messages, "Show us you accept her without hope for the future," and "We have to keep hope or we'll surrender to a self-fulfilling prophecy of no more change."

Sue is supported by her connections with family and a few close friends, yet even for them she feels she needs to be cheerleader. She needs to help them continue to believe in Christi's on-going ability to keep growing. This is another place in the Forest's journey where the absence of a coordinating case manager who carries hope hurts them, causing further self-reliance. In my work as a psychotherapist I'm very familiar with bleak times and the need for the therapist to hold steady with hope and hold that flame so the person can fall into the emotion of despair and come out the other side.

Absent a believing case manager, there isn't enough safety for Sue to let go into her own feelings. The danger that Christi will be dropped is too great. A few times though Sue confides in me as I'm coming or going. "Don't they think I know what her condition is? I feed her, bathe her, and get up all through the night. If I don't have hope how can I have the strength to do these things day after day?" When Sue shares this I think again of my role as a psychotherapist and the patience it takes to work with a client for three years, ten years, through dry spells where neither of us can tell what change is slowly accumulating. The healing comes from the consistency of showing up as much as it does from whatever words are spoken. Personally I understand Sue because faced with crisis I too would be dogmatic in my insistence on hope and determination.

Understanding Sue doesn't mean I don't also know the edge that some of the therapists are up against. Although we always seem to have work to do when I come to sessions, I have the feeling Christi isn't using me as much as she was. I notice that the background chatter in my mind is increasing -- maybe I should work fewer hours, or I'm boring her, or since my mind sometimes wanders off course in our sessions maybe the quality of my work with her isn't good enough. It doesn't seem like Christi has receded, but that she's quieter in a different way, as if she's resting on a raft in the center of a backyard pool, ever so gently swaying but not moving anywhere.

When I'm away from Christi spontaneous questions arise. I think about the balance between the outward sympathetic nervous system and the inner parasympathetic system. Naturally in our development, from infancy through adolescence, there are cycles where one system is dominant over the other.[xvii] I wonder if a change like that is occurring. Or perhaps one system became dominant during her survival and now room is being made for the two systems to come into balance again, as if she's moving from a singular coping mode to a two dimensional system. Maybe a nervous system balance change is why I perceive more complexity of feelings coming from her. She can be quietly processing a sorrowful feeling like leaving Willamette (usually associated with parasympathetic system) and be in anticipatory excitement about Colorado (associated with sympathetic system). I don't know how to look up answers to my musings, but there's a sense of rightness to them.

The team meeting that takes place in late June is one I do attend. Change needs to happen with Sapphire. As the different therapists speak many are near tears. The situation is bleak. No one can come up with the next plan. Although community services exist for patients with mild and moderate head injuries there aren't any for those with a severe injury like Christi's. Sue and Terry take the weekend to talk things over. They decide to continue with all the Sapphire therapists but on a reduced time schedule.

The "alternative" treatment providers - Debra, the chiropractor, the naturopath, and me - continue as before. And the rehab aides continue, with Sue's supervision, to do the exercises they've watched the Sapphire therapists do. Throughout early summer Christi continues to make microsteps of progress. I run into Sue and Terry at Saturday morning farmer's market. Terry greets me with an ebullient, "we're tubeless in Montana." Christi is taking in enough fluid and nutrition so that this morning Dr. Seagraves made a house call and took out the gastro tube. Christi has even begun a regimen of sitting on a commode and the catheter is removed once and for all. With her new freedom she spends the weekend being out and about- visiting Rockin' Rudys (the local hip music store), being wheeled through McClay flats for a whiff of nature, and sipping her own drink at Rattlesnake Gardens.

When I see them on Monday, however, Sue is a bit more serious. Last night, and again this morning, Christi had tears on her cheeks. She is having accident flashbacks again, especially at night or when she's lying on her side. Sue perceives intense frustration that Christi couldn't talk to anyone at the accident scene. Sue gets an image of a lot of sound, confusion, and other people around her. When I greet Christi she doesn't give me an overt signal but I'm drawn right away to place one hand over the area of her spleen. It feels bound tight and bloodless. I place my other hand on the right side of her head, sensing a connection to a mid-layer in her brain. (A few days later I ask a neuropsychologist in my office what territory she thinks I was "in" and she tells me the temporal lobe area, which relates to sequencing and speech, a remarkable congruence independent of her knowing anything about the story.)

Each time the rhythms of spleen and brain come into synch with one another Christi startles and raises an arm or leg, pointing and flexing her foot. What I'm most aware of under my hands is cerebrospinal fluid and what I presume to be the energy of chi. I continue to listen with my hands to the ebb and flow between spleen and brain and the description that occurs to me is that there's a back and forth dance between inhibiting nervous system signals and allowing them to flow through. I know nothing about the importance of spleen in this exchange. Yet I sense a satisfaction of deeply knowing and savoring. Despite the intimacy of listening to rhythms I don't feel the personal connection with Christi that we once had. It seems like she is reserving some measure of privacy. The next night I dream again that she is speaking: this time she says a complete sentence in a clear voice. On waking I regret that I can't remember the words.

Not every session I conduct with Christi takes place in her home. Once I meet her at the hospital for a routine EEG exam to monitor possible seizure activity (thankfully there was none). While her parents take a break I sit with her, listening hand on her leg, helping her remain calm through the process of placing electrodes on her scalp and recording signals for half an hour. In late July, I join Christi and her parents in Dr. Gardner's waiting room to help her rest into centered calm before the hole from her trach is repaired. The doctor promises that someday it'll be visible as only a slight crease. As I wait with her I think about the research project I was once slated to start with Dr. Gardner. Although that didn't happen circumstances have led me to this same spot. When it's time for the procedure he invites me into the office surgery to continue hands-on work. Dr. Gardner and his assistant set themselves up on her right side, Sue sits on her left, and I sit at the foot of the table, my hands on her feet.

I listen to Christi throughout the procedure. I hear her floating calm, again on the raft we practiced during her early hospital days, as the process is explained and begun. Each time I feel her fluid quality begin to freeze, like little ice crystals adhering themselves into a skimmed pond surface, I silently remind her to let go back into the movement of fluids. When Dr. Gardner finishes trimming the edges of the hole and begins the stitches, I feel a surge in Christi's lymph system. Several times I blanch and redirect my gaze to the floor or focus exclusively on her feet because seeing the blood and the stitching makes me queasy and distracts me. The stitches take a long time. Christi's equanimity falters, her anxiety surges. I feel it beneath my hand like a bright metal stream down the front of her ankle. For the first time I speak aloud to the team. "Her anxiety is increasing, can you let her know what is left." Without skipping a beat Dr.

Gardner speaks to Christi. "We're three quarters done, maybe ten more minutes." It's enough for Christi to regroup her concentration on floating, on gently moving fluids.

Mid-August the reality-hope standoff finally ends. The decision brings relief as much as disappointment. Sue, Terry and Christi are mentally and emotionally prepared. There has been incremental gain. Mary and the speech therapist both report they are able to read Christi more. Vocalizations and a raised eyebrow help them understand her response to a question or movement suggestion. However, motor initiation continues to be a problem. Only if the movement or verbal request is particularly meaningful to Christi is time delay significantly shortened. Therefore, the Sapphire treatment team decides the gains don't sufficiently reflect the time investment. In-home speech and occupational therapy services come to an end. Mary, the physical therapist, is the only staff member from the team who will proceed. She will come twice a week because she sees that micro-changes continue to accumulate. Also her warm teasing relationship with Christi has an intimacy she's not ready to walk away from.

When I see Christi after this decision she seems relaxed. I place one hand under her sacrum and the other on the back of her skull. I can feel energy flow from her tailbone through her skull. I sense how the spinal cord nerves travel fountain-like up to the brain. They fan outward and tuck themselves under in the sensation of a tidy packet. A comfortable feeling of assurance, of containment, that everything is in its place, enters my mind. The contrast to the accident arises. I can't fathom what it must have felt like to be flung in all directions. I imagine how a liquid tossed carries with it all the "hard" pieces. "Scattered" enters my mind as a singular, all- encompassing word. Then a question, "Have you begun to feel cohesion again?" As a response I perceive softening, release, and an ease that expresses confidence, that "all of me is here." Later when I think about this I have the image of Christi as a puzzle. It's not that pieces are being put back together with an external plan. The puzzle itself is pulling the pieces together.

The Forests deal with the team change setback by taking a weekend away. They decide to travel to Spokane to see a play at the Opera house. For years they've had season tickets and have gone four times a year. The weekends have also included shopping at Nordstrom's and sampling restaurants. Now one of the caregivers goes along to be Christi's roommate and assistant. Christi's eyes are closed for much of the performance but she seems comfortable being there, her body relaxed in her wheelchair, only tightening slightly as she is wheeled in and back out through the crowd. The most fun, though, is the shoe shopping at Nordstrom's. The young man selling shoes speaks directly to Christi as he holds up shoes and waits with Sue through the pause, open to perceiving the slight ripple of cheek and eye widening that signals interest or disinterest.

Refreshed from the weekend away the Forests begin to make a new plan. It is obvious that Sue will need to continue her high involvement with Christi's care and treatment. Returning to teaching full time at the University will have to be delayed. Earlier in the summer it had seemed that Sue could begin to be more independent. Now the kite that was flying further from home has to be reeled back in. Sue is disappointed, yet stoic. Interviews are held to reconstitute their caregiving team. They decide on two new aides who understand that their responsibilities will include routine care, showering and grooming, as well as facilitating stretching, vision exercises, and muscle strengthening. The new hires come in forewarned of the long-term commitment this will be. Even so, they go through a stage of unconsciously hoping their enthusiasm will elicit a miracle and help Christi pop out. As fall progresses they drop the fantasy and engage with the simplicity of daily repetition. All of us on the team know Christi's changes are coming one centimeter at a time.

Throughout the fall there are minor ups and downs. There are days when Christi is more alert and then more asleep. There are weeks when accident trauma memories come in clusters, interrupting sleep, and moans escape like puffs of steam from a volcano. And there are weeks of renewed optimism. She makes a throaty noise to signal that a contact lens has become dislodged. Or she spends a Saturday afternoon at the movies with her peer-aged caregivers. Christi even goes downtown on Halloween night to be part of the revelry.

———— ♦ ————

Candace

Through September, October and November I spin through the same stages of hope and simplicity the caregivers experience over and over again. In my journal I express tension between ambitious goals and accepting the "enoughness" of whatever I'm doing right now. The temptation to grasp dreams of who I might become permeates all aspects of my life, not just my work with Christi. I'm trying to refine my research ideas. I want to incorporate into my research what I've learned about movement development in BMC but I struggle to figure out how to put it into an objective measurement instrument. My primary advisor returns from sabbatical and encourages me to figure it out, believing I'm trying to articulate an understanding valuable to the field. But others on my committee caution me to scale back my ambitions and "hide" the BMC perspective because it'll be considered suspect and distracting in academia. My perceptual system plays tricks on me repeatedly. Instead of seeing solid objects, like books on the shelf, I see everything as spinning molecules. Quantum physicists might tell me I'm seeing objective reality, that in truth everything is always in motion and solidity is an illusion. But I find the experience unsettling. At first I have a primitive reaction, making myself motionless, holding my breath, closing my eyes. Then I consciously begin relaxing and breathe fully while the visual phenomena passes. It makes no conscious sense to me, yet I believe I'm undoing an old fear and reflexive response.

As I write about hope, my understanding deepens that I create fantasies about what may be to sustain myself instead of just being with what is. Filling myself with possibilities is like air puffing itself up, pretending it is substance. On my disillusioned days I feel like an unlucky person who isn't at the right place at the right time. Sorry, the train just left. No, the prince didn't see you when he looked into the crowd. I am the one never picked. I have gold inside me no one can see. My trust that God is guiding my path wavers as I feel lost in the tangle of trees, unable to perceive direction. Pulled by all the possibilities of what I might do I'm disappointed when I can't bring them to fruition. There aren't enough outside supports. I long for a mentor and no one appears. I dream that I go to see a teacher who tells me, "I can see that you've been looking for someone to mold you, shape you. It's ok for you to just let your organism shape itself." I leave the teacher and become lost on the streets of a big city. On the days that I'm confused I plaintively write, "Where is the destiny I imagined I was created for?"

On my clearest days I can almost touch the dream without grabbing tight. For a glimmer I know I'm already living my destiny. I surrender, stop striving, and land on the soft ground where there's satisfaction that each step is in order, faith that they're adding up to the right direction. I see that to be the most skilled aide to Christi's healing process I must find in myself, over and over again, the fullness of my own daily action instead of judging myself as deficient, endlessly waiting for some future accomplishment to prove my value. I need to do this for Christi because it helps me stay connected to the full value of who she is now, in her quiet state that's more about being than doing, instead of subtly conveying that her value will be achieved at some future date when she can walk or talk. If I am quiet enough in myself I find where Christi teaches me the substance of being.

In late fall I begin to want more space to move with Christi. I want to fully stretch her arms or roll spontaneously. The team puts mats on the floor so that we can work from the safety of solid ground. Now that Christi is able to coordinate increasing complexities of sensory input she and I begin working with music that Tom has sent for her to listen to. For many years I've used music in body-mind psychotherapy movement exploration groups. Different sounds elicit different movements. Specific sounds invite diverse body systems to come forward into expression while other systems remain in the background. The music also provides the structure of beginning, process, and ending.

The first week of December when I arrive for a session I put the "Healing Chords" CD in the player but within the first 5 seconds realize it doesn't feel right. I replace it with Waves I by Gabrielle Roth.[xviii] This is a journey, about a half hour long, through five musical evocations: flow, staccato, chaos, lyrical, and stillness. Because the music is providing structure I am free to follow Christi's process without holding that linear framework myself.

As the flow segment begins I reach for Christi's right arm like I have so many times before. She pulls it back from me in a manner I read as, "I'm in charge of my own arm movement." Surprised, yet pleased with her assertion, I focus on her torso and legs. I facilitate slight twists of her torso and bend and stretch her legs. It's like stretching after getting up from a nap or in preparation for a walk through the woods. The transition to staccato music brings on muscle tension. It's as if her motor signals want to send her moving into space but her body can't respond so she is bound up. When the music switches to the middle chaos section my focus spontaneously changes to her glandular system. Without rushing I move my hands around in different combinations, touching one point on her torso and another on her leg or arm. The muscle-bound sensation dissipates and I feel space between the tissues of her body. There is a multi-directional quality to the space even though there are still no external movements coming from Christi. I begin to feel like I'm winding through a dark passage with her, following her turns in a black night maze. When the lyrical music takes over I feel bone marrow flow through her left femur, tibia and fibula, and into her left foot.

In the last section, stillness, Christi opens her eyes. She shifts them slightly to the right, as if she is looking in memory. She does not seem distressed. Then I perceive blackness again. I sense it opens into a clearing. There is black night sky with no moon, yet mysteriously we can see. For a few moments there is only emptiness. And then an image appears in my mind. Christi is lying on the ground. I am beside her, on her left side, as I am in real life. She is also a distance away from me, elevated in the air, five figures fanned along her right side to the top of her head. It seems like the accident scene but there are no other images to confirm this, as if the concrete realm is implied but not visible. A silent communication of understanding is taking place between Christi and the figures. Then the figures look across her body, directly into my eyes. I know them and they know me. Despite the deep familiarity I can't describe their features, as if form is of little relevance, seen yet transparent.

I know without question that they have entrusted Christi back to the ground, knowing I am there beside her, along with all those I represent in that moment. They vanish. Within the blink of an eye we are again just on the floor of her room. When the music ends I sit close to her for a long time. There is a feeling of rest and a bit of residual awe at the truth just exposed. After a bit I'm moved to say aloud to her, "I promise to help you find the language to tell your own story." At that moment Christi feels very adult to me. Later I write in my journal, "She has taken ownership of living her own story."

For many years I think about this experience. How did I recognize the figures around Christi and they me? How did they know in advance how much help Christi would have? What does it mean for spirit to embody bones and water, the flesh of human form? Christi too seems to process this vision over the next several years. The awe of almost leaving the earth alternates with anger that she has had to return for such a difficult journey. Even some therapists and caregivers helping Christi in the years ahead find themselves angry at these "angels," incensed that they required so much from Christi. Perhaps because I have the memory of their eyes seeing into mine I never feel the anger, just the intensity of mystery that I hope will someday be further revealed.

> A wonderful painting is the result of the feeling in your fingers. If you have the feeling of the thickness of the ink in your brush, the painting is already there before you paint. When you dip your brush into the ink you already know the result of your drawing, or else you cannot paint. So before you do something, "being" is there, the result is there. Even though you look as if you were sitting quietly, all your activity, past and present, is included, and the result of your sitting is also already there.
>
> D.T. Suzuki
> Zen Buddhist Scholar

Christi and Sue

Sue and Terry end the year 2000 with extremes. On the uplifting side they spend a night together away for the first time since Christi's accident a year and a half ago. It's not completely unencumbered because Sue has to organize staff before they leave and she constantly carries her cellphone in her pocket. But demonstrating that it can be done means forward progress to both Sue and Terry.

On the down side, just weeks after they return home, Terry suffers a heart attack. Fortunately he immediately receives excellent care. The surgeons are able to make repairs with a stent. While Sue waits in the hospital family area I sit with Christi on her mat at home. Christi's left inner ear seems to be straining, as if it's an antennae for her body, tuned to an invisible station across town. When the phone call comes from Sue that the surgery was a success Christi settles down deeply. Even without an externally visible movement it's clear she has taken and released a deep breath and her tightly focused attention. For the second year in a row the Forests' holiday week is dominated by resting at home.

As the New Year starts Christi seems rather restless. The idea arises to try a dance class. As a young girl Christi was a dancer, particularly loving her creative dance classes where invitations to float like clouds or beat down like a rainstorm were channeled into movements. Serendipitously, a dance class facilitated by University instructor Karen Kaufmann and student volunteers is beginning specifically for people with disabilities. Christi seems intrigued with the idea. Although her range of motion is still very limited we know she can move with flow if the movements are facilitated like they are in PT. The plan is made for Miryam, her primary caregiver, me and a rotating third caregiver to attend the class, purposefully giving Sue a break and encouraging Christi to have an expressive activity independent of her Mom.

The night of the first class we all arrive early, excited by the brand new challenge. In the hallway everyone sheds winter coats and shoes. The dance studio is a small rehearsal space, only 30x30. Twenty-one of us arrange ourselves into an irregularly shaped circle; ten class participants, five UM dancers, three of us helping Christi, two group home staff members, and Karen, the lead teacher.[xix] Karen tells us this class is about having fun, exploring ideas through our bodies, and expressing different kinds of feelings. We warm up with stretches familiar to Christi from PT and that seems to help us settle into the class, reminding us of the foundation we already have.

Although we're in a group class, exploration of movement is individual. Karen stirs our movement explorations with suggestions. Can you move in straight lines? What about squiggles? We move as fast as we can and as slowly as we can. We make big shapes and little shapes, on the floor and while we crisscross our way around the room. We expand, stretching tall or wide, and shrink small as possible.

Each of these movement explorations creates challenges for those of us helping Christi. How do we translate the experience of speed? We move her limbs quickly. We wheel her fast from one side of the room to the other. We wheel her backwards and around in circles. We help her out of her wheelchair and onto the floor for big stretches and curling on her side. We try to feel the movement in our own bodies while simultaneously helping Christi feel it in hers. Christi is processing lots of sensory stimulation. She feels familiar and unfamiliar hands guiding her movements. She perceives her own body moving and other bodies, known and unknown, moving around hers in the space.

The class isn't about building new friendships yet a special click occurs between Christi and Leah, one of the UM dance student facilitators. Leah picks up Christi's subtle expressions, recognizes the presence beneath the stillness, and looks directly into Christi's face. She's not just facilitating movement with Christi, she's engaging in an intimate dialog. It's like intuitive parenting when a Mom perceives and amplifies an infant's impulses. It's easy to imagine this replicating one way our brains develop the neural network linking internal perception and desire with external action.[xx]

Miryam and Leah form a particularly compatible facilitation team, their voiceless communication and synergy enabling them to amplify Christi's range of movements. The class series ends in spring, but Leah continues by coming to Christi's house for private dance sessions. She brings mutuality. She's a college level peer with a love of fashionable apparel and music. Sometimes Leah invites friends who are percussionists to come play while they dance. This is the closest Christi comes to being at a college party.

Although it's barely perceptible, like the blip of a pulse, Christi begins showing the first hints of initiation. Leah is so enthused she invites Christi to "go public" by taking part in a summer community dance concert with lots of alternative performances not typically seen in a dance concert. On the night of the dance the curtain opens to Christi and Leah on opposite sides of the stage. They are dressed alike in black pants and pale pink tops. Leah begins moving, floating arm undulations. Christi sits still in her chair. Probably few in the audience know that her ability to sit quietly, holding her own head steady, is a major accomplishment. Leah crosses the stage to Christi and gently helps lift her right arm. Leah is an extension of Christi. She spirals into Christi, a tender touch of inward sweep, and then reverses, carries a wide reach lightly into air, a flowing arc through her own body. As the line in the song "who knows God's plan" plays, Leah switches to Christi's left side. Before Leah picks up her arm Christi turns her head slightly towards her and moves her arm the first inch or two, up and out, all on her own. Sitting in the audience I almost gasp. Christi's movement is tiny, perhaps even missed by anyone not paying rapt attention. But it's profound to me because it's a demonstration of memory and what we all hope will be the growing power of independent movement. After the concert Sue, Terry and a team of caregivers, each one beaming, cluster around Christi and Leah, presenting them with the traditional recital gift of flowers.

Because Sue and I share background in developmental psychology, we often talk about Christi's progression in developmental terms. We watch, noting micro-steps, as Christi increases her ability for complex sensory processing and physical control of posture and movement of her limbs. Sometimes I think we are watching in slow motion what happens, non-consciously, in early infant development. A month in an infant's life is expressed as a year or two in Christi's.

One of the important tools facilitating Christi's movement recovery is the family hot tub. It is just big enough that Christi can lie diagonally across it with room for Sue to hold her head and shoulders up from behind. Other caregivers easily fit in alongside to help support Christi's torso or legs. In many cases Debra or I join them in the hot tub, conducting our Body Mind Centering movement facilitation work in the water. In addition to the good feeling of floating, the warmth invites tense muscles to release. Freedom from normal gravity allows Christi to explore an expanded range of motion and gentle rocking. She even begins to take her first tentative pushing off "steps" from the side of the hot tub, later transferring this to work in the large therapeutic swimming pool at Community Hospital.

Water as a treatment environment makes a lot of sense. It's become commonplace for runners to use it when rehabbing an injury because they can continue to work their muscles without the pounding impact of running on land. It also makes sense because the water realm, in utero, is where we first practice the foundations of human movement. We kick, push off, roll side to side, even somersault. At one time scientists categorized all this primitive movement as random, as if it were merely a discharge of energy. However, beginning in the 1970s, Hofer and others re-conceptualized in utero movements as integral to development of our neural networks.[xxi] In other words, thumb sucking, kicking and tumbling are developing circuitry in our brains. Movement triggers organization of sensory and motor patterns. Internal and external information is registered and motor responses generated, such as physiologic regulation expressed as swallowing, yawning and sucking. The stepping motions of a growing baby swimming inside Mom are developing the same muscles that kick the air when diapers are changed and eventually propel crawling across the floor and pushing up to standing.[xxii] The common stereotype is that the brain directs all movement, but in reality control develops secondarily; movement experience sets the infrastructure the brain uses later in directing intentional movement. Understanding the importance of in utero movement in brain patterning has led developmental specialists, most prominently Heidelise Als, to advocate radical changes in neonatal intensive care units. Als has spearheaded modifications in incubators and staff-infant interactions so that premature babies can more easily continue their development. In her method the babies can balance rest and spontaneous movement, thus lessening the secondary complications of learning disabilities many premature infants develop.[xxiii] Perhaps someday these insights will also apply to the environment we provide coma patients.

This is over simplification, but a clear image. In crisis, Christi's body reverted to the baseline pattern of development, a developing fetus curling inward around the center point of abdomen. Her arms were bent at the elbows, hands fisted, spiraling inward to rest against her chest. Scientists once talked about early reflexes as disappearing, but now understand that our brains build themselves on a process of reflex inhibition. Full expression of primitive reflexes are modulated and remain as underpinnings of more complicated movements, visible within the diving reach of a baseball player and the arched back of a runner crossing the finish line. Bainbridge Cohen refers to primitive reflexes as our movement alphabet.[xxiv] As we grow they become the makings of complicated words and sentences but never lose the individuality of each unique letter.

Because of the extent of injury to Christi's brain, she has gone all the way back to distinctly expressing the beginning alphabet. Entering the hot tub and learning to float, really float in rest, is a process that takes over a year. At first the procedure of getting Christi into the hot tub creates so much tension and contraction that the session primarily focuses on guiding her towards relaxation. As able-bodied adults we "throw on" a swimsuit and step into the hot tub, as if all the individual steps are part of a single gesture. But for Christi this is a slow deliberate process. Each arm is stretched to enable enough flexibility to put her arms through the top of the suit. She is lifted to standing so the bottom of the suit can be fitted. Then she's carefully moved back into her wheelchair. Shoulders, feet and head are strapped for safety, and finally she's covered in towels for warmth and rolled onto the porch. Once she is beside the hot tub there's another multi-step process. She's guided into a half stand so the basket of the hoyer lift can be placed beneath her and cinched for security. Then she's raised into the air, care given to help her keep her head up and back instead of dropping forward. The lift is pivoted, swinging her over the water, the basket slowly descending into its warmth and the waiting arms of at least one caregiver and most often two. Even though the water is warm, often Christi's first reaction is to flinch, reacting with tension to a new sensation. With words and touch Christi is invited to rest. We whisper to her to drop the weight of her head into Sue's hands and to release the tension in her torso because her rigid muscles and organs seem gripped like a fist. We invite her to let her legs and arms float lightly near the water's surface. Sometimes her arms curl up, exposing them to the cold air and we dribble warm water over goose bumps until she's relaxed enough to let her arms float.

Especially in the early months of using the hot tub, as soon as Christi begins to relax, a cough erupts. Swallowing a natural amount of saliva requires her concentration. It's not yet something that happens beneath her conscious awareness. Christi's coughs are whole body coughs, folding her like a book snapping shut, her navel the center point. Sue, infinitely patient with the repetition, talks Christi through the process of cough and swallow. Her voice is calm, the reassuring parent, as she describes aloud the whole sequence. "You had some phlegm in your throat... it's ok... now you've coughed, cleared your throat... you can swallow... breathe." We start back at the beginning, inviting Christi to relax into floating. It takes nearly a year for Christi to spontaneously swallow her spit and inhibit the impulse to gag and sputter. It's a year of repeated practice to learn to cough using the differentiated action of diaphragm, throat and mouth, omitting propulsion from arms and legs. As she masters this Christi's brain is re-strengthening the neural pathways of physiologic regulation, like those we first lay down in our in utero floating.

Developmental psychologists talk about critical windows of learning. This doesn't mean these times are the only times a skill or pattern can be learned, just that it's the optimum time. At any other time it takes longer and is perhaps more awkward, like inserting a big heavy dictionary beneath a tottering stack of smaller books. As an adult Christi is outside the critical window of mastering and integrating primitive reflexes, but with patience beyond what most of us can imagine she methodically accumulates the kinesthetic knowledge that's a foundation for all types of learning.

Candace

Looking back through my springtime journals I notice I write the word "choppy" multiple times. One reason is because, although the routines of home rehab are going along steadily for Sue, Christi, and the team, there are short bursts of discomfort. Tom has continued to send Christi DJ'd CDs, but they now speak of his struggles with drifting apart. He tells her he's still confused by the conversation they began in Oregon, months before the accident. The talk about, "dating, waiting and all that complicated stuff...I won't be able to figure it out until we get to talk some more or someone else comes into my life. It's so hard 'cuz I get so lonely and I want someone to fill that empty space and then I think about you and what we had and how much I love spending time with you and after that I'm back to square one. But regardless of the outcome, I want you to know no matter what I still and always will love you." He tells her, "I hope these messages aren't coming across as pressure. I'm trying to inspire you, to let you know you're not alone. There are people you can't see or hear all sending love and compassion your way." Slowly, Tom is becoming one of the people sending love from further and further away.

My own work with Christi is interrupted as I travel for several family trips and focus on getting my first round research articulated. The language and statistical format to express what I want to analyze keep eluding me. When my classmates talk excitedly about disproving someone else's findings with their own research I feel increasingly alienated. Academia seems more and more like a one-upmanship contest, one that I don't want to play. In my work I make adjustments by combining psychotherapy and consulting, but my attempts to re-ignite the passion I once had fall short. The one idea that does intrigue me is taking a journalism class to learn how to write stories about the science of development as well as "something about alternative medicine." However, I can't imagine any way to fit this into my crammed schedule or where it could lead professionally.

I'm uncomfortable with my inability to find direction. I write in my journal, "I'm like a compass that is bobbing in a circle with a loss of the necessary magnetism to lock in a direction… I am waiting for resonance. For the deep yes that says this way… Plants must wait for the right alignment of warmth, light, softness of earth to begin their growth. Like them I'm waiting for the conditions to pull me forth. And perhaps the commitment I'm waiting for is the one to myself. To recognize my own core more deeply and support its emergence. Please guide me, God."

During this time period Sue's directional course is also challenged. When she takes Christi to Denver for a re-evaluation with the vision specialist he says he's seeing progress. Yet, he believes Sue needs to stay home full time with Christi in order to get maximum results. On top of this Mary again brings up lack of progress and drops back to only one session per week. This means Sue must work with the caregiving team to replicate the best they can what Mary was doing. And finally, the chairperson of the psychology department tells Sue she needs to come back to work full time for the sake of the program she runs. Sue has tears brimming in her eyes when she expresses how helpless she feels to meet all the demands, to keep everything afloat. She has her own discouragement about Christi's slow pace of change yet has to stay positive for everyone else. When we talk I remind her that Christi made the choice to live, it wasn't something Sue forced. Neither of them could know how difficult the journey would be.

On Memorial Day weekend the death of Dudley's Aunt Florence knocks loose more of my preconceptions about spirit and embodiment. We aren't with her at the moment of death. That happens in a frantic commotion of relatives and paramedics. During a family dinner party Florence chokes on a piece of food and the loss of oxygen causes her heart to give out. The family calls us to meet them at the emergency room. When we arrive Florence has been dead for over an hour but she is still lying at rest on the examining room table. The family is sitting, shocked into immobility, in an adjacent private room. I'm not sure why Dudley's cousin wants us to see Florence, but she insists.

Dudley and I sit down on either side of Florence, completely unsure what to say or how to act. I touch her arm, inanimate and impersonal stone. That feels like no kind of goodbye so I lay my other hand on her forehead. Startled, my eyes lift in surprise. I inhale sharply because I feel the sensation of swirling, a bit like a spiral staircase wending its way upward. I say aloud to Dudley, "She's not all the way gone, you can still say goodbye." He must know what I mean because he leans forward, touches her shoulder, and with bowed head enters a prayer state I've seen him adopt many times in church.

I switch my right hand to her forehead and place my left behind her head, letting the sensation of swirl touch me. In BMC we describe the tactile experience of glandular activity as something halfway between air and water and this is the texture I experience in Florence. My left hand is on the upper third of her skull, a resonating touch point for the pineal gland. A back and forth rhythm ping pongs between my hands. A mini shudder shakes the pulse and I sense the startle of choking. The part of my mind witnessing my experience wonders if needing to release this shock has slowed down her spirit's leaving. Then the intensity of the swirl increases, bouncing into my left hand. It begins to pass through my hand and beyond into some other dimension of time space. It's like it is slipping through an open seam into a hidden pocket, not entering the ER room. The moving energy feels huge, like a storm, yet nothing is moving in the room itself.

Outside the room I can hear the nurses and doctors laughing, talking about parties planned for their holiday weekend. I am tempted to peevishly call out "keep it down, don't you know someone is in here dying." But in the next instant I realize their laughter is the cycle of life. Florence is exiting amid continuity. In BMC perspective the pineal energy is an exit point and loops around and re-enters as life force at the tip of the tail, the coccygeal body, the red root chakra. I consciously ground my body down onto the chair to feel my own tail support. Oddly, once I embrace the camaraderie of the staff's chatter their sounds disappear in my perception and I sense only the privacy of our room.

My eyes are open, yet slightly unfocused. I begin seeing as if dreaming. I am in completely open prairie, like the Wyoming prairie where Florence's family homesteaded. Florence, as a very young and joyous girl riding bareback on a fast horse, enters my vision from the left and passes in front of me. She doesn't fall, but gracefully slides backwards off the rump of the horse, then continues through my left hand where it rests on her skull. She disappears into a dark seam opening while the horse continues to gallop even faster across my field of vision, freed from its burden of carrying a child. The swirling sensation and image vanish like a dissipated cloud. All of Florence is as still as when I first touched her arm.

Simultaneously Dudley and I look up. Without saying anything we get up and leave Florence. As we enter the family room everyone rises. Someone says, "Let's go back to the house," and like automatons everyone moves. Once we're back at the house I don't feel like talking so I wash dishes, marveling at how precious and full this task feels. I look down at my hands in soapy water, recognizing the sameness in them in supporting a spirit's passing and washing dishes. I'm too spacey for conversation. The left side of my head feels fuzzy and buzzing so I'm relieved when Dudley drives us home. I fall deeply and dreamlessly asleep in the comfort of my bed.

Christi and Sue

Summer is a quiet time in Christi's rehab. When her 21st birthday comes Sue and Terry take her out to dinner and serve her a glass of wine. Christi doesn't drink it all, but that's not the point. It marks the event in a traditional way. I write in my journal that it's "not the emancipation of a 21 year old, but on-going rebirthing."

In the month that follows Christi lapses into increasing passivity. Her caregivers still help stretch her arms and guide her hot tub relaxations, but Christi is disengaged. Unlike her earlier depressions that seemed weighted with negativity, this phase is characterized by collapsed, flat energy. It's as if she doesn't even have the energy to be negative. I wonder to myself if a response like this typically occurs in rehab. It's one I'm familiar with from psychotherapy with long-term clients. When they feel lost amongst the trees and unable to imagine a big picture, they stop even looking about. In my sessions with Christi I hear absent silence when I touch her, as if no internal impulse is being transmitted. Many on the caregiving team feel like Christi doesn't care if they're there.

A shift starts to happen around the end of August. Since Christi isn't initiating much, I decide to add guided meditations to our work. I combine touch and spontaneous verbal visualizations based on whatever arises in my awareness. One day when we're doing this I have my hand over her right kidney and ask her to visualize a cell. As I invite her to imagine all the components, we hit a feeling of suspended shock around the nuclear membrane. For a momentary flash I feel an electric wire static charge. It feels entirely split off in the dimension of air, and has no relationship to the transforming power of bodily fluids. The feeling vanishes without any resolution.

In the night Christi wakes up and stays on alert for nearly four hours. Sue describes it as "charged lightening." Usually Sue can help soothe Christi back to sleep, but not this time. In the morning when Debra arrives for a session Sue and Christi are both exhausted. Debra quietly touches Christi, inviting the softening of fluids to enter her mind. She talks slowly to her, helping to normalize the feeling of fear that can take hold when all our reflexes respond to distress. Finally, Christi's breathing begins to deepen and she falls into sleep.

A few days later Christi, Sue, Miryam and I do a session in the hot tub. My hands are on Christi's head and right shoulder. An image arises of settling onto thick cushioning moss. As I gently encourage Christi to yield and settle into this cushion the image changes. It seems now as if the cushion is the uterine wall and Christi settles briefly and then pushes off. Like I'm tracking undulating rhythms I follow the flow of sinking into and pushing off for several minutes. But then I start to become confused by another movement signal. I feel the environment contracting and inhibiting her movement and the fluid space around her. My hands listen to a jumble I can't decode or direct. There's sensation without an accompanying story. Then a strong sensation of CSF (cerebro-spinal fluid) flowing down

Christi's spine. Even though she doesn't move it's like I feel her rock down and back along a long vertical tube.

Then Christi's relaxation seems to deepen. I become aware of the calm emanating from Sue and Miryam and an open-ended feeling like nothing needs to be rushed, we have all the time in the world to just be. After several minutes of quiet floating the end of the session comes as a pre-arranged time rather than an impulse arising from any of us. Still, it feels as though Christi has entered another stage of inner journey. It is glacially slow. In my journal I describe it as "watery composting, a fueling regeneration." When I return later in the week and we work on the mat I note that the right side of Christi's brain feels the most full that I've ever felt. Habitually, like a weighted ball, her head has rolled left whenever she's lying on her back. For the first time her head rests turned to the right throughout our entire session.

Candace

The gentle progression of Christi's work is jostled, for her and everyone else, when the 9/11 catastrophe hits. Fear and uncertainty are deeply stirred for most everyone in the country. Even newscast reporters talk from behind shocked eyes. A day later when I'm working with Christi my attention is erratic as I drift in and out of perceiving my own fear. At the end of the session I have a moment of clarity with her. I realize how many souls are probably hovering near the border of embodiment because they left life so suddenly. I tell Christi that she might perceive that since she so recently was on this side of that border. Her slightly furrowed brow in response makes me think she knows what I'm saying. I encourage her by saying someday the wisdom of her experience may be something she uses to help others who experience trauma. She knows how suddenly what you knew can change. As I leave the house I caution the caregivers to limit how much of the non-stop news shows Christi watches in order to limit secondary trauma. As I drive home I nearly have to pull my car over because the beauty of the light on the hills is so magnificent and captivating. I feel a strong wave of the presence of love and am comforted.

For the next several months my focus is dominated by my psychotherapy practice because all my clients are deeply affected by 9/11. Some are rocked by the resonance to life long fears and experiences of maliciousness. They don't sleep well at night and startle easily. Some become hypervigilant to sound. Rational reasoning doesn't resolve the fear and our sessions depend on using the same tools I've practiced with Christi all year. We breathe together, imagine fluids and the structures of bone. I keep guiding them toward the confidence to yield and rest.

For other clients the tragedy is a wake-up call that life must be lived fully because there is no guarantee. The work for these clients is to hear what passion they've been tamping down. We do lots of breathing into organs and aligning their support. We examine the fears that keep them from acting on what they've longed for. As they become more aware of self-limiting beliefs about what choices they've considered allowed or un-allowed and explore new options they also discover newfound energy to literally move their arms and legs. There's energy to break through their kinesphere. My clients commit and un-commit to relationships, return to school, and move to new cities.

In my own world I'm living a combination of the experiences of my clients. Before 9/11 my life was already in upheaval and disorientation because Dudley and I were mid-way into a major remodel of our house. For months we've camped out in a tent while most of the old house was pulled apart. We're literally redoing the bones and fluids of home. New rooms are being created and for the first time we'll have year round running water. Aligning with my heart's desire we've added a kitchen filled with light and a room for my art and studying. I struggle to maintain a small semblance of order and progression in the whole process but unwieldy chaos frequently knocks both Dudley and me off base. As if it's a daily mindfulness practice, throughout fall I'm re-grouping to find my embodied centerpoint, my solid connection to him, and then the action path out.

Late in the fall Christi shows me her awakening connection of inside to outside. As our session begins, she seems deeply internal. This isn't in a withdrawn manner. Like a swimmer way down in the water she's engaged in moving within deep body currents only perceptible to her. A question arises in my mind about how deep currents connect to expression in words, gesture and movement. In Christi I feel a wide dark gap between the two. Then my awareness is drawn to bone and the sense that oceanic marrow is infusing the honeycombed structure of compact bone. I ask if it'll come all the way to the surface of bone and connect to muscle but that intention isn't here today. The pervasive feeling is a peacefully dreamy state and I drift in that space with Christi. Finally as the session comes to a close I get a glimmer of how a wave forms in relation to deep current. Seen from above it looks unconnected, as if riding over the depth independently. But looking from Christi's perspective I feel momentum rising from below, direction that will ultimately shape a wave.

———◆———

Christi and Sue

In early December Christi goes through another stretch of flashbacks that relate to her immobility right after the accident and during the hospitalizations. What's new about this series of memories, however, is that they seem less about reliving the vivid experience than about finding a place to set each event down in time and place. It's like when a 3 or 4 year-old wants to hear the story of her birth over and over again. The child wants to hear the words out loud, in sequential order, giving definition and structure to an experience that resides unbound by time in sensory awareness.[xxv]

Just before Christmas Christi awakens at 11:40 PM, the same time last week's flashbacks roused her from sleep. Sue wakes up at the same time and goes down to Christi's room and lies down beside her, matching her breath to Christi's until they both fall asleep again. Sue feels herself merge into a shared dream of the accident where Christi is mouthing, trying to call for help. The striving wakes them both up and

Sue reassures Christi that everything is ok now. Sleep pulls them both under again. Now Sue feels herself in a dream on the edge of Christi's dream. Christi is far away, meeting a lover. Sue isn't seeing it explicitly, yet knows it's a deep love. Christi then melts back, deeply relaxed. When Sue tells me the dream the next morning it sounds like astral travel, going across space-time instead of inside personal body-mind. I wonder if union with a beloved gives Christi direction or reassurance at a time when she needs it. Or if it reminds her that someday the feeling of pleasure will replace the memory of trauma.

> "If I pay attention to what is happening inside, what wants to open next, it will always intensify. And as I sense each new capacity, I also discover what is in the way, preventing my opening. So if I sense my compassion is growing, I also encounter the doubts and resistances that stop me from really living in compassion. Acknowledging this becomes the next step in the process of opening."
>
> Jack Kornfield, After the Ecstasy

Candace

Even though I desperately want it, cohesion and advancement elude me. Our six months of major remodeling has ended and we're living in our house. Still, there are countless tasks that drag on. It takes three months to get my cook-top burners all working, the carpets in, and the bookcases installed. I continue dreaming of missed airplanes. Dudley and I can't get to the gate at the same time or I lose my shoes or luggage and miss getting on board. As if the displacement from re-modeling isn't enough, in January we discover the psychology office Dudley and I share is infested with mold. The mysterious illnesses we've all had the past two months start to make sense. Within one week we find temporary space and move. I start going to the doctor to figure out why I'm so fatigued and dizzy. The only thing they identify is that my immune system is stressed and they start me on a month of medications. During this month we also tread through fears that calcifications that show up in my mammogram are cancerous. It's an enormous relief when the biopsy shows all clear. Spring brings the opportunity to move into new offices with our good friend and we imagine a fresh start. Dudley gets accepted to an April artist's residency at Ucross and immerses himself in his photography. While he's gone I make progress on my research project examining interactions between Moms and their six-month-olds. My preliminary analysis of the data does uncover what I hoped to find regarding infant movement and increased social interaction.

My body, however, lags behind the fresh start I envision. I'm not so comfortable in my skin. It feels like there's sandpaper just beneath the surface, scratching me with every movement. Hypersensitivity makes me search my closet for the softest clothes I own to wear to work. Sound that comes from two rooms away irrationally feels like invasion. I close the door to my room to keep sound at bay. I dream I'm bit hard three times by a rattlesnake the size of a 10 year old. The rattler is upright in the middle of a street. Cars are pulled off and drivers yell warnings. But I don't hear them and never see the snake until it strikes me. I wake up in shock and for days have a hard time shaking the dream. On many days I'm sad. There's no discernible cause, just sadness. All the effort I expended to "keep it together," to make it through months of upheaval, have left me exhausted. The bones in my shoulders and ribs feel brittle and like they're cracking open. I re-frame this in my mind as spring. I write, "Does the earth feel this way when a bud pushes through? Or the husk of a bud when the blossom begins to unfurl? Cracking open in this benevolent universe let me trust all the nourishment of support." Nourishing support is my longing, not yet felt experience.

Throughout spring Sue and I talk a lot about new ideas and support. Sue is still working part time at the University and on a start up grant for Early Head Start. But she and I both long to find a way to expand on the ideas that open as we work with Christi. Independent of the sessions I do with Christi I start meeting with Sue. Each meeting gives us the opportunity to step back and begin re-telling and categorizing the stories of the last year. Sue and I know we'd love to talk to other families and patients to find out if they experienced anything similar. Maybe our stories together can make a difference. How have they dealt with combining allopathic and alternative therapies? How have they navigated costs and agencies? Have they had unusual sensory experiences? Have peers stayed involved? We start looking around for grants that can support our efforts to explore these questions.

Christi and Sue

Sue is expansive about new ideas because Christi's healing work progresses relatively quietly through winter and early spring. Only one brief glitch occurs when a hand specialist they consult recommends fusing the bones of Christi's wrists so that her hands won't continue to curl inward. The doctor reasons this will let her have more functional use of her hands because they'll be turned outward. Sue and Terry don't agree. They see the progress Christi is making in gaining conscious control over her arms.

They believe the softening that's begun in her forearms will eventually spread down through her wrists, and someday all the way down to her fingers. They reject the medical intervention and keep up intensive stretching exercises.

Mary continues to come to the house for physical therapy once a week and on the other days Sue and the caregivers repeat the routines Mary designs. Vision exercises, chiropractic adjustments, Body Mind Centering sessions and hot tub relaxations fill out the schedule. There are so many therapies to keep track of Terry installs a larger 3'x4' whiteboard calendar on the wall next to Christi's mat.

Once a week Christi dances with Miryam and Leah. As her flexibility and coordination increase their dances become more complex. Using Miryam on one side, facilitating, and Leah on the other, Christi can move both arms at the same time. Her arms can mirror one another or go in opposite directions. Leah begins introducing set choreography rather than spontaneous changes. Four times they circle the arms right, as if tracing the rim of a huge bowl sitting on Christi's lap, and then circle four times left. The next set is four waves, one arm bent in to the waist and the other extended to the side. Sometimes Leah forgets the routine and Christi is the one who pulses the start for the next direction. Christi's body-mind is retaining pattern memory.

In late April I have a session with Christi that illustrates how hard she's working to coordinate incoming and outgoing signals in order to express herself in movement. On the day of our session Sue tells me that Christi was awake in the night. She had exceptionally high tone all the way up to her face. It took Sue an hour of talking and comforting her for the tension to ease. As we begin our work I'm drawn to place my hands on her torso and under her back. My hands are positioned as bookends for the space taken up by the top portion of her liver. After a few minutes of silence I begin to feel a build up of something I can't put my finger on. I exhale long and audibly. Christi exhales strongly in reply, repeating my sound. Then her face takes on the shape of sobbing. Hard sobbing but without sound or tears. When this subsides I put into words the sense I perceive, that she's "tripped up by a domino of confusion, overwhelm, and scared anxiety." The confusion begins with too many sensory signals and time disorientation. The phrase I hear back from her is she's been "hurtling through space/time." I can't tell if space and time are two separate words or a single perception since I hear it as space/time. I begin talking to her about internal perception and outside expression and action. In my mind's eye I see a gap between the two. Unlike other times when it's been a void, this time it's like thickened polluted air. Christi withdraws, pulled down by some internal dreamlike imagery. After a brief minute she startles awake.

I say the word "demons" but I know it's not exactly the right word. I can't think of a better one to express what I mean about overcoming something negative as part of our inner journey. For today, Christi's demon is the polluted fog between inner and outer which traps her far away from others. I talk about aloneness and being connected like I would talk with a psychotherapy client. I acknowledge how alone she is when facing whatever she experiences down deep inside herself. And I remind her she's surrounded with people who love and care about her. The journey to connect our innermost selves with a caring outer world is a mythic one for most people. Our community has an "Art of Healing" show Christi is scheduled to see the very next day. I suggest to her that she look at it with attention to how each artist depicted inner experience. Christi does not yet look directly at objects with sustained, open-eyed focus. I think, however, she does register visual stimuli and I assume she'll take something away from the art experience.

By mid-week Christi begins to show something new in physical therapy sessions. When she is sitting upright and begins to falter, her head and body righting reflexes begin to kick in. More spontaneous movement is elicited by situational context. For instance, when her ankle is unstrapped from the footrest she initiates forward movement to place it on the ground. Christi appears to be more emotionally frustrated when she can't move on command. It's not that she is actively scowling or making sounds of exasperation. It's "just a feeling" many on the caregiving team get. During this time period Christi sometimes appears in my dreams in two positions at once. She is standing by the window looking out and also lying in her bed. I think this expresses what many of us feel being with her. Christi's intention would take her all the way to standing. But her inability to coordinate motor patterns leaves her barely moving. She is "locked in" and understandably frustrated.

In May Sue resigns from both of her part time jobs. She needs to leave her job at the University because the program needs her to be full time and neither her heart not her energy level will allow that to happen. The Head Start job requires too many committed hours when she still needs flexibility to respond to Christi's daily needs. The financial loss will be difficult for the family, but the emotional demand to give more than she has takes an even more damaging toll. Miryam, a key caregiver for Christi whom Sue really trusts, needs to return home to Canada and will leave them in the late summer. Sue knows this will require her to hire and train a new person and that will seriously limit the amount of time she can be out of the home. Christi displays consternation with a continuously furrowed brow for a few days after the decision. After one of our sessions Sue and I talk with her together, assuring her that she is not wholly responsible for this decision. Sue is leaving as part of her own career evolution, something that eventually would have happened even without this rehab detour.

Sue quits at the beginning of summer to give the University time to hire someone new. She also wants to leave on vacation unencumbered. Sue, Terry and Christi are taking their first post-accident vacation. For ten days they will be without any caregivers. Their trip takes them to Denver for a short re-evaluation at Craig. Christi's favorite speech therapist is still there and tells them she still believes Christi will talk someday. She just needs to keep relaxing and let it come.

The rest of the vacation is shared with family at the bi-annual reunion. Christi has a cousin, Erin, just a few days older than herself. Sue and Terry don't shy away from the unspoken comparisons. The girls have grown up together and the Forests see no reason the changed circumstances should disrupt their ties. Erin's success is in college and Christi's is in the micro steps of rehab. For Sue and Terry what's most important is maintaining loving ties and continuing traditions that supported them over their life span.

Candace

While the Forests are off on their trip I give myself the end of semester gift of attending a meditation retreat. Eugene Cash, the Vipassana teacher I worked with before, is returning to Montana to lead the group. I think it'll be exactly what I need to soothe my fatigue and sorrow. My friend who is serving as retreat coordinator knows my tenderness and arranges for me to be housed in one of the tiny cabins that will be extra quiet. As the retreat starts we're asked to sign up for two jobs, like ringing the bells to announce meetings or helping the cook, all of us together building the support structure necessary for five days. Uncharacteristically I allow myself to underperform and only sign up for one job, a cooking shift. I know I can't commit to support any structure outside myself. Intuitively I know that what's required of me is letting go of chronic orientation to what is going on around me. My body-mind has been stuck in the open position too long. I'm ready to discover more deeply the direction that will emerge rather than striving to fulfill set expectations. Even though the order of each day is simple- sit, walk, sit, walk- the time for each vanishes from my awareness. I read the schedule over and over without retention.

After the first two sitting periods I am settling into the gentleness of the retreat center. We're practicing sitting still, feeling the ease of head perfectly balanced on the spine. I breathe deeply. I'm imagining with relief the days ahead with extra naps during the breaks. I anticipate spacious quiet nurturing me. I even hear the distant churn of a motorboat on the lake as perfect union with our meditation instead of rejecting it as a sound intrusion. However, rather than continuing to slowly settle into calm, by the third sitting period I descend into sensations of manic activity, like I'm ready to run for hours without stopping. Internally I feel a wild jungle without paths. My bones are freezing cold in the center. The marrow is quaking. I feel unfamiliar to myself and this generates even more physical fear and panic. Arising from the bones themselves I sense the experience of terror. No words, sounds or images. Just terror unleashed from an underground cave in a flurry of wings. I become even more panicked, wanting to grasp any habitual orientation. Every cell in my body seems to be striving. Deep within the cytoplasm of each cell there is a self trying to remain upright, as if I'm a drowning swimmer trying to keep my head upright where I can breathe. This is more primitive than sight. It's my ears, everywhere in my body, desperately trying to reference gravity.

My internal speed is so off-kilter with the slow walking meditations that Eugene encourages me to walk faster whenever I need to. I go up the steep hills behind the retreat center, taking rapid, tiny breaths into the place of panic. One breath I hear happiness, birds rustling, calling to one another enthusiastically and to the sun because spring has finally arrived. One breath I want to flee, as if a firestorm is raging somewhere close and every instinct says go without looking back. I lose more and more reference to time. Thanks to the time-keeping bell ringers and pull of the group's deep internal rhythmic clock, however, I continue to show up for each dharma talk and sitting meditation.

Eugene tells me to practice kindness to myself. When I come back from walks I wrap myself in layers of blankets even though they offer little warmth to the deep frozen fear. In my mind's eye I imagine laying kindness down next to the chilled bone, not to change it, only whispering "I'm here with you." Eugene sees that the whole group needs the gift of self-directed love and together we practice loving kindness meditation. When the part comes to offer kindness to ourselves I begin crying. For the rest of the weekend every time we do this meditation I cry in sorrow for my fear and pain. Even as the sweetness of love grows and enters, thawing the ground of my being, it reveals deeper and deeper layers of hurt.

Few words or stories come to me. My analytic witness persona has temporarily vanished. One insight does land on my doorstep though. I see that I'm anxious about fulfilling the right action or expression for my life. Will I do the work I'm called to do? I don't doubt that down deep I have a true nature. I just don't know how it will be expressed. I want to trust that as I am ready the timing of the universe will make it come to pass. Paradoxically, I worry that once my full capabilities are called upon I might not have the ability to support myself well enough to succeed.

On the last morning of the retreat I dream I can hear the bells calling me. I open the door joyously, gratefully, to welcome the sound of the bell. Instead of beauty, evil enters. I awake profoundly saddened. In the first sitting meditation I think of the dream and the recognition comes, "this is the moment I lost naiveté." Even though it was a dream I feel it as memory. There was a time I threw the doors of myself wide open and learned I wasn't safe. I tempered joy and trust with vigilance and wariness. Now I'm being given a chance to correct the pattern that became imbedded as reflex. One summer of BMC training Bonnie repeated the phrase, "how do we feel safe in an unsafe world?" I haven't solved that conundrum, but I know for the sake of my deepest self I need to.

By our last sitting I am still wrapped in a blanket, pulled close over my head, still trying to warm my chill. I cry again when we practice loving kindness meditation. As we face one another to begin talking, breaking our days of silence, I sit opposite a dear friend and let tears be my half of the conversation. I choose not to artificially collect myself into a happy ending. I thought coming here I would find glue to put myself back together from the hard year. Instead I saw the falseness of trying to be my own glue. My greater task is to trust the cohesion that exists as a law of nature. Randomness is part of the whole of creation. My mantra becomes "discover yield; find the release that supports knowing who and where I am."

I reflect on this experience many times throughout the year ahead. It's not a surprise that bones are such an integral part of my inquiry. Bones are the levers that move us into space, into action in the world. Bones have both the life force of blood and the density that provides structure and stability. Serotonin and oxytocin, neurotransmitters usually associated with feeling good and bonding with others also affect bone function.[xxvi] At other times in my life when I've opened the door to deep sensory inquiry I have felt fear. It used to show itself as whirling chaos or as the sound of shattered glass. The inner fear experience has repeated so many times I've even asked my mother if anything happened when I was an infant, suspecting I might be non-verbally remembering a true life incident. "Maybe," she muses, "there was the time when you were little there was a hurricane." It probably doesn't matter if I ever know a factual story. Maybe there never was a real incident. Maybe I just remember disorganizing sensations I had as an infant because of energies moving inside and outside myself. Whirling and shattered glass are just image descriptors. They are examples of what Dr. Daniel Stern in *Diary of a Baby* calls "storms."[xxvii] What is important is that I stop trying to urgently keep my head upright, flailing like I'm afraid I'm going to drown. Sometimes it's important to lay your head back and let the current take you.

———•◆•———

Christi and Sue

Early summer already carries the shadow of fall. Not only is Miryam moving away, but also by September Leah plans to be living on the west coast to pursue more training. The dance trio that's worked so well together is ending. To finish on a celebratory note the three of them construct a Hawaiian themed dance based on the circular arm movements they've practiced all spring. Their dance concert is in the basement of the Forest's home. About twenty-five of us attend, sitting on the floor and in chairs in a staggered semi- circle. Some of us are from the treatment team, some neighbors, and a few professional colleagues of Sue. Miryam and Leah help Christi dance her arms in slow motion hula dancer gestures. The three of them are so seamless it's like a movement beginning with Miryam travels through Christi and out the other side into Leah's continuation of the gesture. Their dance conveys the soft wave of tall grasses in gentle breeze. Christi's dedicated effort to reclaim movement is applauded by all of us. As everyone chitchats before leaving, however, there's discomfort in the pauses. No one says they were expecting more but the sentiment is there like a ghost in the room. The subtleties in the dance - Christi participating in directing her arm, of finding internal fluidity in gesture instead of dry pushes - was only faintly felt by those of us in the audience. What we see in the backdrop is the distance the recovery journey still has to go.

A long distance runner who competed in the Badwater Ultra-marathon once told me that one of the most daunting parts of the race is "seeing the road ribbon 40 or 75 miles ahead." The grueling 135-mile race goes through the heart of

Death Valley in July. He says he'd rather run an equally difficult trail without being able to see so far ahead or behind. "In Badwater," he says, "you run for two hours and the distance in front and behind all still looks the same." I wonder sometimes if Christi feels like this runner. She works incredibly hard, yet the landmarks of progress aren't clearly distinguished and the distance to go extends so far ahead the end point vanishes.

On a good day the treatment team surrounding Christi cheers her on, celebrating the amazing feat of being in the race. But on bad days we too look down the length of road and we're discouraged. Like in the Badwater race, it's an endurance event for the support team too. Friends who mean to be supportive ask us questions about our work with Christi. These questions usually come in the form of, "How's she doing? Is she _____, yet?" It's always a hard question to answer. How do you convey meaningful change when you say, "there's so much more life on the inside of her forearms," or "she made a spontaneous sound the other day when her Mom teased her about showing off for guys." Most of us on the treatment team are fine when we're in the session with Christi because in that instant we're sensing awakening and subtle shifts. But sometimes outside of session, like in the mixed group at the dance performance, we see through the eyes of success measured by generally observable landmarks, like the ability to move your own arm independently. We all can see this skill is still somewhere far down the ribbon of highway. This is why the basement dance performance ends with an unstated undertone of "is this enough?"

The undertone was there, too, when Sue and Terry drove away from the family reunion. Family members want to be swept into the magic of incremental steps, but they ache for the big visible signs. After the dance performance a neighbor of the Forests says the slow journey is too painful for her to watch. She wants to go back to her memories of Christi in high school. Even though she's just down the street a divide settles between them.

The mood in the room at the end of the dance probably also reflects the sadness about change in the caregiving team. Miryam has been a key person of the heart. Her presence offers calmness and loving regard for Christi and her parents that infuses all the routine tasks. Miryam is exceptional in her ability to give fully, yet know that the story being played out belongs to Sue, Terry and Christi. She's clear her role isn't to second-guess them, but to support wherever they are on the path. We all know her generous steadiness will be missed.

After Miryam's departure Christi enters a bit of a funk. It's like she slows down and retreats inward. For Christi's long time friends and family, seeing her distance herself like this isn't unusual. When Christi had a problem or feelings she wanted to work through she often wanted to be alone. She'd go for a drive or hike and think things through. One of the challenges for any individual, especially a highly autonomous person like Christi, who becomes one hundred percent dependent on others, is that she can't just go away for an afternoon of solitude, at least not physically. Many times in her recovery process, during times of change or particularly daunting obstacles, she seems to travel away in the only way she can, by removing her engagement with those of us in her helping world. Rather than an engaged, participatory partner, we're met by passivity and apathy.

Debra, who has known Christi through many years, is very sensitive to Christi's need for space, but also the need to find her way back into connection. In one of her sessions she helps Christi onto the mat placed on the floor. She guides Christi onto her side, legs and arms bent, her back rounded into a curled position. Debra murmurs encouragement to rest, to feel the support of the mat beneath her. She curls herself behind Christi and holds her.[xxviii] After a very long pause Debra begins to tell Christi how much she's seen her grow, how much she admires her strength, her courage, her as a person. Debra's not sure how Christi receives these words, but she herself feels greater ease for having spoken them aloud. Later Sue calls Debra to say, "I don't know what you did today but there was a big effect, Christi was really there in all her afternoon therapies." For Debra, key moments like this help her know she makes a difference, and keep her journeying on the long road with Christi.

Early summer Sue intuitively feels it's the right time to introduce another treatment method to help Christi relax. Although Christi is gaining more mastery over flexion reflexes, an undertone of tension and gripping remains. Sue decides this is the right time to try EMDR. We're fortunate that in Missoula there is an experienced practitioner. Nancy Errebo, a Clinical Psychologist, works extensively with traumatized war veterans and professionally trains others in the use of EMDR.

EMDR, Eye Movement Desensitization and Reprocessing, is a technique used in psychotherapy. It has a well-documented clinical record of helping patients resolve trauma experiences. Under the guidance of a trained clinician, the patient goes through a process of re-categorizing and integrating the traumatic experience. This is accomplished by helping the patient to stay grounded (oriented) in the present and to revisit the imagery and sensations of the traumatic event in short bursts of intensity. It is called an "eye movement" therapy because while processing the material the patient moves her eyes right and left. This helps the brain reorganize the inner network of perceptions and associations. In some cases, however, instead of eye movements the patient uses another form of bi-lateral processing, such as external cues of sound or tapping. Because Christi can't yet command her eyes to move quickly side to side, the choice is made to use tapping as her cue.

Sue, Christi and I decide that I will accompany them to the first few sessions to help facilitate communication. No one knows how Christi will respond so our first session is set up solely to explore how we will work together. We meet for the first time on a cool June Saturday morning. Nancy sits facing the three of us. Sue and I have our chairs pulled up on either side of Christi's wheelchair. The office is small, comfortably plush with richly textured carpet, dim lighting, and art in muted tones. Our knees aren't more than two feet away from Nancy's. Even though the room invites nestling in, cushioned safety, I don't feel the downward rest this implies. The air tastes like cold tin, like we are close to an unseen danger, that something will break open, break apart into chaos. I try to focus intently on Nancy's directions to Christi to feel the safety of "home base," the place she'll always come back to. Christi's rest spot is the floating raft she used before her surgeries. Nancy shows Christi how the tappers work, placing them beneath each thigh, testing out the right intensity. Christi probably would not have been able to do this treatment before now because she wouldn't have been able to multi-task attention to both sensory input and focused image. I instruct myself to settle into the restful room, Nancy's even voice, and today's practice of the formula of EMDR: grounding; a positive self statement; just a peek into the disturbing memory; and letting the taps help dissipate the memory into a new form of physical-mental integration.

Slow trial isn't Christi's style. She's a warrior. She may as well be saying, "You've given me a new tool, now I'll use it fully." If I had paid attention to my own sensations instead of trying to squelch them with reason, I would be ready for the flashback images that come next. In books like *Peter Pan* and *Harry Potter*, one gets from common reality to the supernatural by holding onto the hand or garment of the one who is transporting. That's how it seems I travel into Christi's inner world. My hand on her leg, I fly through this dimension of time and space into her nightmare. I lose track a bit of the order but I know the first memory fragment is the accident aftermath.

Deafening silence. The emptiness feels like physical pain inside my ears. It's absolute. There isn't peace because it's clear there is something wrong. We've become trapped behind a triple-walled concrete layer. Then silence vanishes and sound swirls like a waving streamer, so loud it's incomprehensible, impossible to decode.

There is a momentary bit of relief as quiet stillness emerges. As if seeing from a single pair of eyes, Christi's eyes, there is vision of her form seen from a distance. Then there's the sensation of trying to get back to her body, straining. I don't feel like I'm literally seeing. The experience is more holistic and singular than vision. Christi is exerting fierce effort to get back. I assume I'm witnessing a life/death moment.

I sense someone beside Christi speaking into her right ear even though I can't hear any sound. I think this is Christi on the ground at the accident scene and that whoever has reached her first is offering comfort. Then there is sound again, loud and undecipherable, and shadow shapes of other people moving quickly. Sound becomes muffled and I feel sensations of swimming. We're someplace deep beneath the surface. Nothing above us is visible. We are in endless time. I feel an inkling of fear from Christi that she will be lost in coma. Perhaps this is what begins to separate me from the shared experience. I say aloud to Christi that her safe "water place"- the agreed on phrase for EMDR- is different than the coma water and invite her to compare.

I'm aware of myself and the sensation that my brain is scrambled. I can perceive but I can't create a thought. I feel frustrated, crabby. I want to tell Nancy to be quiet, I don't want to hear any more of her "stay with it," "good job" words. I don't know if I'm only feeling myself or if I'm still mirroring something of Christi's. When I look at Christi she seems more restful, like she is regrouping in the quiet water place. I'm not resting. I'm agitated. A blunt edged phrase, "I've had enough" comes into my mind.

Nancy asks Christi her level of disturbance at the memory now. Nancy counts off a scale of 1-10 and Sue and I simultaneously say we see Christi's acknowledgment of level 9. Inside myself I feel grating, the phrase "of course it's disturbing." I'm aware that although some of the charge has been lessened, the reality of her life remains changed. Nancy asks, "Do you feel less blame?" Christi arches. Sue says something that feels soothing but I don't decipher the words. I add, "Do you appreciate how hard you fought to get back?"

Objectively I know the session has been a success, that Christi will be able to use Nancy's help to process the trauma of the accident and the resulting beliefs and feelings. But I am too cranky to have any conversation. I practically run out of the room, get in my car and drive home as fast as I can. My neck is in so much pain I want to cry. I crave being upside down, as if it's the only thing that will soothe me. I go directly to bed, laying my back over several pillows, hanging my head over the edge. I feel empty and cramped all at the same time. After awhile some perspective comes. I think about muscles. I remember the summer we studied muscles at BMC School. Everyone was tense, bound up in excessive deliberateness, demanding that his or her own unique needs for the learning environment be met.

Sometimes Bonnie would stop all the requests for more and more specific information and tell us to lie down on the floor and do nothing. I realize I can't figure out consciously what got me so distressed and cramped up in the EMDR session with Christi. I have to let all effort go.

Over the next week lots of emotions wave through, perhaps each with a grain of truth, but also unreasonably exaggerated, bigger than what I really mean. The first emotion through is resentment toward Nancy for being able to calmly observe the emotional storm, commenting from the safety of shore while I got rocked with images. This emotion tumbles into anger. I feel invisible and taken for granted as an inanimate tool. I feel unsupported in my role. Rationally I know that neither Sue nor Christi can be my support system because my role is inherently unequal. Christi is the patient in need. Sue is the parent already stressed by her dual role as 24/7 caregiver and rehab coordinator.

Guiltily I think how much worse it must be for Sue to witness the accident images with her own daughter. When I talk to supportive friends about my experiences, I hear myself recounting a story that I wouldn't believe myself if I weren't living it. Within the same breath I believe and disbelieve myself. Then defensively I feel anger that my life has been changed by something that was none of my business in the first place. I dream about death and grief. In the dream my mother, sister-in-law and nephew are killed in a car wreck, but none of my siblings will acknowledge the loss. I feel urgency in the dream, but upon awakening I write in my journal, "Death is propulsion of life forces, not an ending but the continuity of direction." I don't even know what I mean by that but I find it soothing, trusting that some wisdom beyond my conscious mind is working things out. By the end of the week I finally arrive at compassion for myself, and for the fatigue I feel from the intensity of supporting Christi's journey. I even begin to have some gratitude for all I'm learning from the experience. I am amazed at the unlikely circumstances that pulled me in to be part of this life-altering path.

By the time a month passes and we go back to Nancy's for the next EMDR session I'm ready to accept whatever happens. We begin by working out in advance what the schedule of sessions will be so that Christi and Sue know the rhythm. When Nancy asks what the starting point is, Sue and I hear different words. I hear "choice" and Sue hears "control." However, we take the same meaning, that Christi is expressing that she can consciously decide to enter a memory or not. Then when Nancy asks about today's target, we hear "something different than the accident itself, right afterwards." Nancy turns the tappers on.

Christi pulls Sue and me into her memories of the hospital trauma. Out of the corner of my eye I see Sue tilt her head slightly down, a frown on her face. Later, Sue and I compare our experiences of the session. It seems we alternate images in five or ten second clips. This reminds me that for trauma psychotherapy clients there is often a time when sharing explicit memories is more appropriate in a group session. Multiple people share the discharge of intensity instead of the single therapist witnessing and passing it through. When Sue calls Nancy after the session, without knowing what each of us "saw," Nancy says she had the impression the session was about the surgeries, "the throat and some other incision."

As my perceptions swirl with Christi's, sometimes I see images, but most often there is no sight, only sensation, as if I'm again inside her body experience. I feel her inability to make a noise. She is trying to move her tongue and shape her lips but nothing happens. I feel tingling in my scalp around a halo line and feel pain in the back of my neck. There is pressure in the throat, the spot where the trach will go in. The tappers become louder to me and merge with the sounds of the breathing machine in the hospital. I see the jolts shock her body to keep her heart beating. I hear the doctor's voice say, "Are we going to lose this one?" I feel her determination to enter back in. But entering in there is pain and she arches back. An increase in sedative comes.

There is a feeling of drifting and then an insight. Christi remembers that she didn't come back to wait for her parents. She came back for herself. Her consciousness chose this for her. Simple words can't convey how profound the moment of this realization feels. Christi curls her arm into her chest, not as a sharp reflex, but with tenderness, touching herself over her heart.

There is a long quiet pause. Then the memory of "waking up," discovering the extent of her injuries. There is self-recognition, a palpable sense of "me-ness," yet an inability to will any movements.

In the real time of Nancy's office Christi becomes more aroused. She reaches back with her head as if she is striving toward ownership of movement. There's no time to follow this gesture because we've reached the artificial construct of time and the session needs to come to a close. I remind Christi to use her strength to rest into support and ease instead of trying to overcome. Nancy reminds her to think of positive self-messages, like "I am strong."

I leave the session with sharp, clear thoughts, but each one seems disconnected from the next, like stepping stones strewn across the lawn in a pattern I don't recognize as a path. I'm awestruck by what Christi is doing in the EMDR sessions because it's so far outside the norm of what's assumed possible for someone with injuries like hers. I wonder what it will take for our culture to fully respect body memory. Experiences like this with Christi keep challenging my understanding to go deeper. I don't know where this will lead me. Will I use my expanding perceptions to directly help others like Christi? Or will my role be to explain the phenomena to others? Now that my own beliefs regarding what's possible have widened, what responsibility do I have? Certain as I am while I'm in my sessions with Christi, an unsettling uncertainty about both direction and capacity creeps in. I question if I'm capable to fulfill what is needed.

When I wake up the next morning my mood has worsened considerably. I feel a cry of abandonment aching to erupt. I write in my journal, "I keep hitting the wall of God, why are you so silent when I pray for help?" An image I've had before reappears. I am a toddler on one side of a door I can't open and I'm calling for help. Feeling forgotten I want to collapse in silent despair and frustration. This morning I think God is the parent who doesn't come to the door. God is outside me, not within participating in the unfoldment, having compassion in human disappointments, opening doors to more objective truths.

I stay somewhat miserable all day. I'm not exactly sure what my despair is about. I feel defeated in a way unusual for me. True, I'm frustrated that even though I'm ready to change my work, nothing has materialized. But that's just a scratch on the surface compared to how let down I feel. What makes my feelings stranger, however, is that I also feel more ease. Months ago at the meditation retreat when I sensed cells letting go of endless upright striving, I felt fear. Now each cell feels full, unconcerned about direction. I trust there is basic glue holding everything together.

When I see Christi the next day it feels best to sit quietly with her. I don't hear anything in particular from her body. Just before we end I feel inspired to say a few things aloud. I tell her, "You are already whole. Everything you're learning to do again is about expression, not wholeness." I suppose I could be talking to myself as well, reminding myself that I'm whole even if I don't reach some imagined potential.

When I go upstairs to leave I stop to talk with Sue. I find out that yesterday was a terrible day for her as well, that she "hit bottom." She felt self-doubt and loss of faith in their journey. She wanted to call me and ask if I was withholding the truth from her, that I saw their situation as more negative than I was letting on. She wanted to call Mary and Dr. Seagraves and ask the same. It's not that Sue has never had these questions before. A year ago when she felt unsure she thought she'd put self doubt to rest. Yesterday her feelings were deeper, more filled with despair. It felt absolute. No magic will come into their lives. This morning she feels better and calls Nancy. Besides sharing her observations about the session, Nancy tells her that it's "normal for some kick-back afterwards when stuff is unfinished."

I leave the Forest house knowing that Sunday's meltdown was both personal and impersonal. Walking through my own feelings of abandonment and silent betrayal was probably important. I don't know if Christi ever prays. Perhaps I will ask her sometime. My impression though is that their family's relationship to God isn't that overt. I hope that having walked through this deep darkness we will emerge on the other side into greater expansion. And I hope that the expansion will be in manifest form: that Sue and I will obtain funding opportunities for our research ideas; and that Christi will acquire new skills. I don't want any more insights, just the prize. How many steps it will take to get there I don't know. I remind myself I need to keep cultivating steadiness.

Weeks of steady work carry on. Christi has several great sessions with Mary where she's able to keep her right leg relaxed throughout. Sue and Terry start thinking more about travel and Terry considers looking for a travel trailer. I notice that in my journal I keep writing variations on appreciating "accumulation." Just as when a tide changes, the momentum and direction are different, but it takes a slow accumulation of waves to come all the way into shore. I start saying, "Christi is a cumulative miracle."

I dream about Sue, Terry and Christi a few days before the third EMDR session. Christi is moving around a room, her limbs shaping graceful arcs as if she is a ballerina. Then she is putting on her sandals to go somewhere and I hear her talking. I cry because what has happened is so profound. But sharply the dream changes; someone is trying to kill the three of them. The hit man has been sent by an unknown person. He is hateful to all those around them.

In our next EMDR session the flashbacks pick up where they left off. It's strange really. It's like we're in a movie where the reel stops at the end of one session and then a month or so later continues. I rejoin Christi's imagery, although this time there is more separation between her experience and my perception. It's more like I'm gliding along with her, a distinct separate form, instead of being merged with her sensations as I was in the previous sessions. The scenes begin with a disoriented lament.

"Where am I?" She's waking up in the hospital. There are flinches of pain that seem to be held behind a dam before they can finally pass through. Then her form blurs, fades away. She is suspended in deep water, like the place of coma I saw in the first session, but not so deep this time. Periodically everything lightens, like the first hints of very early dawn, and Christi seems aware of people around her. It viscerally feels to me like her room in St. Pat's even though there are no visual cues. Each moment of awareness is fleeting. She goes back to deep water. It feels as though sensations held within her body are releasing, rising, allowing themselves to be known by a wider field of consciousness.

Then there's a direction shift. It feels like there are fragments of beliefs and feelings about the accident that have been floating above her that are now beginning to settle down into her body. There are two levels of consciousness. One is based in the body tissue, the one we've been working in all year. The other is high up, not quite conscious thought, more like clouds, each a snippet of thought. Now the clouds are weighted by gravity and settle toward the rising body consciousness. A middle area of consciousness is emerging that will integrate the two by interweaving their previously separated threads.

I sense that Christi is aware that time has been taken away from her. I see an image of time as an evil force that has spun her into an eddy, a current that won't release her. I mumble some encouragement to Christi to "take charge of timing," knowing the phrase is inadequate. I feel my brain trying to generate words but every word dissolves before I can grasp it. The part of my consciousness that's my own state wonders if I am mirroring Christi's experience of being unable to move her body to action or her cognitive brain to form words.

I've ended our other EMDR sessions charged from the intensity, but this one I leave feeling spacey, as if I'm floating in the gaps between thoughts. I probably shouldn't even be driving because every gesture feels slowed down, like I'm in time-lapse photography. At home that night I can barely make any conversation. I'm relieved to passively watch a movie that requires nothing but coasting along in someone else's creation.

I go to sleep and wake up the next morning with the phrase "I don't understand your workings, God." I may have picked this up from the session, but it feels personally mine. Dudley and I are past our limit of dealing with stressors. I pray for help but we only get more discouraging obstacles. I can't understand any meaning. On the verge of tears I write in my journal, "I can't see your hand here, God. Don't break us any more, God, we need healing. I pray for the tide to lift us higher and feel crashed against the rocks instead. I cry because you feel silent to me, God, at the very time I am actively praying the most for help. I see glimmers- pausing yesterday to be awe struck by the beauty of sunbeams on hay bales sparkling with droplets from the night time rain; I open the trash drawer to throw something away and there is a shiny new penny on top of the bag and I smile despite my discouragement. God, I want you to know I'm tired- please give me a sign of hope."

Dudley and I go for a long walk up in the mountains. I tell him about my stress, the crush of responsibilities that seem to prevent me from moving in a new direction. As I say it all out loud I feel a presence of God, behind me and to the right. I keep walking, noting my desire to push the presence away. I'm a sulking child, acting out the words, "You weren't there when I called so now I don't want your comfort." Just watching this silly play for what it is forces me to laugh at myself, allows my petulance to transform.[xxix] I know in my heart I haven't been deserted by God.

Several days later I learn from Sue that Christi has been having bad nights and difficult spots within each day since the EMDR session. It seems to Sue that Christi wants goals articulated. Sue suggests some and Christi relaxes a bit, but Sue perceives her suggestions are only in the ballpark, not yet on the mark. I tell Sue my feeling at the end of the session that I wanted to express something but I couldn't find the words. I confess feeling as if I were letting Christi down by not summarizing, but I just couldn't get my brain to perform. I think about what my Dad has told me about Parkinson's and how words are often there at "the tip of my tongue," but he can't get them across a threshold that'll let them out. I wonder if Sue and I are both mirroring Christi's state. I wonder if it's why I feel the obstacles in front of me rather than a pull toward something. The shape of the idea, as well as the words to express it, lies fallow on the ground. I'm aching for forward movement. Within each human cell the molecules of muscles, actin and myosin, sit waiting and I wonder how to propel them into expressive action for Christi, for all of us.

As adults we see the toddler's transition from a wobbly stand to solid walking as fast. For the child there are a million fall-down moments. With the perspective of time I look back and see this period of my life as condensed, no more than the days it takes a baby to move from standing to walking. But while I'm falling down again and again it seems interminably long. I keep waiting for my own miracle and endlessly remind myself to drop all fantasies. I must accept my own accumulated miracle, just like I accept learning to walk.

When Nancy and Sue talk again Nancy tells her that she believes Christi is through the trauma part of memory, at least for now. Nancy believes the new focus should be on the qualities Christi wants to strengthen: qualities like confidence or independence. She doesn't think it's time to set observable goals, like walking or talking. Later Christi can begin to determine how to express the qualities in action. Sue agrees. And Sue reaffirms for herself that pulling back from her own career was the right decision. She fulfills her final training obligations for the Head Start program and heads into fall with no work commitments.

Nancy's help through EMDR continues for the next five years. Sometimes monthly, other times quarterly, she assists Christi in recovering from post-traumatic stress disorder symptoms. I don't attend any more sessions because Christi trusts Nancy and seems confident with her own capacities to handle the process. Nancy balances her experienced knowledge of trauma thoughts and processes with her feelings, instincts and being "kind of like in a trance with her." Even when Nancy can't see evidence in a single session that something works she maintains trust that the method facilitates processing and is comfortable in not knowing the details.

Sometimes their work is very specific, as in: particular accident-related arm and throat sensations that impede Christi's progress in eating and arm mobility; and the sensation of landing on her left side, the jeep on top of her, that is getting in the way of rolling onto her side to rest.

Other times their work is more general, like processing feelings about friends or caregivers, or controlling her capacity to sustain attention. The Forests buy Christi an EMDR tapping system to use at home. They also use it when they travel long distances in the van to help reduce her tension and her startle response at braking. This is very successful and Christi is increasingly able to travel without upset and with greater attentiveness.

Many times they return to Christi's decision to live. Nancy is alerted to the need to address the topic because of a spontaneous flashback Sue reports to her. One of Christi's caregivers, Suzanne, trained with the Chalice of Repose program and often plays the harp for ill or dying patients in the hospital. She and Sue plan a quiet Sunday afternoon intended to deepen Christi's relaxation with soothing and nurturing sound. The room is warm and dimly lit with candles. Suzanne begins playing her harp. Just moments after she begins Christi curls into a ball and looks as if she's experiencing intense emotion. Sue has a visual image of Christi following "five figures" towards a light. Sue's instinct kicks in and she immediately interrupts, touching Christi, reminding her where she is now. "Christi, open your eyes and look around. You are in your home. We're in your room. Suzanne is playing the harp for you." Christi is able to immediately open her eyes and relax. It appears she sees Suzanne more clearly and her face softens in apparent enjoyment of the music. Although she has a flashback, Christi's EMDR training helps her re-orient quickly to current time.

In their next session Nancy follows up with Christi about the memory of "coming back." She helps her process both the kinesthetic memory of the event and her thoughts and feelings about it. They work on Christi's questioning of her choice. This becomes a subject for multiple sessions. In one of them Nancy feels an anger reaction about "being sent back with so little support." She says this aloud and Christi pushes out a big exhale and vocalization that Nancy takes as resounding yes. They even work on Christi's memory of the doctor who said, "Let her die," diffusing the complex trauma bit by bit. Each session a hyper-alert fragment melts back into becoming part of the whole. As if they are incrementally releasing air out of an overfilled tire, Christi's overall body tone begins softening.

Scouting Voyages

In order to see birds it is necessary to become a part of the silence.
Robert Lynd

Candace

I take an August canoe trip into the southeast arm of Yellowstone Lake with Dudley and two friends. It's not an easy place to get to. Early in the morning we load our canoes and enough gear for five days onto a motorboat ferry in West Thumb marina. We squeeze ourselves in amongst the mounded piles and the captain bounces us over three foot waves to the opposite side of the lake, dropping us at the north end of the non-motorized area. The sound of his motor is long distant by the time we reorganize everything into our canoes and push off for our designated campsite a few miles away.

Uncharacteristic north winds raise rough waves that push us back no matter how hard we paddle forward. Being on the water is dangerous and we turn sharply to shore, finding shelter on a curved 40-yard stretch of white beach. At first we laugh at being marooned, sure we'll leave in another hour when the winds die down. One hour becomes two, then four, as we keep scanning the sky for a sign that the wind will relent and allow us to cross. It's not just the wind we're fighting. It's all the expectations we have about our agenda, of where we anticipated we'd be, and our capabilities to get there. We tell stories, lie on the sand, bask in the sun, walk aimlessly, then restlessly. There are only so many times we can walk up and down this tiny beach. Our space is restricted by thick brush, spindly Doug firs, and a steep hillside that prevents us from traveling further than 15 yards inland. At various times one of us advocates re-loading the canoes and trying to advance our position, but we're never unanimous in taking the risk. We reluctantly surrender to the reality that this obstacle is too big to overcome. We yield to nature.

After spending the night on our tiny beach we launch early the next day. We choose not to wait for the sun to warm things up just in case that brings wind. We paddle past Molly Island, home sanctuary for a breeding colony of white pelicans and set up camp just west of where the lake disperses into marshland and forest. We are in one of the most remote areas of Yellowstone Park, thirty miles or more from any roads. A distant airplane is the only sound we hear that speaks of civilized life. Otherwise we're in nature's long silent pauses between the sounds of birdsong.

Yellowstone reminds us we live in geologic time. The lake we've just crossed was formed by volcanic eruption 600,000 years ago. Remote camping slows down our rhythms. We stop telling time by our watches. We hike the area behind camp, bringing back armloads of kindling and firewood. We sit on logs, binoculars trained at the marshland, scanning for signs of the moose we know must be there hidden by tall grasses. We stand still and tilt our heads to hear the chattering of ducks as afternoon melts into evening. All around us is the slow, whisper-like work of life; the incremental decay of last year's grasses, a moose's big hooves stirring up the silt, trout laying eggs among the reeds. We are unhurriedly rejuvenating.

I remember this time in Yellowstone a lot when I reflect on the block of time between years three and seven in Christi's recovery process. Interestingly I start calling them the middle years, the delta years, even though I have no idea what they're in the middle of. The changes in all our lives seem clumped in slow seasons, accented with a few momentous days.

I feel that the chronic frustrations in my seemingly stalled career change are like those on the day I was marooned. They are more a product of comparison to expectations than a reflection of what is happening. My discouragements are like paddling against the waves and barely progressing no matter how forcefully I pull the paddle through the water. All progress is too slow for what I want and creates uncertainty about ever obtaining my goals.

———•◆•———

Christi and Sue

Christi and Sue seem under a similar spell. Sue tries to restart her career without unduly impacting Christi's rehab, but she's only successful in fits and starts. She begins, as a consultant, conducting evaluations for families with children with disabilities. She tries to mold herself into a credentialing program in clinical psychology that promises on-going flexibility, but after a year of knowing it's not in sync with her future she finally gives it up. Sue has a sense in her heart of what she wants; she just doesn't see the definition.

Christi is like the marsh. We all know there is deep transformational work going on, but we only see flashes of "wildlife movement" within seemingly static form. Some of the flashes are satisfying bright spots. Christi's third evaluation at Craig encourages everyone because the speech therapist there remains positive about language, speech, and eating chunkier and chunkier bites of food. Terry and Sue begin traveling more with Christi- an annual vacation in Canon Beach, family reunions in the Dakotas. They even go to Arizona to attend Tom's graduation from college. A year later Tom and his new wife come to visit Christi in a symbolic tug for her to mesh past with future.

Holly honors her friendship with Christi by including her as a member of her wedding party. Christi works hard toward a goal of participating. On the day of the wedding Christi is dressed in a gown that matches everyone else's. She succeeds in sustaining posture and attention, with no leg extensions or arm contractions, for the whole length of the service. However, the magnitude of this achievement isn't known by most of the wedding guests. Sue and Terry, though, are very proud of Christi and tell her how terrific she was during the service. They all go to the reception, despite difficult wheelchair access issues. They stay only a short time, however, because there's not much to say to Christi's other old high school friends once past the superficial, "how are you" exchanges. Besides, Christi is very tired from the effort she expended at the service.

Despite their efforts to stay connected, both Holly and Tom's married lives take them off in new directions. Communication slowly becomes more and more occasional. Sue and Terry see this as a natural change in life beyond high school and have no hard feelings about it. And although it causes them some sadness, they too have to accept changes in their own friendships. Their closest friends have ushered children off to college or into independent lives and are gaining freedom. These friends use newfound disposable income and time on cruises or European tours. But the Forests can't go along. Their world has gone in the opposite direction, becoming more introverted and centered on home. When they do get together with friends Sue and Terry invite them to talk of their adventures and the successes of their children, but it's awkward. Friends feel guilt at their own pride, discomfort with their own ineptness in relating to Christi, and they begin to drift away.

My work with Christi goes in cycles. Sometimes we explore movement in the hot tub and sometimes we work indoors with her on her mat or sitting in her wheelchair. The location shifts are sometimes caused by circumstance, like sub-zero weather or a malfunction in the hot tub water jets. Most often though there's a vague accumulation of feeling that we've reached a limit and an impulse arises to try a change in location. It's like sitting around the dinner table with friends, the meal over and conversation relaxed. Maybe a slight pause comes into the conversation and one person suggests moving to the living room. Simultaneously everyone assents because, without their being consciously aware, it was on the tip of their tongues to suggest the very same thing. That kind of synchronicity happens over and over. Sue or I make the suggestion, but Christi participates equally.

On one such occasion we return to working in the hot tub. On the mat we've been doing a lot of stretching of arms and legs, deliberately bending and extending. We've been reminding Christi verbally and with touch on her hand, forearm or shoulder to release the reflexive bend in her elbow. Once she is settled she can deliberately place her arm down. It's a movement less about reaching into space than consciously inhibiting the inward reflex. Each time she releases her arm it's an invitation to orient herself vertically, up and down in relation to gravity, rather than into a ball. She begins to slowly move her right arm in an inward-outward rotation with the beginnings of differentiation and activity in her fingers. On this particular day once we've settled into the hot tub she points us in a new direction. Like the conversation shift that happens in the change from dining room table to living room, the new builds on what took place before but not necessarily in a linear fashion.

In the hot tub I'm at Christi's left side with my hands beneath her torso. Before today I often sensed she was holding herself up, not fully releasing the weight of her body into the water and my waiting hands. Now it feels as if she has settled, like sand fallen through an hourglass. Waiting, listening, we feel a new impulse from her to roll side to side. Sue and I are on opposite sides of Christi and we help rock her a quarter roll left, then right, very slowly, gently. After many repetitions of this, including rest stops in the center, the impulse arises to go further. Once we help Christi initiate just a little more movement she picks up speed so fast that she's propelled all the way over onto her belly. Sue and I fumble to reposition quickly enough. A last second save by Sue, inadvertently knocking Christi hard on the chin, prevents her from dunking face first. Our spontaneous "whoa" is celebratory and slightly scared.

"OK, now we know what you want to do. It's great. But a little slower this time to give us a chance to figure out our part." Perhaps Christi is as surprised as we are. Her expression is like that of an infant who is reaching for some object beyond her fingertips when abruptly the extension and weight shift turns into a flip. We continue facilitating Christi's roll left to come back to resting on her back. We repeat, beginning the roll this time to the right. Repeat is the operative word. For weeks, and months, we continue helping Christi roll in the hot tub, our facilitation becoming smoother, although not perfect. Several times her head does dunk under and she comes up sputtering. This too is celebrated because Christi can recoup her breath and swallowing without contracting even after such a startling surprise.

Over the next several months Christi becomes so adept that she repeats the rolls quickly and so many times in a row that those of us helping become slightly dizzy. Perhaps our dizzy feeling reflects Christi's experience of confused processing of information from her inner ear. Ears send us the phenomena of sound but also, perhaps even more importantly, reference information about where we are in space. They help tell us where we are in reference to earth and to the people around us.

The nerves to the inner ear are among the very first to develop (myelinate) in utero, which indicates their importance in setting up patterns of movement and brain development. The otoliths, very tiny calcareous particles deep in the ear, contribute information about where we are in relation to gravity. Think of them as slow moving, settling like falling clumps of color in a barely warmed lava lamp, and defining orientation. The three semi-circular canals, each in its own unique angle, register movement. They give us information on speed and direction, how we're flying through space.[xxx] They are anticipatory. Ideally, otoliths and semi-circular canals work together to give us a balance of information. Interestingly, one theory of human emotion holds that all states boil down to be primarily about either orientation or anticipation (moving toward or away). The consciousness of ears is about relationship, safety and alarm, rest and excitement.

Bainbridge Cohen hypothesizes that one location where our bodies say "stop- too much" to sensory overload is in the thalamus. Instead of sending signals off to different parts of the brain (its usual function), it acts like a kind of circuit breaker by tripping the switch when it can't decode the rush of information coming in. A sensation of too much information can be felt as pain, as if the million bits of data turn from benign tickles to hurt. The dizzy feeling I have while helping Christi roll in the hot tub, makes me wonder if the overwhelm of information coming from the inner ear at the time of Christi's accident- the spinning of the jeep, the impact of landing- caused a thalamus "circuit break." By beginning to use a spinal movement to slowly roll in the hot tub Christi is doing more than learning a sequence of muscle movements. Another "breaker' is in the spine, in the dorsal root ganglia where the communication arc begins between sensory and motor nerves. In the hot tub Christi is likely literally opening up the traumatized motor pathways at the spinal level and reprogramming her brain to receive and direct information from the inner ear.

This re-training process, gently introducing a movement in slow enough steps that it becomes a safe part of the movement repertoire, is similar to the procedures used by sensory integration specialists to help a child who has vestibular (motion-balance) sensitivity.[xxxi] The sensitive child may try to remain still and upright as if he is fearful that he will tip over and spill something precious and cause unrecoverable instability. Or in some cases the opposite occurs. A child is so busy turning upside down and sideways that there's no time to land into stillness. In each case learning is inhibited and interpersonal relationships are negatively affected because so much inner non-conscious attention is allocated to positioning in space. Two years from this point in the story I'll meet another severe traumatic brain injury patient, Nick, who will remind me again how important it is to heal inner ear chaos.

Over the last ten years I've practiced an ear awareness movement exercise I learned in BMC training. After hundreds of times I still learn something new each time I practice it. The simple rolling side-back-side sequence is also a gateway to perceiving nervous system patterns related to inner and outer perception and action. The exercise goes like this:

> Lying on one side we yield to inner perception, eyes closed, otoliths settling, arms bent inward, feeling the bond to earth. Listening to hear our own impulse of desire, we follow, rolling onto our backs, semi-circular canals registering our shift in space. Eyes, arms, legs open; perception of the outer environment is welcome. Finally, satiated by openness, the roll continues to the opposite side, settling again into bonding, digesting.[xxxii]

Most of us find spots where we become stuck, either habitual places or expressions of a particular day. The depth of the exercise comes in really listening for movement cues arising from our bodies, instead of imposing external timing. I usually find transitions are the hardest. Resting down into the earth I want to stay a long time, comfortable in my introverted proclivity, not compelled by authentic desire to roll into external engagement. Yet once open to what's going on outside me I can get stuck. I'm reluctant to stop tracking everything around me to re-connect with downward rest. I focus so much on the external I forget to be aware of the support that's still beneath my back. My transitions are often generated by gradations of vigilance and saturation. I pull myself out of the internal by "reaching" with my hearing perception, much like Christi did when she "listened" for how Terry's heart surgery was progressing across town. And I release my outer focus when I've become so saturated that I can't absorb anything more. I startle towards and withdraw away. I practice this exercise infinitely, seeking gentler transitions.

Around this time in my work with Christi I am also curious about cellular and interstitial fluids, the ocean inside the cell and the ocean the cell swims in. Bainbridge-Cohen differentiates between the mind state characteristics of these two fluids. Cellular, which makes up 65% of the fluid volume of our bodies, is expressive of present, moment-to-moment experience. It feels like home with "nothing to do and nowhere to go." Characteristic qualities are, "presence, beingness, absolute rest." Interstitial fluid, connecting all our cells together, is the foundation for vitality and flow of power. Mind characteristics are "activity-oriented, active involvement with the outer environment."

At the meditation retreat I had a flash of understanding: awareness of the inherent multi-directional quality of cellular fluid is important support for letting go of staying upright, vigilant, controlling. I sensed myself supported and at ease within a sphere comfortably oriented in space no matter what direction it turns. Intermittently I get brief glimpses of how interstitial fluid connects everything together in seamless flow. Stillness and motion are equally balanced. I wonder about deepening my embodiment of transitioning between the mind of the two fluids instead of leaping from one to the other like I do in the rolling exercise.

Christi isn't making distinct facial expressions yet, but it becomes easier for her caregiving team to read nuances of emotion and thought. This is something Christi's chiropractor, Pat, notices during a visit to her office. (Pat Skergan has been a weekly member of the treatment team since the first anniversary.) As they are leaving, the rehab aide pauses and turns Christi's wheelchair toward a vase of lilacs set on the table. Watching the aide whisper something to Christi, Pat says it was clear that the signal to turn came from Christi's impulse. The aide amplified the intention, sequencing it into action. Pat wants to cheer seeing Christi express desire to engage her environment. And she feels gratitude that Christi is surrounded by caregivers who perceive and respond to her subtleties.

Despite these small signals, Christi lapses into long periods of what feels to those of us on the outside like passivity. It's Christi's version of the rolling side-back-side exercise. Her energy is internal and curled downward. Nothing entices her to open outward. It is frustrating to Sue, Terry and many on the treatment team. It's also confusing because we don't know when to choose patient acceptance and when to agitate the status quo. Like in the marsh, when is the ground doing its best work as resting sediment, and when is life more stimulated by the moose tromping through and mixing things up?

Many of us working with Christi primarily express the energy of reaching toward her. She can feel the benefit of connection without needing to initiate toward us. The pattern was set in the beginning when Christi had such a high level of need that we each needed to go deeply towards her with all our nonconscious perceptions. Sometimes during bouts of her minimal engagement I think the imbalance goes beyond her lack of motor skill. She accepts contact from others, but it is half-hearted engagement, like eating vegetables that are good for you but you don't particularly like. Her passivity is more like depression than restorative rest.

During one of the extended passive episodes Sue and Terry weigh again the possibility that Christi has physiologic depression. They contemplate a trial run of anti-depressants. There is some clinical evidence that medication can also help with generating movement. One of the most famous cases of anti-depressants helping restore movement and interactive awareness is the Buffalo, New York firefighter who "wakes up" from a traumatic brain injury after a decade in a nursing home. According to news reports the treating physician credits a new mixture of stimulants, anti-depressants and Parkinson's disease drugs. Interestingly, however, the family credits the hours his parents spent with him each day, especially his mother's rehabilitation routine of "singing, hugging and constantly talking."[xxxiii]

Sue and Terry decide to stir up the status quo by adding various homeopathic remedies to boost brain function instead of anti-depressants. Sue follows her intuition regarding timing just as she has for integration of other complementary alternative medicines. And, like the firefighter's family, she continues to follow her conviction that strong family and friendship relationships are essential keys to Christi's incremental recovery.

Paradoxically, as Christi's skill at managing the sensory stimulation of public places increases, her ease decreases. She can maintain her posture on a shopping trip through Target even with lots of sound and movement around her. She can sit beside her parents at a restaurant table and swallow tea or a few sips of wine. She even eats bites of custard or mousse without coughing. Still, there's a growing aura of self-consciousness. With Christi's growing sensory integration capabilities it seems she's shifted from almost exclusive focus on postural challenges to also perceiving how others are responding to her. We would be celebrating this increase in perceptual skill if it didn't come with the price tag of negative self-consciousness.

Sue and Terry are more self-conscious as well. They still go out to dinner, but only to small family-run places where they feel welcomed. They've had enough of awkward moments as diners move to another table when Sue begins spooning food into Christi's mouth. They shop more in catalogs for Christi's new clothes because as they wait for her to indicate her choice with an eye blink they don't have to notice the sales clerk surreptitiously staring.

As a culture we have a long way to go in terms of integrating people with disabilities. We have wheelchair ramps that allow each person in, but there's not much help to cross the divides of awkward or absent communication. One member of Christi's treatment team, reflecting on things she's learned, says she looks at a person with a severely limiting disability, someone she might have ignored in the past, and knows there's "someone in there." She's more likely to approach the person and caregiver rather than pretend she's too busy. Adding to our cultural discomfort with disabilities is the prizing of autonomy, beauty and the power of rational thought. We turn away from Christi because we can't imagine ourselves living within her limitations. We don't want to admit how scared we are at the thought of losing whoever we take ourselves to be.

Despite the increased self-consciousness, Christi and Sue try another big step. We all know Christi needs intellectual stimulation. We want to find subjects that will encourage her to think, that will be intrinsically appealing. Even though she watches the daily news, we want something more active for her. Arrangements are made for Sue and Christi to audit a discussion-focused class on forgiveness at the University. It seems like a good idea. It's a small class with a gifted teacher where Christi can hear an interesting discussion about a subject surely within her own heart. The professor tries to include them. The other students try. Sue and Christi try. But they never reach harmony. Christi often falls asleep halfway through class, either from fatigue or avoidance, we don't know. It's like there's a cut-off switch between what she takes in and what she can express out. It's too complex. Christi can communicate a single chosen flower of impassioned thought, but not a whole bouquet of flowers. They fall out of her hands and back onto the ground before she can gather them securely together.

———•♦•———

Candace

Periodically I'm confused by the quality of my relationship with Christi. I reason that I need to treat my work with her like I would a long-term psychotherapy client. In psychotherapy a phase often occurs where the person uses our relationship as a comfortable rut instead of actively engaging. Artful therapists know when to support active rest into the shelter of protective positive care and when to nudge, using the support of relationship as leverage for change. I don't always know if I'm putting too much or just the right kind of energy into my exchanges with Christi.

Interpreting Christi's passivity is made more confusing because it could be a medical issue. Sue has to use all of her intuition to perceive when this is true. When Christi has a bladder infection she becomes more lethargic and won't rebound until antibiotics are administered. And in a couple of instances the shunt becomes clogged and she falls asleep repeatedly during the day. After one of these episodes she needs to be hospitalized again to move the shunt into a spot with less scar tissue. The only bright spot in that hospitalization is that the doctor offers encouragement. He sees evidence that her brain is continuing to heal and says there are "no limits."

As my father's decline with Parkinson's disease continues, I see similarities between Christi and him. Two falls, a year apart, result in Dad breaking each hip. He tries hard to follow the rehab therapist's directions to regain independent walking, but the progression of Parkinson's makes it too difficult to direct his feet to move the way he wants. He needs a wheelchair full-time. It's impossible for my mother to physically take care of him at home so he moves to a nursing home. She eats dinner every night with him, first sitting with him as he feeds himself, and in the later years feeding him each bite. My oldest brother brings him home on Sunday afternoons to watch a Patriots or Red Sox game on television, an old favorite activity he seems to enjoy but doesn't watch on his own.

When my other siblings or I make the trip to Florida, we take Dad a mid-morning treat of a mocha Frappuccino and muffin. We know he loves this. He licks his fingers for each crumb, sucks his drink down to the bottom, and answers our queries of enjoyment with a satisfied "mmmm, yuh." But we no longer see him smile. He replies to our questions with half sentences or single words and asks no questions of his own. The disease has robbed him of nearly all his ability to initiate.

Even though we still have him, we miss our Dad. Sometimes we want to jostle him into paying attention to us. Our heads know he can't engage but our hearts sometimes believe he won't. What does catch his attention seems random, obsessive, or surreal. On one visit my sister Laurel and I sit with him and I get up to speak with the nurse at his doorway. I am talking to the nurse but my attention is still half at the table. He continues to speak to Laurel. Gesturing at my empty seat as if I'm still sitting there he tells her I'm in a trance and snaps his fingers at the imaginary me. It's as if I have left behind a configuration of molecules that he still perceives as me. Although his comment is bizarre it's also truthful. It reminds me of the dreams I have of Christi where I see her in two places at once.

Episodically he believes that my mother is dating someone else. We tell him that's impossible; she visits him twice a day. She spends every dinner with him. He makes us promise we'll tell him the truth if she begins seeing someone. We chalk his obsession up to his fear that he can't hold onto her anymore, that he can't compete with someone else. She is factually not dating. But in her own private thoughts she has begun to wonder about her own future, if she'll always live alone or if she'll share her later years with another man. She doesn't share these thoughts with anyone but he seems to know.

My siblings and I each have occasional experiences with Dad where, seemingly out of the blue, he focuses fully and his words slide easily across the wide gulf between inner experience and expression. And strangely, what he chooses to say to us, in direct and blunt terms he wouldn't have used pre-Parkinson's, is on target with undercurrents in our lives that we haven't overtly talked to him or anyone else in the family about. On one trip when I stop to say goodbye before going to the airport he surprises me by firmly admonishing me, "You have to quit stalling and get your work done." I believe he's talking about me finishing my doctoral degree. My frustration with how slowly it's going, as well as my lack of enthusiasm for it, has been on my mind on each beach walk I took during this visit. I want to finish while he is still alive because I know it's something that'll make him very proud. I will be the first person in the family to reach that level of academic success. But I also think if I finish school I will complete a goal he's holding onto. Irrationally I think if

I finish he'll die. It's grandiose childlike thinking but this awareness doesn't stop the reticence from creeping in.

When I see Christi after visits to my Dad, I am extra careful. I don't want my sorrow of incrementally losing him to cause me to push her. I caution myself to have patience. And I stay available for those times when we connect about the heart of a matter.

Some days when I work with Christi I feel strongly that she is steering the recovery process from an internal place. It's palpable, like a deep ocean floor current picking up grains of sand and carrying them in the distant direction of land. The phrase "accumulating density" comes to mind. Conversely, circumstances reveal the opposite of this with Dudley's cousin Carol. For her the current is drawing away from land and her body is divesting itself of grains of sand. Carol, dying of breast cancer, asks me for hands-on help because of what she saw with Florence. I spend one session, much like I did in the early days with Christi pre-surgery, helping her find restful peace floating on water. The water she floats with isn't clear as it was with Christi, however. It is murky, opaque to my listening hand.

A few days later we're together in her hospital room. Moments after I place my hand on her arm she begins traveling far from the room we sit in. Although I don't associate her with wilderness I see her as a pale oval of light traveling beyond two layers of mountain peaks on the horizon. Her tone is clear and sure. She seems deliberately, happily, headed someplace those of us she leaves behind can't see. Her family isn't ready for her to leave them so quickly. They request one more medical intervention. The doctor complies, but finds me in the hallway and tells me I have to tell the family it's time let go. I say nothing to him, but know I won't do it. That is not a job I'm willing to take. As I walk away from the hospital I sense her pulled back into the room, as if her spirit is a kite reeled back in hard. I feel the thud of it in the back of my own skull. I mentally offer her a silent prayer of support and apology that I can't help her fulfill her own timing. My regret is softened though a moment later when I perceive her willingness to wait, to gift her family with the time they need. When Carol dies a few days later I feel a wash of contentment flow over me. And then a spark of curiosity blooms about where she traveled.

In BMC School Bonnie says, "Change is only a membrane away." I know it through Carol and Christi. Bonnie invites us to understand that our job as helper is to return to the edge of that membrane, a thousand times if need be, to be ready for the moment of crossing over. We don't bang on the door. We simply stand next to it, offering opportunities, until it opens of its own accord. I don't know happens on the death side of the membrane. On the living side the entire human cellular system is built on sliding back and forth between equilibrium and disequilibrium. A density of fluid or chemicals builds up in unequal portions on one side of the cellular membrane or the other, creating disequilibrium, until a righting action occurs that causes the cell wall doorways to open, equalizing inner and outer. When I feel sensations of density and current with Christi I imagine I'm sensing the down deep dance of fluids and chemicals in and out of cells. Knowing her physical self is engaged in life processes according to it's own wisdom it's easier to wait patiently at her side for the saturation point that will spontaneously create change.

When Christi is in long inward phases I have time for meandering questions and contemplations. I think of the words of Hanus Papousek, pioneer developmental doctor. He wrote that it's important to respect how busy the young infant is with developing the lymph system and digestive processes. We can't expect focus on outer engagement while this is occurring. When I intuitively feel the importance of waiting through long stretches of lessened engagement with Christi I consider she is perhaps busy in the realm of lymph and internal digestion.

Lymph is a fluid system I am intuitively drawn to explore. Traditionally we think of lymph primarily in its job as defense system of our bodies. In BMC perspective, however, I resonate with the qualities of mind in this system that are about specificity, clarity, and flow of delineation. Lymph cells recognize patterns and act accordingly. I think of lymph as the slow geologic time I experienced in Yellowstone because it has its own timeline that requires patience.

I'm intrigued whenever I read about lymph. It's like being at a party and over-hearing someone talk about a person you know. You want to lean toward that conversation to learn more because it seems related to you in both a tangential and personal way. For inexplicable reasons I keep highlighting every scrap of information I come across hoping to perceive the meaning beneath the particulars. In my stack of highlights are facts. Glial cells, the infrastructure trellis supporting the brain's neuron network, are embryologically linked to lymph. Candace Pert discovered that glial cells, the lymph system as a whole, and the digestive system communicate with one another through the same neuropeptides.[xxxiv] Recent science has discovered that in Parkinson's patients the inability of glia cells in the brain to "clean up" errant proteins, as well as digestive problems, predate the symptoms that expose the condition.

Also in my highlights pile are interesting wonderings. For instance, neurosurgeon Dr. Frank Vertosick, Jr. discusses how the 3-D memory system of the immune system is an emergent property of the lymphocyte ecosystem. He considers evolution and asks, "Why did the immune system grow in complexity in concert with the advancing complexity of the brain?"[xxxv] In conclusion he states, "I believe that the immune system is vastly more intelligent than we realize, but since we don't speak its language, we tend to deal with it only through violence... A more thorough understanding of immune networks may allow us to speak to our immune systems..."

Words like his strengthen my resolve to hear more deeply. What would it mean to speak a system's language well enough to gain perspective from its point of view? Once in my doctoral graduate studies I gave a class report on Pennebaker's work that identified T-cell (lymph) changes when we write about meaningful events in our lives.[xxxvi] After the formal report part of my presentation I shared with the class the question that interested me the most. What if his findings weren't cause and effect? What if asking an internal question caused the entire system to simultaneously, ala emergent network intelligence, create the words that flowed out on the page? What if the immune system change is participant in thought creation, not outcome? No one in the class said a word. I sensed instead the energies of my classmates pull back. They meant no harm, it was just the question that stirred my passion was too much a foreign language.

In my pile of highlights are my own long-term questions. How is the lymph system itself, with its three-dimensional pattern intelligence, part of synergistic thinking? How does communication between lymph, digestive system and nervous system via peptides create awareness? How exactly do thoughts emerge from the whole of our organism rather than coming from linear connections between neurons? My work with Christi makes me curious if traumatic injury damages glial cell infrastructure and how that affects her ability to interact in movement as well as thought. Did Christi sharing trauma memory correlate with lymphatic system changes, just like writing about memory does? As always, I have way more questions and maybes in my mind than answers.

Sometimes I'm far from infinite patience when I work with Christi. Often this happens when Sue too is ready for more action. I'm aware of how we are all part of one system. I think about how the birth process is mutually created by mother and baby, both of whom are ready for release from the overcrowded body. My readiness, or Sue's readiness, to change and move is part of the necessary input to help Christi move more autonomously. The action urge is sometimes as simple as increasing the speed of stretching or varying the locations where the rehab aides take her for a walk. At one of these times Sue arranges for a visit to the UM based Montana Technology Assistance Center. They introduce a new command device to Christi. It's a switch she can tap with the side of her knee to turn things, such as the lights in her room or her stereo, off or on. The idea is a good one, but it's premature. Christi cannot consistently direct her movements and the effort to do so is increasing her tone. High tone negatively affects her ability to sit in her wheelchair and stretch her limbs. The idea is shelved.

Sue and I channel our restlessness by writing grants to various foundations to fund research into how other families with severe TBI survivors navigate the complexities of long-term rehab. Even putting our ideas and plans down on paper, however, is often difficult for both of us. Sue is frequently interrupted by demands to address Christi's rehab needs. I continue to juggle school and work so I too am unable to meet numerous submission deadlines. A grant that we could write in a month if we focused takes us four months because of interruptions. Unfortunately, our efforts bring no results. We don't find anyone interested in funding our ideas. Perhaps our timing is off. It's like my dream of trying to get on an airline flight, but I'm not able to get on board. Realistically right now neither of us is free to conduct the interviews we want to undertake even though we wish we were. And we begin to admit that neither of us really believes that analyzing data from multiple families will convey the heart of what we have learned from Christi. No matter how comprehensive the interviews, the study we envisioned is unlikely to create the changes in public and scientific understanding we are both hoping for. Maybe, like in my dreams, I'm not finding the right gate for my flight.

Sue and I decide to tackle something smaller. We create a short workshop for nurses translating the Papouseks' work on intuitive parenting into attuned caregiving for patient care. We offer a second version at a symposium for parents of severely ill children. One father confides in us that he sometimes feels guilty that he's closer to his son who is too ill to communicate than to the boy's twin brother. Once, sensing that something was wrong, he followed his intuition and called home from work to ask the caregiver to check his son's temperature. The fever she discovered confirmed his perceptivity even though his logic told him he couldn't have known. When we see how relieved he is to express this story to someone who understands, we ache even more to be able to change the isolation parents feel in this culture that has few words or science to validate their experiences.

Another step I take to satisfy my urge for new direction is to sign up for a journalism class on magazine writing. It takes me eighteen months to actually work it into my schedule. I want to hone my ability to convey my thoughts in a story. I've always been drawn to non-fiction. In all the art forms I've dabbled in over the years I've consistently loved most the practical; the woven placemat, a pair of mittens, a bed quilt.

The class exceeds all my expectations. I have an excellent teacher and my passion for writing is reignited. But the passion has an unexpected downside. I'm re-awakened to a dream for myself that I don't see a way to fulfill. I write in my journal, "I've been on this track of letting go (of my psychotherapy practice) to become a researcher. But that is probably only a half truth- I've been letting go in hopes of being a writer."

For months, years, I fill up pages in my journal about my longing to write and my fears about earning money. Of course I have other common fears about being good enough or knowing how to make it happen. But the most consistent is money. I need to earn a living and that leaves little time and energy for writing. And I don't see a way to earn money writing. I'm not self-promoting enough to become a freelance magazine writer.

My obsession about enough money is only partially true. Practically I do need to contribute to our family income. But I also have a more primitive fear that there aren't enough resources to support me. The me I saw so clearly at the meditation retreat, struggling to stay upright, is also urgently determined to always be able to take care of myself. I got my first job at fourteen and have worked ever since. Just the thought of relying on someone else to support me turns into instant anxiety.

My primitive fear is also entangled in my Dad's decline. What is undone in his life will now be forever undone. In the first three years of my life my father chased many dreams of his own. The biggest was his desire to be a pro golfer. But with a family to support he gave it up. For reasons I logically don't understand I feel like it's too selfish of me to take a chance on my dream when he didn't get to chase his.

And what of Christi's hopes and ambitions? Or Sue's? When I'm conversing with many people about Christi's situation I see that their awe is followed by an instinctive cringe. It isn't about her. It's imagining themselves in a situation of that much dependence that they'd consider intolerable.

I dream again I'm missing airplanes. I am on a flight that is forced to land and I have to get on another plane. I wander all over the tarmac. I can't find my way to my connecting flight and know I'm running out of time. I call out in exasperation. In the morning when I record this dream my call comes out on the page as "I can't find the write plane!" I have to laugh at how clearly I named my dilemma.

Sue

As 2004 comes to a close Sue is more frequently discouraged. It reminds me of late winter when we're all tired of cold and dark. We know spring will come but we don't feel it thawing our bones or stirring our blood. Our hibernation has grown stale and feels more claustrophobic than cozy. We scan the skies but no sign of migration announces spring.

Rationally Sue doesn't think we fail to get any grants because Christi's story isn't compelling enough, but emotionally she feels that twinge. If Christi had already had a happy Hollywood ending would more people be interested? Is their journey enough as it is? What if Christi's plateaus are end points, not rest stops? No matter how fiercely Sue clings to her determination to keep moving forward she's not immune to discouragement and judgment. Even when she tries to ignore them, she sees the expressions of pity when she and Christi are in the aisle of a store.

Sue's heart is also breaking because her mother Bea is showing the first signs of Alzheimer's. When Sue isn't focused on coordinating Christi's full time care she's monitoring the day-to-day safety of Bea's independent living situation. As Bea begins to regress, getting lost when driving and making mistakes in her finances, she becomes more dependent on Sue. Bea even begins resenting the time Sue is devoting to Christi instead of to her. Sue is pulled apart between them. She plaintively shares her ache with me. "I don't have my mother and I don't have my daughter." How impossibly agonizing to pour herself into supporting them both and receive so little back in return. Sue draws strength from Terry's support, but he can't relieve the burden that rests on her shoulders or the grief of loss. Pulling the covers over her head and crying isn't an indulgence Sue can afford. There's too much work to be done. Work made especially hard when it seems that winter will never relent.

> Man is the only animal that laughs and weeps, for he is the only animal that is struck with the difference between what things are and what they ought to be.
>
> William Hazlitt

Christi and Sue

2005 begins as a season of rough choppy water. It feels like waves are slapping against one another from different directions like they were on the day we were stranded on the beach in Yellowstone. Windswept waves and the lake's swells collide, setting off even more crescendos. It seems like there are no openings we can align ourselves with to create a way through. Each in our own way, Sue, Christi and I appear thwarted.

Christi is in the geologic time of the marsh. She seems accepting if not content. She isn't agitated about time. I hear her wisdom when I ask her about the Terri Schiavo case that's all over the news in March. Schiavo suffered a brain injury and is the subject of a fierce dispute between her husband and her parents. Schiavo's husband wants to disconnect life support. From previous conversations with her, he understands that she wouldn't want to live under these circumstances. Her parents want her to continue life in the nursing home, believing she does respond to them and therefore there is hope for eventual recovery. Their legal battle captures the national spotlight and diverse groups animatedly weigh in on the matter.

I can't tell what Christi sees when she watches the newscasts about Terri Schiavo. She may see a reflection of herself. She and Schiavo share the bent inward arms, a perpetually open jaw, and eyes opened wide in a somewhat startled expression. I know a newscast of Christi wouldn't convey all the life force and subtle communication we feel from her.

In one of our sessions I ask Christi what people should know about the case. Her two answers come in the form of questions. She wonders if Terri is lonely and if anyone is able to read and work with her internal signals. Christi knows first hand the gap between the deep inner self and the outer self. Her second question is whether anyone really gets how hard it is, how much time and dedication it takes to come back from this level of injury. The sustained effort and periods of loneliness can lead to despair, making a person want to give up. Christi is six years into her journey and the progress she's made by external measures is minimal. Gradual recovery takes a huge amount of time. Just because you *can* do it doesn't mean you *have* to.

Christi's compassionate perspective on choice touches me deeply. Even though her choice was made in a split second, Christi chose life. And I think she would defend another person's right to make a different decision, especially with personal experience about how hard it is. I wonder if a neutral person has asked Terri again what she wants. And what a weighty responsibility it would be to convey that answer to her loved ones.

Several years after this conversation I read a story of a mother riding in the life flight helicopter with her injured daughter. The Mom says she senses her daughter going away even as they fly toward help. She feels her daughter is fully at peace with leaving. This makes it easier for the Mom to not pursue heroic measures when they arrive at the hospital. Instead she signs the papers to donate her daughter's organs so that others can benefit. This story reminds me that non-tangibles drive the decision regarding exceptional medical efforts. There never will be an objective criteria list.

Sue is affected by the Schiavo story as well. She hopes to someday help families make the decisions they need to in the hospital, but has limited energy to expend on a future vision. As the aura of endless winter surrounds Sue there are problems with some of the caregivers as well. A treatment team member from the first few years meets one of the newest caregivers in a bar one night and drunkenly tells her she's naïve to believe Christi will ever get better. When Sue hears this she wants to throttle her. It's hard enough keeping everyone's hopes up without someone undermining the effort. Boosting this caregiver's spirits back up just requires more of Sue's emotional energy.

Christi is making incremental progress. Without being cued, she initiates a slight lean forward in her chair when it's time to transfer to the mat. Once seated, she fans her elbow outward the first few inches toward the mat to settle herself onto her side. She's demonstrating that she can be both stable in her position and begin movement. Although she can't chew hard foods she is eating chunks of soft foods like cooked apple and squash.

What Christi can't do yet, though, is give back personal acknowledgment to her caregiving team. There is no spontaneous smile of reciprocation or obvious overall response to their ministrations. For instance, on a shopping trip with peer-aged caregivers she blinks to indicate her choice between two items. But her body can't express laughter or curiosity. Christi can't direct, she can only respond. On a few occasions the caregivers forget their role of facilitating continuous stimulating engagement. Sue finds out from a friend that the caregivers park Christi in a corner of the store while they do their own shopping.

Several of the peer caregivers have their own unmet needs for parenting. Once they're comfortable in the Forest's home they turn to Sue. Seeing her dedication to Christi they imagine she's the perfect mother, one who knows how to be fully attuned. While Christi is resting they pour out their school and boyfriend problems to Sue. A few even seem to become jealous of the attention Sue lavishes on Christi. They hint they'd like Sue to make their favorite food for lunch or buy them a specific gift on a shopping trip. Without directly saying it, or perhaps even being consciously aware, the message is: "Christi can't even appreciate what you're buying her and I can so you should give it --your attention, your special holiday gifts -- to me."

Sue isn't immune to twinges of deep envy. They don't come often but cut hard when they do. For instance, when some of the young caregivers blithely tell her about calling their Moms to see a play or go out to lunch they don't notice

Sue's sharper inhale and held breath. Sue can't envision that she'll ever be the recipient of her daughter's reach back toward her. She is lonely for Christi even while being with her every day.

Even though we can't see spring's approach there is a gentle thawing underway. Sue and I plan to present a workshop at a somatic conference in June. For it we write a short article on the intuitive caregiving relationship. Instead of writing in a single academic voice as we've done in our grants, we convey our message through alternating perspectives. Sue writes a first person parent perspective and I write as a somatic therapist. This is significant because Sue merges her professional persona into the power of a parent's voice instead of vice versa. And I begin to more distinctly articulate my experience from my unique professional perspective.

Leah comes back to dance with Christi on several occasions throughout the late winter and spring. Their duets are to songs that are Leah's recent favorites or something she's heard that reminds her of Christi. In May they decide to videotape a performance for Sue and me to take to the conference. Sue, Leah and Christi costume themselves in matching tan pants and white stretch tops. Christi sits in the wheelchair and they guide her arms in even bigger arcs than in the previous show. One arm rises up while the other sweeps out wide. All on her own Christi does a solo dance, lifting her right knee a few inches, moving her foot up and down, pausing, then side to side. They place Christi down on the mat and help her move opposite arm and leg, her two limbs waving and folding like sea kelp. This time no one applauds or judges. They perform only for the video camera, marking another slim step in the long journey.

When Sue attends the conference in June it's the first time in the six years since the accident that she spends a night away from Christi. She even shuts her cell phone off for 12 hours of complete off-duty time. Sue wriggles the tie between her and Christi a tiny bit looser.

———◆———

Candace

I have my own reasons to be excited about our conference paper. I am entering back into the world of somatic studies after my exceedingly long detour through graduate school. Throughout winter and spring I spent endless hours in the lab coding tapes of interactions between mothers and infants. My task was to determine if Mandarin Chinese mothers used the same intuitive parenting repertoire as a group of US mothers. The desired goal was to add to evidence that the individual skills of the repertoire vary slightly in frequency, but as a whole are cross-culturally universal. In the process I've learned that the painstaking examination of second-by-second interactions that research requires is not a match for my personality.

The end of my dissertation process is stormy. In early May, the week I am to defend my dissertation and graduate, it explodes. Even though my advisor has approved my work, my committee members have been too busy to pay attention. When they finally get around to reading it, they object. They decide to require more explanation. I won't be allowed to walk in the graduation ceremony. My advisor, also shocked by the committee's reaction, tries to mediate. She says the committee members all want me to succeed and to have a quality product, but her words are hollow to me. My resiliency is gone. I completely fall apart in tears. I push back, wailing "they care nothing about my ideas or success." I was prepared for a B grade, but not a D.

Being blindsided this way is the final straw. It's been years of an ill-fitting match between the University system and me. My passion for learning was squeezed out over and over. My enthusiastic questions were often met with disinterest. In the spring as I struggled with the dissertation stats I was turned away by two professors who said they had no time. They suggested I find another student to help me. I was expected to achieve in an environment with little help and constantly changing or unspoken rules. On bad days I interpreted my teachers' lack of enthusiasm and attention as a statement on my value as a person. After years of this double message from faculty - we want you to succeed and we have little time or energy to support your work - I am at a breaking point.

Cooler heads prevail and a compromise is reached. Although I will have to do additional work on the dissertation, I am to go through the graduation ceremony for the sake of friends and family who are literally days from flying into town. Dudley and I don't tell any of them how close it was to not happening. I go through graduation focusing on the meaning to my family. I wear my grandmother's college graduation gown from 1907. As I sit in the crowd of other graduates I feel her passion for learning and my parents' aspirations come into fruition through me. I am numb to the University bestowing anything on me. I feel instead that I take hold of something I won with the support of those outside the University system.

Even though I'm not technically finished, in early June I celebrate graduation by going to a workshop with my long-time BMC teacher, Bonnie Bainbridge-Cohen. We explore our deepest origins of being by tracing embryonic development from conception to our initial primitive home embedded in the uterine wall. Over and over I reach for supportive home base. It's the place that offers me nurturance. I feel the simultaneity of a mother's hormonal welcome and the embryo's reach.

We investigate the deep origins of breath. With our awareness we drop through the layers of breath; lungs, capillaries and cellular exchange. Going deeper we listen for the long and slow undulations of expansion and emptying, intermingled with life force energy deep in the belly.[xxxvii] I place my hand on Bonnie's belly to use her perceptual precision to amplify my own. As if coming to me from a great distance I hear deep sound, like an Australian didgeree-doo or the whoosh of a seashell held to my ear. It's strange because even though I say I hear it, it's more like I'm hearing the echo because the original sound is outside my range of hearing. Perceiving through Bonnie I sense the mystery of a force that is part of all physical systems yet distinctly none of them. Language doesn't exist.

My experience at the workshop feels deeply nurturing and profound, yet as I drive away the specifics melt into the background. I don't consciously think about it again until late in the fall. Instead I focus on getting to the workshop in Tucson with Sue.

Disappointingly, only a couple of acquaintances attend our presentation. Even though we wish our work would interest a larger group, we aren't bothered. I think we both need time away more than we need recognition. We sleep late and relax poolside. I attend other process-focused workshops, like authentic movement, but avoid lectures heavy on content. I need time and motion to shed the last year of drive and emotional upheaval. I don't find any new doors that seem to open into my future. I feel like Christi. I respond adequately, but no motor pathways open to propel me forward.

Perhaps, like Christi, I need more time to finish the work of the marshland. Throughout the summer my final dealings with my dissertation committee are like a business transaction. I want out of a bad relationship. I just want them to tell me what is required and to let me go. One professor wants history, one wants another tangent of thought, and another a certain page count for legitimacy. I make each addition as interesting to myself as I can, but I don't care about the product as my own anymore. When I finally defend my dissertation and officially pass I feel more defeat than success. Other than my advisor, not a single person on the committee expresses any interest in the value of my work. I feel like a little kid who finally calls out "Uncle" so the bully stops pummeling her. I am getting out, but I know I'm damaged. I don't believe their stamp of approval has anything to do with me. Only the hug from my advisor the day I finish, tinged equally with enthusiasm and relief, has real meaning.

I have to admit that my intense negative emotions about the lack of meaningful support are fueled by other situations as well. I feel frustrated and helpless looking at the stress on Terry, Sue and Christi from a medical and social service system that has a limited view of recovery. And, for the last two years I've had a job at a non-profit organization where the demands far exceed the economic resources and Board support. I took the position thinking it would help my transition away from psychotherapy. Although it performs that function, the emotional toll and stress increasingly outweigh the growth in the organization or me. Having stayed in the "bad relationship" of the University for so long I can't repeat my mistake in the work world. I no longer want my capacity for autonomy and challenge to excuse inadequate support. I understand clearly that this stressful job is preventing me from focusing on writing the story about what Christi is teaching me. In BMC terms, I need to let go in order to take hold.[xxxviii] In August I give two months notice. Coincidentally my last day of work is also the day I finish the dissertation process.

The origin of the Yellowstone River is a day's hike from the place we camped when we took the canoe trip into the SE arm of Yellowstone Lake. Up on the Two Ocean Plateau the melting snow forms intertwining rivulets, combining and dividing multiple times, then accumulating into two creeks that turn decisively in opposite directions, one ending up in the Pacific, the other in the Atlantic. I backpacked there with friends a few years before the canoe trip. We tried to find the exact point of origin for the Yellowstone up on Younts Peak. Although we didn't find it we were very satisfied to sit on a hillside imagining how this entire corner of the park participates in beginning such a powerful river. The Yellowstone River cascades down from the wilderness and spreads itself out into its namesake lake. Each year the lake rises and falls four or five feet, slowly tumbling the water toward the outlet. The water we watch dump into the marsh will journey for 10 years through the lake. This is three years slower than the time required for our human bodies to reconstitute. Just past Fishing Bridge the river is reformed, beginning a run 700 miles north and east, the longest of any undammed river in the lower 48 states, before joining the Missouri River.

 I contemplate the mysteries of origin. I ask questions out loud, but I'm not really looking for an answer. The fun of the question, of seeing something so intriguing, is more compelling than learning the scientific answer. I'm awed by the difference between a snowflake that becomes part of the Pacific and the one next to it that joins the Atlantic. In spring I'm fascinated that even though the ground seems still asleep, in a single week an eruption of Glacier Lilies and Shooting Stars pokes its way up. Their petals fling open like joyously outstretched arms. What is the unseen moment the flower bulb, after a winter of condensing and conserving, reverses direction and begins expanding? I want to know the magical moment when holding on becomes breaking through and reaching out.

———◆———

Christi and Sue

In the fall of 2005 I'm thinking a lot about Christi's choice to live. She is like the Glacier Lily still underground building its core. I know if we keep paying attention she will teach us about the process of coalescing. In order to grow we endlessly cycle through periods of chaos. DNA strands release their paired twist and float through the cell replicating themselves to form the foundation of two cells. The intrinsic order that exists is inexplicable to the human eye. I trust that Christi is engaged in an equally intrinsic process of deep change even though we can't perceive the progression clearly. I know if we're patient she'll show us the decisive moment of turning to the Pacific or Atlantic, the moment DNA binds together again in expansionary growth.

Coinciding with these musings, I invite Annie Brook to Missoula. I know Annie from our studies together in BMC. I ask her to teach a workshop on the fundamentals of pre and perinatal awareness to a group of psychotherapists and movement practitioners.[xxxix] The idea that experiences in the womb and in the birth process begin building non-conscious beliefs, emotions and coping strategies that affect future behaviors, has been gaining credibility in the psychology field. Theories about how this can be true given our minimally developed brains, especially before the third trimester, differ widely. I think the ideas are intriguing enough that I'm eager to explore them further with my local colleagues. In Annie's private practice in Boulder, Colorado she offers water-based sessions that combine her knowledge of BMC, pre and perinatal work, and Watsuu (a water based healing modality). Annie also offers to meet with Christi to see if her perspective can add something to the healing experience. Because Sue met Annie when she attended the somatic therapy conference last June she is comfortable taking a chance.

The Saturday of Annie's session with Christi is a quintessential early fall morning. Although there's the promise of a sunny and warm afternoon, the morning has a sharp edge of coolness making it perfect for soaking in warm water. Debra joins Christi, Sue and Annie in the hot tub to help facilitate the process and to increase Christi's comfort. The elongated sighs of "ah" as they settle into the warmth express the mood of ease. I sit beside the hot tub, in a witness position, or as we say in BMC, "holding the field." My job is to participate and support by keeping my attention on the whole. This essentially creates an invisible bubble around everyone else's experience, allowing them to explore more freely.

Submerged to their shoulders, voices crisscrossing softly, Annie gets to know Christi and Sue with words and touch. She asks questions about the healing journey, meandering slowly back to questions about conception and the birth process. Meanwhile she gently touches Christi's right arm, shoulder, and the back of her neck. Debra alternately supports Christi's sacrum and feet. Sue holds the back of

Christi's head, her customary starting position in all hot tub work.

Christi is attentive, her overall tone awake with vitality, much like the early morning light illuminating the aspens beside the house. Occasionally she sways left or right seemingly in response to Annie's questions. Sue looks curious, balancing her perspectives of objective scientist, watchful mother, and intrigued explorer.

Annie begins to elicit details of Christi's conception and birth. Sue and Terry had difficulties with conceiving and carrying a child to term. Before Christi they lost a child with a miscarriage at 5 months, an event that increased their fears for Christi's normal development. When Christi initiated labor a month early Sue and Terry intuitively believed everything was ok, but their residual grief from the miscarriage caused them to hesitate. The doctors didn't think Christi was "viable" and stopped Sue's labor, putting her on bed rest. As soon as Sue says this Christi begins to roll right and left, as if she's adding her comments. Because rolling is a movement we've done in the past Sue and Debra know how to seamlessly facilitate it by shifting their bodies and hands.

Annie leans her face in close to Christi. She acknowledges Christi's head turns that seem like searches into the space around her, as if trying to find something solid to touch. "You were trying to be born in your own time. You were interrupted, your pushing was stopped." Her voice pauses, her hands moving to the crown of Christi's head. "It wasn't anything you did wrong, nothing was wrong with your pushing."

Sue seems equally ready to express the frustration she felt so many years ago when labor was stopped. Her voice pushes back a small dam of accommodation. "They made us wait and by then Christi was too big for a regular delivery. We had to schedule a Caesarean. When it was finally time we demanded to wait an extra few hours so we could have the one anesthesiologist who allowed fathers into the operating room. We wanted Terry there. It was the one thing we could control." As Sue speaks Debra feels a current move down from Christi's head to the sacrum. Then the flow becomes a trickle wending into the space in front of the tailbone.

"Now you don't need to rush," whispers Annie into Christi's ear. "Take your time so you can feel the transition." Annie changes positions with Sue so that she can hold Christi's skull, one hand on occipital bones, one on forehead. Christi continues to turn her head slowly, to the side and down, as if she is once again rubbing her skull against the bones of her mother's pelvis, trying to find the way out. The expression in her eyes is earnest, determined, yet also shows the effort of scraping against something that's holding her back.

Annie responds to her effort. "They gave you chemicals to slow you down. Now you can feel your blood, your potency for life, separate from them. You can trust your own timing." The area around us on the sun porch begins to feel charged with expectancy, like the buildup when a storm is slowly approaching from the western mountains. Christi's toes float against the side of the hot tub and she points hard, pushing off. She spirals to the left.

Christi's body seems to hum in a unified vibration, like the air under electrical wires except denser, traveling through water. Early on Debra and I worked with her on bone marrow quieting the sputter of nerves. Today seems similar but is more systemic. I imagine Christi's entire bloodstream enlivened with awareness, dispersing within itself the charged air of glandular arousal, supporting her nervous system's integration of this experience. Sue steadies herself. She is the persona of bones, supporting the building surge in Christi and also nourished by it. Unseen by the group in the hot tub, Terry chooses this moment to look out from the bedroom window. I smile at him and give the barest of nods to let him know all is well.

Christi comes to a restful floating place on her back again. Annie continues to hold Christi's head. They both turn their gaze to Sue. "You can tell Christi what you couldn't then," Annie invites.

Sue looks Christi in the eyes. "Back then there wasn't anything we could do. The doctors were in charge. I'm sorry I couldn't protect you differently. They told us then you weren't viable, just like in Idaho. But this time we're proving them wrong. We're doing it our own way."

There is a long, long pause. Annie, Sue, Debra and Christi all seem suspended in time, like Morning Glories opened to the warmth of the sun. The stillness makes each second seem a minute long, each a round pearl strung together into a necklace. We're on the edge of restful infinity. And then silently the moment ends, the flower petals close. Everyone's nearly simultaneous exhale conveys settling more than discharge. We gently move into transition- dropping the hoyer basket into the tub to warm it, fastening it around Christi, and lifting her to the waiting heated towels. A state of quiet envelops everyone in the Forest household throughout the afternoon. Christi takes a two-hour nap, sleeping deeply.

Whether Christi actually replayed a series of birth turns, or visited a memory of birth initiated and stopped, isn't in the forefront for the Forests. What matters most is whether engaging in the process with Annie's questions and support contributes to her overall healing. Does it help unravel self-limiting tendencies or beliefs- perhaps ones that go all the way back to patterns established in the birth process? Certainly the repetition of the question of "viability" is compelling. At other times in Christi's work we've experienced a pattern of a burst of initiation followed by an impeded ability to carry an intention through smoothly. Since the doctor and the Forests chose not to allow birth when Christi initiated it we can't know what would have happened. Would Christi have been fine in terms of normal development? Would the prematurity have led to a disability, almost as if Christi had a destiny to teach us about inner presence and the human form of doing? Was the birth experience a skill-building precursor for what everyone needed when this emergency struck? How did the experience at birth, where Terry and Sue overrode their own intuitions, influence the decision they made with Christi at her hospital bedside? Reflecting on the session we have more intriguing questions to ponder than answers.

A few weeks after this hot tub session my friend Peter tells me about his post-accident coma experience when he was a young teen. He remembers lying in the hospital bed, listening as the doctor told his mother that they were "uncertain if he'll make it." He says the sense memory is still vivid. "I wanted to tell her I'm fine, I feel whole. But I couldn't reach beyond to tell her that." On the surface he was immobile. Many years later he was seriously wounded in battle. Again he experienced wholeness within a broken body. When I hear his story I wonder even more deeply how the traumas of birth and injury help us build skills for future challenges. It is rather like the theory that pregnant women have nightmares as a physiologic rehearsal for the adrenal surges of the birth process.

Because I'm finally finished with my academic training, over the course of the next few years I have more time to dig into the research that interests me and take long walks to muse about the questions working with Christi raise. I think a lot about the greater issues illuminated by the session she had with Annie. In the big picture the question of in utero and birth memory isn't an esoteric one because the medical and psychological implications are enormous. The question affects our understanding of memory and consciousness. I begin to understand more clearly how what Christi is teaching us can have an impact on how medicine is performed at both the beginning and the end of life.

Take, for instance, the question of when pain is experienced. Just twenty-five years ago it was standard procedure to operate on newborns with only a paralytic to keep them still, but not anesthesia, because doctors didn't believe babies perceived pain. Observations by medical staff, however, led to numerous research studies and ultimately a growing consensus among medical providers that organism level responses to highly noxious procedures begins around 20 weeks gestation. Now today's high tech surgery on a fetus includes anesthesia.

Still under debate is when we define physiologic responses as an experience of pain, not just reflex. Some believe this doesn't occur until 29 or 30 weeks when higher levels of brain activity begin. The prevailing view that consciousness resides in the cerebral cortex, however, is being challenged. For instance, observations of young children with hydranencephaly show smiling, laughing, crying, and alertness to what is going on around them. These are children who possess a functioning brain stem, but no cerebral cortex.[xl]

There isn't consensus among psychologists regarding how far back memory goes. One line of inquiry investigates spontaneous stories from toddlers that detail birth injuries, medical complications and people present at a delivery that are later verified by others as factual. Adults also access birth memories during facilitated regression. For instance, in one study the subjects were able to remember the head and shoulder position of their birth that were later independently corroborated by the obstetric record.

Reports of fetal and infant memory are catalysts for new theories of memory and consciousness. No agreed upon consensus exists yet. Some argue that memory is in the central nervous system, and therefore limited by its stages of development. Others believe memory is biochemically based, and exists throughout the body, encoded someplace like in RNA. Some theorists believe that physical expression of memory is temporary, that consciousness is an emergent phenomena arising from collective neuronal or cellular activity. And finally, another subset of theorists believes there are parallel forms of consciousness, one within physical structure and one transcendent. The transcendent consciousness, it is theorized, is an experience of self unbound by form. This consciousness can be within the form of the fetus or external, "seeing" the mother or others in the environment with a visual capacity that supersedes the infant's anatomical vision capacity and physical laws of space. Observations of adults who describe this experience in a regressed state suggest that the transcendent consciousness merges with the physical self either sometime during the third trimester or within days of birth.

When Christi shared her accident experiences with Sue and me was she in a transcendent consciousness? Were we somehow tapping in to biochemical memory that had nothing to do with her central nervous system?

My questions deepen when I consider the way Jill Bolte Taylor, a neuroscientist, describes her experience of two self perceptions that occurred when she suffered a severe cerebral hemorrhage. The stroke caused blood to flood the left hemisphere making her unable to use language or visual symbols and intentionally move. "…my conscious mind felt so detached from my physical body that I sincerely believed I would never be able to fit the energy of me back inside this skin, nor ever be able to reengage the intricate networks of my body's cellular and molecular tapestry." During the period when the right hemisphere was wholly dominant she, "…no longer perceived myself as a single, a solid, an entity with boundaries that separated me from the entities around me."[xli]

If consciousness is cellular, transcendent or even brain stem based then medical and end of life decisions, such as what Christi faced when labeled "brain dead," will need to be handled differently. What if like Peter there's someone in there feeling whole, or Bolte Taylor feeling in union with all? What if what was once labeled only physiologic distress is consciousness in pain? Even when an individual or family reaches a decision to discontinue life support, pain medications will be used with greater respect to minimize physiologic distress. If we understand that spirit timing is distinct from the body's cessation, our institutions will likely set up different environmental conditions, more like those in Hospice centers, for a spirit's passage into death.

———•———

Candace

My elation at finally being unencumbered by school and a job collides with the accumulated toll of the effort I've expended. My body aches all over, as if I'm bruised, and instinctively I want to retreat into a safe, quiet den. Yet, like the wind, my mind is restless. I imagine myself standing on shore and looking out across the water. I want to travel somewhere new and be restored by nature. I want to resume my own journey of curiosity. I am fatigued from multitasking. Now I want to narrow my focus. I want to connect with my personal life's purpose. Faith tells me it's a current somewhere underneath the surface. My nighttime dreams change from not finding the right flight to arriving on a race course too early. Volunteers want to assist me but no one is clear enough about the course to offer any tangible help.

I begin to articulate a new vision for myself, one with my artistic expression at the forefront instead of on the periphery. I want to find a means to pursue writing this book. This is an idea that was planted very early in the journey with Christi and Sue. I'd like to say I feel exuberant about this. Truthfully, it's physically unpleasant. When I speak my vision aloud I feel the membranes around the cells in my body shrink and tighten. They feel as though they're embedded with glass shards like those cemented on top of a protective wall. I don't know if the shards keep me in or keep intruders out. I breathe slowly, deliberately, avoiding the temptation to pick a fight with Dudley so I won't have to tolerate the sensation of threatened shredding.

Because I have time off, Dudley and I go to Florida to visit my parents. A few days before we arrive we receive the news that my paternal grandmother has died. This isn't unexpected since she's been bedridden with congestive heart failure for several years. When Mom tells Dad about her passage he seems to understand and nods. However, by the time we arrive he is confused and anxious. His brain has transferred the word "mother" to mean *my* mother. When Dudley, Mom and I join him for dinner he drifts back and forth between two realities.

In one reality he gives me a weak smile of welcome and hoarsely whispers "hi, honey" as he accepts my kiss on his cheek. My mother sits next to him feeding him his umpteenth dinner of mashed potatoes and pureed mystery meat. Every meal he's served now is white or grey. Dudley and I sit on the other side of the cafeteria table chattering about events from our normal lives. Stiffly he turns his head to look at her and us, seeming to at least nominally track the conversation.

And then his agitated reality takes over. He ignores my mother completely, as if she is no longer there. In tight words, faster than he ever speaks anymore, he tells me, "Your mother is dead." With his left hand he holds up an imaginary piece of paper. He runs his hand across the lines on it that only he can see. "I'm stuck here in this place. You have to call these people right away. I've made a list. They have to know. They'll know what to do." He looks into my face but I'm speechless, temporarily unable to generate any response other than blankness. "You have to call John Bryant first. He'll take care of all the arrangements." I know he means the owner of the funeral parlor at the end of the street of my childhood home. A year and a half later, when my father dies, we do go to that funeral home.

I steer Dad back to the reality of dinner. "Mom is right here, Dad. See, she's helping you with dinner." He looks left and after only a slight pause continues eating his dinner, although with no observable pleasure. Mom talks to him and holds his hand, acting as if he hasn't even spoken to me. Once he's finished eating, though, his urgency returns and he writes on the phantom piece of paper. Now he's ordering me. "I can't get out of here. You have to make the calls." He's aggravated with my slowness, my lack of compliance. I reach out for the imaginary paper. I'm too distressed and rattled by how upset he is and how bizarre the scene is to generate more than a weakly voiced response. "I'll make the calls while you go back to your room with Mom." He sees no discrepancy as Mom removes his napkin, unlocks the brakes, and heads toward his room. "You do it now," he commands over his shoulder.

Dudley and I, too confounded to even talk to each other, wait in the hallway. When we return to his room we see that Mom's turned the television on. It's part of their nightly routine to watch Dad's favorite sports show. I'm hoping he's forgotten, but he hasn't. He seems to be checking my face for the lie. "Did you get your Aunt?" I turn away from him, watch Tony Kornheiser go through a rapid-fire sports news countdown, and say, "Everyone who has to know has been called." Without looking I can feel his stare and his disappointment in me. If I look at him I'll cry. I feel horrible, knowing I'm failing him but unable to do anything differently. What must it be like to think your wife is dead? To believe you're helpless to take care of any arrangements? That even your own daughter won't help you? I can't alleviate his suffering in any way because there is a huge divide between his two realities. One cancels out the other. His real-time sensory bodymind holds Mom's hand, swallows the soft ice cream she feeds him and knows the routine of dinner and television. And his constructed mind, running on sadness and anxiety, keeps putting the wrong puzzle pieces together and believing them to be a fit.

I make my own broken fit. I stand in his room willing my body to be still and pretending interest in the television. I want to run down the hall, out of this stale smelling air, and gasp the cool night air. I know my brow is probably furrowed. Even though I pretend enthusiasm, telling him how glad we are to be here, I am a fake cheerleader. I don't want to be in Florida living this scene. To relieve my tension I make myself numb with an internal fog bank disconnecting feeling and action. But, I can still hear my own cry. I want my father back.

It's weird that Dad's thoughts become actual perceptions, like holding a piece of paper that doesn't exist and writing firmly onto the page. His brain tells his body the wrong things and there's nothing we can do about it. It's typical for all of us to spend time in mentally imagined conversations or events. Usually they remain background, no more than slight elevations of pulse rate and hormones. While imagining such things we continue to function in real time, driving a car or cooking a dinner. Dad has lost an inhibition between thought and action. Once his emotions of loss set an action plan in motion he can't undo it, even when nonsensical. His behavior is locked, like Christi's high-toned leg extensions or curled arms. He can't use current experience to calm his motor plan. Parallel tracks exist instead of crossovers.

It takes my brother Gary's visit the next day to knock Dad out of his confused loop. When Dad tells him "mother died" Gary uses his locker room chiding voice. "Your mother died, my mother is still here. I'm taking you over to her house right now." Gary's jostling wiggles whatever wires had broken down in Dad's brain and he recognizes his mistake, saying weakly, "I thought it was your mother." I can hear both the residue of the pain he felt while living in this mistaken reality for the past two days and his embarrassment at being so wrong.

By the end of fall my restlessness insists I set off in some direction, no matter how limited my vision of where it'll take me. The most logical place to start is with the idea Sue and I have had for two years – find out what other families are out there. Since no grant source expressed interest in our idea, Dudley and I decide to take an equity line of credit on our house. It's kind of like funding my own sabbatical. My plan is to investigate other treatment programs and write about what I am learning from my work with Christi. By November I'm on my way to Seattle for my first interview.

I begin my investigation of other TBI families and treatment programs with a visit to a developmental movement program in Seattle. This is a logical start given that I chose during my doctoral studies to explore how movement develops and is integral to sense of self. My BMC studies also included early developmental patterns as a central component. Treating brain injury by repeating early infancy and toddler movement sequences dates back to the pioneering work of the Bach-y-Ritas in Mexico during the late 1950s. The father was paralyzed by a stroke. His son George, a psychiatrist, knew his father prized being vibrant and active and would still want to be. He rejected the experts' prognosis that there would be no recovery. Instead he undertook a project to help his father re-learn how to move by assisting him to repeat, over many months, the sequences of crawling to standing that are a natural part of development. Seeing the success of this effort, the other son, Paul, a neuroscientist in the U.S., began a lifelong research interest in neuroplasticity. He became one of the first to challenge the long-standing scientific bias for localization of function and impossibility of reorganization of an adult brain. Paul Bach-y-Rita saw even more firsthand evidence of plasticity when, after death, his father's brain was examined. The damaged brain stem and motor centers had not been repaired. Other areas of the brain had taken over their functions. [xlii]

Nick, a twelve year-old patient I meet at Seattle's Developmental Movement Center, is, like Bach-y-Rita, being coached to relearn how to move by repeating the motions of crawling. He was severely injured in a traffic accident ten months ago, and like Christi, wasn't expected to live. His parents sought out alternative treatment opportunities as soon as he was released from the hospital because of his poor prognosis and limited traditional treatment options. Bette Lamont and Nina Jonio, the founders and therapists of the center, began working with Nick while he was still homebound and unable to initiate any movements. It took five people to help him passively go through the range of motion I see him do during my first site visit.

Nick's mom Jennifer is in the treatment room helping Bette and Nina. Nick, a husky boy, utilizes a wheelchair for most of his day. However, here at the Developmental Center he is lying belly down on a big gym mat. Bette is at Nick's feet, guiding his right leg into a sideways bend. She's a small woman, elf-like in appearance, with energetic enthusiasm and quick strength she uses to outwit Nick's inertia. The ball of his foot fits into her right palm. She places the heel of her left hand on his sitz bone on the same side. On the count of three Bette amplifies the slight initiation she feels in Nick's foot to help him push off. Jennifer and Nina, both strong and solidly built, are no-nonsense anchors, mirroring one another in position at each shoulder. They help lift and move one arm forward and bend the other beneath his shoulder to prop up his torso. Nick executes a jerky version of army crawling. They repeat these same steps over and over to help Nick move the length of the gym mat and back.

Several times over the next six months I drive to Seattle to observe Nick's sessions. Each time he is doing more of the push and moving faster down the length of the mat. His language skills are improving quickly and beyond what anyone predicted given the location of injury. Nick's family are encouraged and despite all the complementary modalities available in their city, they decide to move to San Francisco for several months to participate in a specialized Thera-Suit program that will allow Nick to move in a vertical orientation. They know Nick's recovery will be a long-term process that will require innovation to help him reach his potential.

Christi and Sue

Inspired by my conversations with Bette LaMonte, and Nick's progress, I suggest to Sue and Christi that we begin a modified form of patterning work. For Sue, this makes sense because of her knowledge of early intervention programs. Christi seems intrigued by learning that another person is on a recovery path like hers. Although the exercise itself seems questionable her natural curiosity and trust of her Mom and me makes her willing to give it a try.

For this new treatment approach we move the mat from Christi's exercise platform into the den so there's lots of space. For the first month almost no forward propulsion occurs. Our primary focus is to help Christi relax her arms enough to move them to shoulder height so that she can begin to prop herself up. We stroke her wrists to encourage her to relax the tension so that her hands, even though still fisted, can make contact with the ground. She practices lifting her head a few inches off the mat and turning it side to side. This requires that Sue assist by holding beneath Christi's chin. We help her bend one leg and begin to rotate her foot into a push-off position.

The work we do is a modified form of patterning work based on my training in developmental psychology as well as Body Mind Centering. Rather than focusing on just the form of a crawl in mechanical terms, I'm considering how it meshes with Christi's motivation, mood, tone and the constraints she experiences as a grown person trying to move greater body mass than we do when we're first learning to move. As a developmental psychologist I know that motor development is an integral part of cognitive development. For instance, when infants and toddlers solve movement problems, they're building neural structures they'll use for cognitive problem solving as they mature. There are numerous case studies that document that low-brain re-patterning exercises help a child who is struggling with reading, writing and spelling.[xliii] Today's field of developmental optometry uses movements from early development to address problems in visual focus and attention that undermine a student's academic achievement. Another one of my priorities is to help Christi develop the capacity to push into the floor to raise herself up. Pushing with her arms provides feedback to her torso. In psychological terms, this provides a sense of autonomy. This is markedly different than what occurs when she lies on her back and moves her arms freely in space.

As I work with Sue and Christi to implement a developmental movement program I'm also mindful of Bainbridge-Cohen's conceptualization of the order of development and links to sequential development of the brain. Thinking about the animal kingdom is a handy way to grasp the stages of movement progression. At conception we are like an amoeba or sponge. Then, as we grow, we are like the navel-centered starfish. As our bodies fold and tuck to take shape, we swim like a fish (spinal). Then we develop limbs that move us as amphibians with upper and lower limb movements (homologous). With increasing coordination we move one side of our body and then the other like reptiles (homolateral). And finally we move our opposite arm and leg as mammals do (contralateral). At each one of these stages, utilizing yield to gravity and pushing from earth, as well as reach and pull into the space around us, we build the fibers of our brains that support increasingly complex perception.

Each stage of development builds the foundation for the next stage. In Bainbridge-Cohen's conceptualization each developmental movement stage is associated with corresponding levels of brain development. The most primitive linked to the brain stem and progressing upward to the basal ganglia by the time we reach contralateral movements. One image in my mind's eye is the brain as a large flower. The flower blossom is beautiful and catches our eye. But this bloom can only be there because of the strength of the stem that is supporting it.

As we begin the developmental patterning work I want Christi to begin simply so she can re-strengthen the strong stem supporting her higher brain structures. I encourage her to feel her weight yielding into contact with the mat and to very gently push down into her arms to make space to raise her head. I give her cues to lift and turn her head using internal awareness, suggesting that her nose and mouth guide the turn of her head. Her eyes can rest, staying softly focused. Very early in rehab Christi learned to use the upward gaze of her eyes to virtually pull herself up. That was a capacity she used because she couldn't move her arms and legs independently. Now that she is regaining those movement skills we want to help her release the visual coping mechanism. We're using the patterns to help her find the underlying support, from yield and push, beneath the reach and pull initiated by her eyes.

In August, six months before beginning the developmental pattern work with Christi, I had a dream about her crawling. In the dream Christi was lying on her belly and squirmed her way forward to prop herself up on her elbows. From this vantage point she was looking at some small objects within an arm's reach. She clearly knew what she wanted but couldn't shift her body weight to one side well enough to reach. The scene shifted to shallow water and Christi was moving from the water toward land, as if she were an alligator crawling onto land. A new arrangement of objects appeared, like toys strewn across a baby's blanket. They were enticements that Christi moved toward. At the time I considered the dream to be an indication that Christi was defining more clearly what interested her. I didn't realize until we began the developmental work that the dream likely was a nudge from my own unconscious to instigate a developmental movement series.

Since Christi is responding positively to the developmental movement focus I decide to visit the granddaddy program of developmental movement therapies: The Institutes for the Advancement of Human Potential (IAHP) in Philadelphia. The Seattle Developmental Movement Center where I met Nick traces its lineage back, via Florence Scott, to the work of the Institutes. The program was started by Glen Doman in 1955. In the past 50 years they've worked with 25,000 kids from all over the world, primarily children whose condition has been deemed "hopeless" by traditional treatment programs.

At the Institutes parents are trained to become the integral component in their child's recovery. A staff member serves as liaison between the family and a team of specialists in physical and cognitive domains. The crawling pattern work I observed in Seattle is a foundation of the Institutes program as well as activities to strengthen lung capacity and visual recognition of letters, objects and numeric representations. Twice a year parents attend trainings and child evaluations at the Institutes campus. On these visits the next treatment plan is generated based on the child's progress.

Terminology is highly valued at the Institutes. Each child's achieved milestones are referred to as victories, as in achieving a "crawling victory," "reading victory" or "standing victory." At first hearing these seem silly words to me, yet when I witness the responses in the families participating in the program I see they are potent counterbalance to the deficiency messages families face every day. The word "victory" has likely never been applied to their child before. Before beginning this program most of these families had been to numerous mainstream functional evaluations and come away with lists of deficits, framed as the half-empty glass. But here at the Institutes the glass is always half-full and every increment of gain celebrated. At one movement treatment session I watch the child receives a genuine, enthusiastic "you are fabulous. Look at you," when he takes just two extremely wobbly steps holding onto a bar. Seeing the positive look on the faces of the parents I recognize this encouragement and authentically shared celebration is powerful medicine on its own.

A common question used during the Institutes training is "what is the best way to use 30 seconds of your child's time?" Parents are exhorted to be attentive, engaged and enthusiastic even though many of the children appear hard to engage because of limited visual or aural feedback. For children for whom it seems there is "no way in," parents are encouraged to keep offering an environment so stimulating the child is enticed to find the pathways out. Parents say that conveying a message that 30 seconds counts is antidote to what they fear: a "warehousing" stereotype where a child is parked for hours instead of stimulated.

The families I meet at the Institutes remind me of Christi's family and their determination to not be relegated to an unchallenged, accommodation only, environment. This concern, spoken from the point of view of a spinal cord injury patient, is addressed in Francesco Clark's book *Walking Papers*. He specifically names the bias against improvement he faced from the very people charged with helping him. "They had been taught that my injury was hopeless," he says of his early rehab physical therapists. It wasn't until he entered two different experimental programs that he met rehab staff who were "incredibly enthusiastic and energetic… people who were pushing the boundaries of conventional thinking." In one program Clark was astonished by the simple starting question, "What do you want to do to get better?" Immediately he understood the emphasis was on wellbeing and patient initiated goals.[xliv] The assumption was that he could get better. He felt empowered.

Empowered is a word I hear a lot from the parents in the Institutes program. In traditional physical therapy most parents brought their child several times a week to an appointment and came back 45 minutes later. In this program they are trained to carefully observe and work with their child. They feel involved and that their efforts are restoring dreams for their child. There is no quantifiable measurement for what it feels like for a parent to be active rather than helpless. Looking at the parents around me I can't help but think that reducing their helplessness by providing defined action steps improves the health and well-being of the parents as well as their injured child.

When I leave the Institutes site visit I ache for Sue, Terry and Christi to have the kind of support I see these families have. Christi is not the age this program serves nor would her family probably fit within their highly structured protocols. But Sue would be uplifted by a contact person should could speak to whenever she wanted. The principles Sue has built into Christi's care are so similar. Christi hasn't just been challenged physically, but from the very beginning immersed in a full-living, every 30 seconds counts model. She is included as the family watches the news and Olympics. Peer caregivers read aloud books and take her to the movies. She is shown clothing catalogs and widens her eyes at the new outfit she wants. Sue stimulates her with nutritious meals with diverse spice combinations. And most importantly, Christi is never talked about in the third person, but rather assumed to be present and participating even if she can't signal her own response.

Christi

For the next six years developmental patterning is part of Christi's weekly exercise routine. They are her movement equivalent of playing scales on an instrument before tackling a bigger musical selection. Gradually she is able to push off from each leg and to move her arms with assistance to propel herself down the length of two mats four times in a row. She is able to independently hold her head up and turn it side to side. Her eyes become brighter and livelier. Her back muscles gain strength which improves her stability when she's sitting in her wheelchair. Several times when Sue perceives symptoms congruent with a clog in the shunt, a session of vigorous belly crawling helps re-adjust her system. Perhaps the propulsion increases the flow of cerebro-spinal fluid enough to cleanse whatever was obstructing efficient shunt functioning.

As I visit other programs I am encouraged and gain confidence that our efforts with Christi will accumulate benefits for her. I share everything I learn with Sue and Christi. I carefully avoid comparisons, however, between Christi's speed of change and what I witness with Nick in Seattle or the young child I meet at the Institutes program. I heed the advice from every program I visit about respecting each person's unique healing timetable. Patience, respect and faith are integral aspects within every treatment program and successful family I meet.

Year 2006

> *A mind that is stretched by a new experience can never go back to its old dimensions.*
>
> Oliver Wendell Holmes

Sue and Christi

In the late winter months Sue begins to crack. Fissure lines in her armor let her pain and despair come to the surface. It's the kind of break some on the treatment team wanted to see in the very first year to let them know she understood the reality of their situation.

As I arrive for a session Sue meets me at the door. She tells me about meeting with their Medicaid caseworker. Although she stands erect she's also like a cornered animal with nowhere to flee. "Don't they think I understand the situation? I know what our reality is. They want me to tell them a plan for the future. The future scares me. Who will do these things for Christi when Terry and I can't? I lie awake at night because there are no good options. They have no idea what they're asking when they say *tell me your plan*. Families like ours can't plan, it's too frightening."

There's nothing I can say to make this moment easier. Sue is scraped raw. Even those of us on the team who have been helping for years can't truly imagine the helplessness she feels about the future. Sue and Terry don't believe they made the wrong decision in the hospital. They hate that they had to make it though. From Sue's despairing viewpoint even the medics who brought Christi to the hospital forced her into this awful position. Her own life was upended. What if even after all the sacrifice they still can't provide Christi the kind of future safety and security she needs.

After all the huge crises they've weathered it was a relatively small thing that began to break Sue open over the Christmas holiday. For over eleven months they'd been waiting for the Medicaid system to wend its way through the procurement process for a foam sleep system that will allow Christi to sleep through the night without Sue and Terry needing to get up to turn her. They offered to buy it themselves if need be, but kept being assured that it was in transit to them, only to find out again and again that there would be yet another two month delay. By New Year's vacation they are in despair that this basic support is still unavailable, seemingly without regard to their about-to-hit-bottom fatigue. The system finally arrives and does perform as promised, but it's too late to save Sue from feeling overcome. The truth is she has to push to obtain even minimal support. And it exhausts her because the entire burden to keep things moving forward is on her shoulders.

There were other seeds that contributed to Sue's crack. Last November, Christi and Sue had an emotionally tough EMDR session with Nancy Errebo. The key word "abandonment" came up. Nancy and Sue perceived Christi's anguish and had little to offer her in terms of consolation. Ever since Christi finished the UM class on forgiveness it seemed she was grappling with the impact of her decision to live and re-build her life. Although we can't know exactly what was occurring, the perception several of us had is that she was trying to achieve another level of integration. This seemed to be required because Christi was more conscious of the day-to-day reality of her high dependency. In the EMDR session her demeanor conveyed how vulnerable she feels given her inability to control anything related to her caregivers.

The session was also emotional for Sue. Nancy asked directly, "What will happen to Christi if something happens to you?" Sue lies awake many nights thinking about this very thing. She wrote to me the next day,

> "What will happen to Christi if something happens to me? Who will take care of her? What will happen? I must admit I think for all three of us this is a topic that creates great stress if not traumatic undertones - the options are bleak - and I know this opened up a whole can of dark thoughts for all of us. We know we have to face it - but there are not a lot of positive options out there."

Unbeknownst to Sue, it turned out that Christi's choice of the word "abandonment" was because of a current situation as well as the long-term situation. One of her primary caregivers had decided to quit and had been telling Christi about this when they are alone. Christi was unable to communicate her reactions to anyone. When Sue and Terry were finally informed by the caregiver Christi's anxiety and withdrawal made more sense to them. They were angry that the caregiver put Christi in the position of being unsupported in adjusting to the impending change. In January, when Christi returned to an EMDR session, Nancy commented on the blurred boundaries from caregivers. "I bet they say anything they want to you when no one's around." Christi responded with an immediate strong vocalization. Her sounds were garbled, yet fully conveyed to Nancy a "big yes."

Another wedge pushing Sue into cracking is that she is discouraged by the attitude she hears in some of her peers in the early intervention field. On one of her consulting days her co-workers are derisively discussing the alternative and complementary medicine treatments that families try. She is flabbergasted that even knowing her story, and how much Christi's recovery has relied on innovative treatments, they would talk in front of her in such a discounting "those families" manner. Her despair grows because she observes that even professionals in her field don't truly understand the strain on the families they serve.

Sue has probably felt lonely many times these past seven years, but as she goes through yet another change in staff, the truth that she and Terry are the only stable element is even more blatant. And inadvertently I have added to the problem. Sue has told me Christi "might have some reaction" to my decreasing the frequency of my sessions with her. We don't discuss that Sue probably also feels it. I only see Christi every two or three weeks now. Additionally, I only meet with her as part of a team doing the patterning work. We don't have the intimacy we had for so many years when I did individual sessions with her. When I return from seeing Nick in Seattle and from interviewing other programs, I bring news and ideas meant to encourage them, but the options I'm finding all seem outside their current reach. I know Sue probably feels "left behind."

And she's vulnerable to the inconsistencies that come with a team of volunteers and student assistants. In one horrible week of poor timing in late May all her student assistants leave on vacation at the same time Debra and I are also gone. Because we're a team only through our connection with Sue and Christi, we don't consider coordinating our absences. Sue cracks deeper. She writes me an e-mail saying perhaps I should move on. After seven years and no clear end in sight she is discouraged. The next day she writes again that she "didn't mean she wants me to go." Sue's words are close enough to what I'd be feeling myself that I take no offense. If I were facing difficulties and uncertainty about my supports I would also tend to reorganize in a mindset that I'm alone and would push others a slight distance away.

Besides, I can't say that I haven't thought about my commitment to Christi. I have been volunteering for seven years. Logically I know I've given generously and don't have to continue indefinitely. Yet, I want to help in some form because Sue and Christi are in my heart. I understand that beginning this book is part of carrying their cause forward. Just because it's part of my own journey doesn't diminish that it's also part of theirs. However, our roles are starting to diverge. Christi needs all her resources to rebuild her skills in outward expression. Sue has to coordinate this effort because there is no other rehab person in our community with the faith and fight for their open-ended trajectory. And I need some distance to gain the perspective necessary to reflect on the story.

Shortly after those e-mails from Sue, without anything specifically happening that I observe, Sue's mood lightens. Maybe it's quintessential "darkest before dawn." Sue begins to talk about "just living life." She settles in her mind that the power of their story lies within the reality of dependency and permanent disability.

Christi also shows changes. Her eyes look more at ease and track together. In EMDR sessions Nancy Errebo "sees a shift in Christi's nervous system." Christi is able to self-calm when she's aroused. Sue reports that when Christi awakes in the night she doesn't "reach out" for Sue but puts herself back to sleep. When I work with Christi in July I encourage her to try positions and movements that encourage contact. To accentuate her self-references I help her rest her chin on her fisted hand. I help her move her arm in an arc to push against me or another object. When I place my hands on her head, something I haven't done in at least six months, I notice a completely new quality. The description I use is "ultra busy shuddering." It's like a thick square of jello wiggling on a plate but firmly grounded. Christi vocalizes more than I've ever heard before. She makes a sound like a moan when I stretch a sore spot. Then there's an upward pressure, like a force pushing up a diaphragm in her brain, and finally an ease that sounds like a quiet hum. I feel all these sensations without knowing literal meaning, yet trust that a significant internal change is occurring. A few weeks later when we do a hot tub session I witness the beginning of a contralateral movement. She is on her back and I see that to begin a roll there's an initial flicker between her left eye and a lift of her right hip. Her arms are motionless as her feet float into contact with the side of the hot tub and she extends through the ball of her foot to push off and spirals into a roll. Instead of controlling her head from the back of her skull as she has done, the energy of the spiral travels up from her body through the top of her head.

Even though I don't have language to name the change occurring within Christi, or any idea of what it will lead to, I reflect on the quality difference I'm witnessing. This is a quality change that's occurred over many years. It started with the first roll Christi did that surprised us enough to nearly dunk her head. It was elaborated on in her work with Annie when they touched on a birth memory. And now, nearly a full year later, there's this new spiral roll. The best analogy I can think of is that it's like watching dancers learn a dance routine. In the beginning they go through the moves but you can see their lips move as they count steps, and how they concentrate and place their bodies into pre-determined poses. There is a choppy quality of self-consciousness, an observing self co-creating the action. Over time and repetition the poses and steps begin to smooth. The dance then flows out of them. An internal current propels the action. This is the difference I see in Christi's rolls.

Candace

In the last year of my father's life the gut wrenching sorrowful moments accumulate into an increasingly high snow bank. We attempt to go around it or to sweep clear a pathway to him, but sometimes we can't get past the weight of fallen snow. It dims our words and muffles his responses. Still, my mother, my siblings and our respective spouses and families, continue to give all that we can. Our persistence rewards us with a few blessed moments, and these remain the ones we actively hold in our memories.

I increase the frequency of my visits to Florida. I accomplish this in part because I arrange some of the interviews I want to do for the book in that part of the country. I want to be there more because a portion of my attention is endlessly reaching, listening, for news. It's like I have an internal satellite receiver with coordinates set for Dad. Reflexively I check it every time I awake in the early morning hours.

During my January visit Dad is in the hospital due to a series of seizures that trigger a fever. Then he falls and hits his head. His doctor is somber. He tells my Mom something about "brain atrophy" and the likelihood that Dad won't walk or stand un-aided again. Beyond that he is non-committal except for the caution, "it's just a matter of time before the next infection gets him." He tells us the statistic that 50% of hip fracture patients die within a year. Dad isn't in the hospital for a fracture but he's already had two. I ask the doctor if we are in that year and he shrugs. Even though it's clear to me from the last five years with Christi that doctors don't always know, I want the doctor to give me a factual answer. I want him to tell me how long we'll be in limbo.

I search my senses to give me perspective. When my brother Gary and I walk on the beach an image spontaneously arises of Dad sitting in an oar-less rowboat off shore. In the image the water is more like a smooth surfaced lake than an ocean. He seems peaceful, drifting parallel to where we walk. The image matches what I've felt when I touch Dad. I perceive him busy repairing what he needs to at a subterranean level while the tide is suspended, neither retreating nor approaching.

On a Sunday morning I go alone to see him before I meet my Mother and Dudley at church. He is, per the new usual, sleeping. I just stand by his bedside for a little while, not even touching him. When I go to the church service during the two first hymns spontaneous movie-like scenes float in front of me. Dad is five years old and running through the rooms of his house while an opera loudly plays from a radio. In the second he is a young man, alongside his army pals, laughing about something as they move amongst jeeps in the motor pool. This is different from the way I receive images when I'm with Christi, although similar in that they're not my point of view but his. It's like his memories were misty droplets of water that clung to me while I stood near him. And now they are continuing their passage, evaporating into the air. I have the feeling that I'm witnessing divesting, diffusing. That Dad is letting go of memory fragments that he doesn't need to carry as he journeys through the next phase.

During this year I feel like Christi and my Dad are temporarily balanced at a midpoint, yet headed in opposite directions. Christi is slowly becoming denser and more individually defined. In the beginning she was hyper-porous because she needed us to understand her at the deepest level of being. It didn't matter that her face was non-expressive. But now it matters more. Christi isn't pulling anyone in, yet still can't express outwardly. In fact, some of the stalled feeling Sue and others have had this winter is likely because the intuitive repertoire of caregivers is elicited less even though it's still required. Although superficially it isn't positive, I believe Christi's relative homeostasis is what's made it possible for Sue to finally reveal the cracks she raced past for so many years.

For my Dad, however, we are entering a year where our intuitive caregiving perceptions are called upon more and more. Every month he seems to lose more expression from his face and his response time slows. I try but don't get it right with my Dad every time. During one of my Florida visits with my sister Laurel, she and I go to the nursing home early on a Sunday morning. We light-heartedly bounce into the activity room where he's watching an old movie and cheerfully interrupt, "Good morning, Dad."

He doesn't look at us, no recognition. He's absorbed in the movie. "Dad?" No answer. Unexpectedly, his stoniness pierces my bravado. I match his disregard. I spin away from him, ordering Laurel, "We're not staying."

Nothing in me is nice. I don't even respond to her stricken face before I walk off. I'm all the way down the hall, just in front of his vacant room before she catches me. "Wait, we can't go, we haven't tried."

My cultivated patience to wait and expect nothing has vanished. I've retracted into unreachable cold. "I'm done trying," I tell her. And she is split, on the verge of tears. How can she respond to my obvious hurt and hold onto him. "I have to try again, I can't go without trying."

Scraping up enough generosity for her, not him, I say, "I'll wait." While she returns to him I stare into his darkened room. Somewhere inside me I know there's feeling, some thought or memory or anger, but they're buried beneath the rubble of emptiness. My breath is shallow. I breathe only the barest amount to get by, to endure.

By the time Laurel comes back down the hallway, wheeling Dad in front of her, the sting has abated enough for me to say good morning again, although this time my voice flat, automatic. I'm not proud of sulking my way through the visit but it's the best I can do. It's not until early afternoon when I take a long walk alone on the beach that my feelings tumble out. This morning I was a child again, Dad listening to opera and oblivious to me. Some ache inside me cries, "A thousand times in my lifetime you didn't really see me and now it'll never happen." I harshly judge myself. "It's my fault. I wasn't enough for him. I'm made from the wrong combination of materials."

Over the past two years I've sat beside his hospital bed or beside his wheelchair in the nursing home park gazebo, telling myself silent presence is enough while he keeps his eyes closed for hours at a time. Then flash, my brothers walk in and he opens his eyes to their merriment or the nurse enters and entices him to alertness with a stolen piece of chocolate cake. As the hard sand crunches beneath my feet every jealousy and hurt names itself. Finally I find quiet. The tide picks up my discarded bits of anger and longing. Ocean waves carry compassion inward, for myself and for Dad.

As caregivers and family members I know we're not angels no matter how hard we try. With the wisdom of a birds eye view I know it's important to make time for our own complex feelings of love, generosity, neediness, fatigue and resentment. There must be room for a few pity parties that a disease no one wanted sent us down this hard course. When we're scared by all the uncertainty we need a spot to cry. This doesn't make us unworthy, just honest. Even if only non-consciously, I know Dad will forgive my poor behavior this morning. He'll even benefit from the greater peace I have now that I've spilled onto the beach what I didn't even know I was holding back.

My Dad is becoming less of his personal self and more of his universal self. Sometimes when I'm with him I hear his vibration like the sound a singing bowl makes. Before I never would have described belonging with him as a sound, but as it hangs in the air, beginning to ripple away, I know that my loneliness comes from letting go of this familiarity. Sometimes when I'm with him the sense of the personal is gone and I see only an amalgam of condensed energy beginning to loosen and expand. I want to celebrate what I imagine as his freedom, but I let go reluctantly. Paradoxically, even as I perceive the dissipation of outer density I also feel whatever continues, whether it's soul, mind or essence, as becoming more concentrated. As we labor through the year ahead I wonder sometimes if his personality holds his soul hostage out of fear of letting go, fear of aloneness, or out of habitual survival reflex. And if we as a family, for the very same reasons, do our best to block what is trying so hard to release.

One of the most painful moments I witness in Dad's decline is his last visit with his best friend Frank. Frank and Louise, their paired names patterned into me as if it were a single name, are his friends since high school. Their sixty-five plus year friendship has traversed numerous changes of family size, jobs and residences. Frank and my Dad are from the Jackie Gleason and Ed Norton generation of men. Forever I'll associate Gleason's "to the moon, Alice" with their type of humor about their clash with female sensibilities.

On their very last visit we all meet in the gazebo outside the locked dementia unit. My father's wheelchair faces Frank and Louise as they sit on a bench. My mother has pulled up a chair to sit next to my Dad. We try to make it a festive occasion with coffee drinks and bakery muffins, entertaining as we might have at home. By this point in the disease Dad doesn't gain information by using his eyes much anymore. A periodic flicker of looking seems enough. He appears to me to be listening intently though because his head is slightly tilted forward and down. It seems like his left ear is his central point for contact with the environment. It's as if his exposed ear is nodding, smiling, looking.

Per their usual, Frank and Louise got lost on the way to the nursing home. Louise kept telling Frank how to turn which apparently was getting them even more lost. Frank, in Gleason style, appeals to my Dad's humor. "If Louise does that on the way home she'll be riding in the spot of the hood ornament." It's the kind of line always tossed between the two of them, one my Dad should have amplified with his own quick wit. This time though there is silence from my Dad. The too-long pause is excruciating. Frank falls silent, looks down at the ground. Mom and Louise take up the slack, as women often do. I want to cry as I watch Frank's face register the emptiness in the place his friend once held. A full ten minutes later Dad interrupts the superficial chit-chat with a barely intelligible response to Frank's humor. It is too late. Mistimed, uncatchable, the words fall onto the ground. I want to stop the conversation, tell Frank to pick up the dropped words, see that his friend is still in there, still cherishes him. I feel my stomach clench, helplessly sick on Dad's behalf that he can no longer reach out past his infirmity to playfully touch his friend. Instead of speaking I turn away, stack and re-stack the pile of napkins beside me as if they demand my full attention, tidying an insignificant detail in the face of disintegration.

We all endure the unease for some unspecified socially acceptable period of time before Frank and Louise say hurried good-byes. All of us know and don't say they'll never see Dad again. I hope on their drive home Frank tells Louise about his sorrow and that she comforts him. But given their generation it likely sits un-named between them, expressed later in an extra caring gesture.

By mid-summer I begin finding ease in letting my Dad go. I frequently think about a peaceful feeling I had one summer in the high country of Yellowstone. On that trip I wrote, "this feels to me a place where the earth opens its hands into a palms up gesture to the sky." I begin to feel my heart yield into this open state. By the time I see Dad for his birthday I am at peace. I tell him I say a prayer for him every day, wishing him the experience of boundless love. Without a time delay he hoarsely whispers back, "boundless love."

Christi and Sue

Sue intuits that it's time to add another component to Christi's therapy routines. Christi continues to hold the brush each morning to style her shoulder length hair and hangs onto the washcloth for bathing. However, these functional range of motion activities don't stimulate release of the folded in rotation of her hands. She's had multiple Botox treatments to help relax the muscles but the tension has stayed an unrelenting force. Sue hears about using Bioness hand equipment to stimulate muscle release and sets out to find this resource in Missoula. The quest leads her to New Directions, a specialized gym located on the University of Montana campus dedicated to assisting people with disabilities and chronic conditions. Coincidentally it's a new wing in the building that once housed Sue's office. Unbeknownst to everyone, this begins an affiliation with New Directions that will last for the next six years and lead to unimaginable new skills in Christi's life.

For now though the only goal is to increase Christi's comfort in her wrists and hands. The Bioness device looks like an over-sized splint, the size of a hockey goalie's arm protector. An electrical impulse stimulates, in precise sequence, firing the appropriate nerves and muscles to make the movement of opening the hand. When Christi starts using the system she isn't independently moving her arm or hand in an activity. In fact, it takes several sessions, even with the amplitude turned way down, just to tolerate the amount of sensation the directed stimulation engenders. Sue and the caregivers do everything they can to reduce extraneous sensory input by setting themselves up in a quiet room and keeping the lights exceedingly dim. Christi creates her own modulation by keeping her eyes closed. Gradually, over months, Christi is able to process the sensory stimulation and begin to exercise her hand in a new way.

The supervising Physical Therapy clinician for New Directions, Dr. Sue Ostertag, still counts one of the biggest moments in her work with Christi as coming after a Bioness session. The splint had already been taken off and Christi was readying to transition home. She yawned wide, and for the first time extended her arms out wide instead of rotating her arms inward to her chest. In that instant Dr. Ostertag knew that it was possible to reduce Christi's tone, freeing her for a greater number of potential movements. She also knew the benefits would extend to everyday activities. When Christi put her shirt on each morning she would get more normal sensory input, the kind we take for granted, the sensation of a shirtsleeve passing over our skin.

A secondary benefit of going to the New Directions gym for Christi's exercises is that it gets her out of the house on a regular basis. She's going to a gym, albeit doing her exercises in a private room. It is still a location out of the house. Even though the exercise seems small it is taxing. Christi keeps her eyes closed most of the drive to the gym and back. She has to rest both before and after to have the stamina to engage the activity.

As the year draws to a close Sue has three rounds of intense frustration with the limits of available caregiving personnel. After multiple interviews she hires an aide who seems like she can fit their needs. The first day of training seems to go well and the aide leaves with her schedule in hand. But she never comes back or calls. Another aide is interviewed and works for a few weeks but then falls on the stairs and files for Workers Comp. They find out that they are the third family in a row this aide has had an "accident" with and suspicion is growing about the pattern. The third aide they hire is the worst. After a few weeks of the aide seeming very competent, bruises begin to appear on Christi's arms and legs after her shifts and Sue immediately fires her.

The Forests use their annual New Year vacation in Canon Beach to rethink their situation. By the time they return they've settled on a new course of action. They won't hire any more home health aides. They will concentrate on expanding the team of capable University students already volunteering. These are students who are in training in physical therapy and human performance programs on campus so the work with Christi fits their career ambitions. They already know how to help with tasks like crawling on the mat and range of motion exercises. And most importantly, have the intuitive skills to read Christi and treat her with respect.

Christi's stamina has been increasing and with physical therapy focused volunteers they will be able to add more treatment sessions into the week. Within this decision there's a seed that no one fully recognizes at the time. Over time it will grow and flower. Christi teaches the students that change is possible even where their textbooks say it isn't. She has a growing purpose beyond her own healing. And Sue will realize that she's become a teacher and mentor again, and that she's sending ripples of change through the rehab field.

The greater danger for most of us is not that our aim is too high and we miss it, but that it is too low and we reach it.
                                                            Michelangelo

Christi and Sue

In early spring, when snow, rain and sunshine all come on the same day, Christi too seems to be in a season change. Over a two-day period three of us on the treatment team all have dreams of Christi talking and moving independently. In my dream Christi asks me, "Who are you?" And then she starts crawling everywhere and turns with curiosity toward a sound she hears. Sue and I watch Christi with tears streaming down our faces. Christi continues crawling around the room, yet periodically and referentially looks over her shoulder at Sue and me. The dream reminds me of one of the changes I identified in my research on parent-baby interactions. I found that when the infant began crawling the social exchange changed. Instead of initiating, the mother waited for the infant to begin the vocal exchange and the number of back and forth volleys increased. In the dreams I had early in Christi's recovery she took off as soon as she could. In this one she is maintaining connection while also being more independent.

Debra has a brain-focused session with Christi that feels powerful to her. While she and Christi worked there was an energetic enlivening of an area related to coordinating senses and orienting to the external. Specifically, when orientating is expressed through eye movements initiating turning one's head and going toward sound. It's uncanny how this matches my dream.

Although we don't see Christi instantly making large-scale independent actions, those of us on the team all begin feeling that something has shifted inside her. It seems that all the attention prioritized for internal healing and perception is now at least partly available for external interaction. Christi begins keeping her eyes open longer.

At this same time Christi surprisingly reacts to water. Sue gets the word "blood" but it's not the same as when Christi had flashbacks of the accident. Her reactivity seems perplexing given the more powerful sense of energy she is exuding. We can't know for sure what's happening, but two ideas occur to us. One is that Christi is simply more bloodful. All the exercises she's doing are literally causing more blood to flow to her muscles. The second is that Christi's skin perceptivity is re-enlivening and that triggers release of unresolved startles from her accident. Christi is literally strengthening the membrane of skin. The membrane of skin is where we meet the external world. Unlike Christi's early trauma memories these flashes reverberate relatively quickly and don't cause her to withdraw. In psychotherapy I have worked with clients to let their old emotions discharge by rippling through like spring weather. We share this analogy with Christi. It's not like the early days when we more actively participated in her processing. We know this is a task she can do on her own. We wait for her to show us what interests her next.

"The problem isn't false hope, it's false despair."

The first person I hear say this is Dr. Bernard Brucker, professor at University of Miami School of Medicine and founding director of the Brucker Biofeedback Laboratory. I visit his clinic as part of my research into who and what is out there. Brucker is adamant in his optimism on behalf of TBI and spinal cord patients. The oft-repeated prognosis "no progress after the first two years" doesn't hold up according to Brucker and does a disservice to patients and families. He is frustrated by a system that doesn't collect long-term recovery data. The medical teams who first treat patients and make the most dire predictions don't see the 10 and 15 year trajectories of change. In fact, he asserts, re-training nerves and muscles might not even be able to occur until 5-10 years post accident. Cells, nerves and the myelinating glia, may take that long to repair themselves so that they are available for learning. And learning, ala classic operant conditioning, is what Brucker's work is about.

In Brucker's system a patient is evaluated to determine the best beginning point in muscle training. Electrodes provide signal strength feedback to a computer screen in front of the patient. The person can then work to amplify this signal, obtaining visual feedback in place of the muscle they can't sense or direct. As the patient's ability to amplify this signal increases to sufficient strength the muscle will then fire strongly enough to create movement. Brucker appreciates the depth and intensity of this precise work no matter how small it seems from an external view and therefore keeps treatment times short. Four or five sequential days of training are followed by six-month long breaks for integration.

I'm inspired by the patients I meet at Brucker's lab. Many are five or ten years post accident and continue to work with him to increase and refine their movement capacities. I long to have Christi and Sue meet these families because they would know kindred spirits in the game of patience and celebration of incremental change. Sue would be validated by equipment that reads the almost-ready-to-move-and-gain-control signal she intuitively senses in Christi. And she'd be encouraged by Brucker's confidence in Christi's potential and his understanding that each new skill takes months to become integrated. On days when she feels alone in her faith she'd know there's factual reason for hope.

Sue and Christi

Although the Forests can't envision a trip to Florida to take part in Brucker's biofeedback work, they can implement a new program using resources available in Missoula at the New Directions gym. Since Christi has been successful in processing the electrical stimulation of the hand Bioness equipment they decide to take it to the next level with the ERGYS bikes. On these two bikes, one for legs and one for arms, the electrodes are placed on the appropriate muscles that trigger her muscles to pedal.

Similar to the phase of experimenting with input levels that they experienced with the hand Bioness, it takes many sessions to find the correct placements that work for Christi. Much of the research on the ERGYS system comes from patients with spinal cord injury. The sensory processing issues in TBI are very different. TBI patients are also highly variable in their sensitivities so it's more difficult to have exact protocols. Still, the goals are the same. Help Christi's muscles become more relaxed and stronger. Although the high tone in Christi's arms may look like strength, it's not. She needs her muscles to develop capacity lost in the years of limited mobility. All of the foundation work in stretching and range of motion can now be balanced with building power. There are other secondary benefits to this new exercise regimen. The cardio-vascular workout increases oxygen uptake and heart pumping volume.

Nearly a year passes with Christi successfully using the ERGYS bike. She is gaining strength and endurance, but begins having trouble balancing increased activity with rest. She is falling asleep during the day, yet having a hard time staying asleep at night. Outwardly it is similar to times in her early recovery when she was reflexively pulling back into deep withdrawal but there's a softer quality to it. We wonder if Christi is relaxing "tone" in her attention system.

Bainbridge-Cohen explains attentional over-arousal this way: "If we are consciously (high brain cells) having to deal with HOW do I fall, HOW do I walk, HOW do I talk or keep attentive or chew or swallow or sleep, we are constantly thinking of survival and are not free to be really creative.[xlv]"

Christi's survival and adaptation in the early years of recovery depended on using high brain cells to function. She did have to pay full attention and coach herself with "HOW" to chew, swallow and breathe. Now she's ready to let go of those higher levels of awareness to find the more organic, and low brain, support beneath those activities.

To help Christi consciously rest, with intention rather than reaction, I introduce Sue to a longtime colleague, Serena Early, who teaches Restorative Yoga. This kind of practice, often used to help with anxiety, will support Christi to let go of high brain vigilance to the outer environment and the push to stay engaged and doing. This rest is similar to Bainbridge-Cohen's concept of cellular rest and active yield.* We are awake and present, in contact with the support that surrounds us.

Restorative Yoga was developed by B.K.S. Iyengar of Pune, India. He used props to help people reduce strain as they practiced traditional yoga poses and then discovered that modified supported poses could also help people recover from illness or injury. Judith Lasater, a physical therapist, yoga teacher and student of Mr. Iyengar, further developed and presented these poses to the Western world in her book *Relax and Renew: Restful Yoga for Stressful Times*.[xlvi] Serena, a yoga teacher for over 30 years, traveled to India twice to study directly with Mr. Iyengar. She is also a long-time student of Lasater's and holds an Advanced Certificate in the Relax and Renew system of Restorative Yoga.

---

* In the year 2002 chapter we explored the concept of cellular rest exhibited in a session between Debra and Christi. Rest within relationship is a crucial element of inner and outer modulation.

A year after Serena has been working with Christi I drop by to observe their session. Christi sits cross-legged on her mat with an orange egg-shaped physioball on her lap. Myriah, her primary rehab aide, sits back-to-back with her. Sue, more emotional reference than assistant, sits on the mat in front of Christi. Serena is at Christi's side.

"And now, Christi, when you're ready, can you come any amount forward from here?" Serena's slow and deep-toned invitation to stretch forward implicitly models languorous ease of movement. The stretch she invites is equal parts yielding, letting go of tension, and reaching of the torso. Christi rotates at her hips and slowly drapes her upper body over the ball. Sue and Serena help her continue the forward movement by supporting her beneath her arms, lifting them forward and arranging them on top of the ball in a restful position. Christi's sigh is barely audible. A reciprocal, simultaneous full exhale from Sue, Myriah and Serena is louder and seems to cast a lullaby over Christi. Her head relaxes more fully onto the ball.

The movement Serena guides Christi in today is like a forward and back version of the side-to-side roll we explored in the chapter 2003-4. Instead of rolling side to side as expressions of focal shift, Serena guides Christi in a forward bend pose that promotes inner-focused, contactful rest.

After several minutes Serena speaks. "Now Christi, again, when you're ready, you can lean back against Myriah." Serena asks Christi to go the other way, to open up with her back resting against Myriah's and her chest facing upward. No one needs to help Christi back to sitting. Her abdominal muscles have become strong enough that she can initiate and sequence the movement on her own. Myriah feels pressure against her low back as Christi pushes off to raise herself up. Pushing to raise oneself up is a key developmental movement milestone. As I've illustrated in previous chapters, it contributes to a sense of self markedly different from when we're lifted into a position.

In today's yoga session I observe Christi's control as she moves in and out of postures. This movement articulation is also being expressed in other activities throughout Christi's day. For instance, when Christi stands for a transfer from her wheelchair to the mat she initiates the upward movement with a downward push into her feet. Early in Christi's recovery her standing transfers were more precarious, as if her feet were tentatively, and scarily, balancing on a wobbly surface. She seemed unsure of her connection to the ground and the counter-support of gravity. The quality differences in Christi's movements are a huge part of what the team is celebrating now even though her skill mastery is just beginning to be demonstrated in more traditionally identified markers of progress.

Today's forward bend and back extension with support is the third exercise of the day. Christi has already completed a more active warm-up by doing a supported twist that increases flexibility in her spine as well as stimulating and cleansing the organ system. She's also done lying-down tree pose – one leg straight, the other bent at the knee with her foot resting high up against her calf, arms raised overhead. This pose is an excellent example of how Serena's work with Christi helps her remember the motor patterns of balancing without actually having to balance against gravity. Developmentally we all learn leg movement patterns first in-utero, then in prone or supine positions, and finally take the muscle coordination rehearsals into anti-gravity movements. In the months ahead Christi eventually begins doing tree pose while standing and holding onto two poles for support. All of the poses Serena selects for Christi are helping her gain flexibility and relaxed strength for her increasingly demanding treadmill and gait trainer walking sessions.

The changes Serena has witnessed in Christi's supported twist posture over the course of the year also illustrate the increasing rate of change in Christi's learning curve. In just a few months she went from tensing and contracting in resistance to the pose to self-initiation with a balance between reaching and yielding. In the twist pose Christi lies on her back. She bends her knees and drops them down to the left to rest on the mat. She reaches with her left arm and balances her wrist on her top leg, then stretches her right arm diagonally overhead. Myriah sits behind her left hip to help hold it in a vertical position and gently pushes her right hip toward her feet to help stretch the spine. The twist is always done on both sides. However, the left side has been consistently more challenging for Christi because of her slight scoliosis and because it mirrors the position she landed in after the accident. When Christi first tried this pose Serena, Sue and Myriah observed a panic reaction when her right arm was extended up and out. For several months they worked very gently to help Christi combine tiny increases in the length of the stretch with measured breathing until her body could release the anxious tone and rest into ease. Christi exhibited no panic when her legs were dropped right and the left arm was raised. Early on she couldn't drop her legs all the way to the mat so Serena supported her legs with folded blankets. And, because she couldn't reach her arm all the way to her legs, Serena placed a strap in her hand to extend her reach. Now Christi doesn't need the props and can extend both legs and arms on her own.

For Serena those early limitations didn't matter. She says, "yoga isn't about doing pretzel poses. It's about being present in a given moment with how we are." This is why Serena uses the phrase "any amount" over and over. She is merely inviting breath or slight movement to increase alignment and ease. Fluidity of movement is more important than a pre-determined external shape. In the active yoga poses Serena also elicits fluidity by teasing Christi and expressing her enthusiasm with "wow" exclamations and a fist bump.

Christi seems to have adopted Serena's embodiment of patience and exploration. She appears to savor the pleasure of the stretch and her steadily increasingly flexibility. Christi practices the poses between sessions with Serena (they're listed on the same white board Christi started using in the first year). As she becomes familiar with each of the poses, she becomes more active in initiating parts of the sequence. For example, one of Christi's current stretches is lying on her back, knees bent toward her chest, with hands clasped under her knees. Early on a strap was placed in her hands to bridge the sizeable gap between her hands and legs. It seemed like she was pulling back against the strap. But now when they do this pose she can draw her knees to her chest almost completely on her own and she initiates reaching with her arms. Even when she needs Sue or Myriah to help her complete an action, the quality is of outward direction. She is truly reaching. As pointed out earlier, reach is psychologically different than pull. It's an important foundation skill in going out and in breaking one's kinesphere. It's likely not accidental that Christi's ability to initiate reach is co-occurring with her increasing ability to take faster walking steps.

In today's session Christi has finished her active postures. Now she's ready for one of the longer restorative poses. She will rest in this pose for 15 to 20 minutes. Her three favorites are "Supported Reclining Pose," "Legs up the Wall" and "Side-lying Savasana." "Legs up the Wall" is such a favorite that sometimes Myriah and Christi do it side by side for a companionable restoration break after an active gym session. Today, when Serena offers the choices, Christi blinks slowly at the phrase "Side-Lying." She has been practicing this one since Serena's first visit a year ago. Christi rolls fully onto her right side next to the wall. The team wedges a bolster and blanket between her back and the wall. Her head is supported with folded blankets so that her neck is level and her head is in a neutral position. Another bolster is placed along her frontside, between her bent knees and with her arms wrapped lightly around it. The lights are dimmed more than usual and Serena covers Christi with a blanket.

I see the blanket as a second skin that demonstrably marks the line between inner and outer perception. The first time they tried this, Serena felt agitation in her own solar plexus. She silently repeated a mantra for Christi, "it's ok now, nothing will happen." Part of the exquisiteness of Restorative Yoga practice is that it exposes the edges we all have between arousal and rest, and guides us through letting go of the outward to recuperate fully internally. In today's practice, as Christi closes her eyes and rests, there's a feeling in the room that Serena describes as "even and smooth." It feels like horizontal softening, like a cold stick of butter warmed to spreading consistency. All of us in the room mirror Christi's relaxation, individually resting into ourselves. No one utters a word.

Sue benefits from the restorative yoga practice as well. A few times a year Serena offers a series of Sunday afternoon restorative classes. Sue goes to those classes and attends to her own rest and recuperation needs. For average subjects Restorative Yoga has been shown to bring down cortisol levels and lower heart rate and blood pressure. What an extra benefit this must be to caregivers who spend so much of each day "on." When I dream of a future based on what Christi has taught me, it includes rehab programs that offer special time-out restorative yoga rooms for parents, caregivers and their treatment staff. A half hour daily practice could reduce the incidence of caregiver burnout and illness.

Today's session moves toward completion with the sound of rustling. Christi seems to have her own internal clock and usually, as she does today, initiates coming out of the pose after the fifteen to twenty minutes. She moves very slowly and the team shifts into slow auxiliary action. The blanket is removed and carefully folded. The bolsters are gently and slowly pulled away. In honor of the softening that has taken place there are no quick directives to use her muscles forcefully. Christi is guided into a roll onto her back. Serena says her good-bye for the day, with a soft nod and words of "good work" and "thank-you." Sue and Myriah step away from the mat and begin preparations for transitioning Christi to her next activity.

Candace

In the week my father dies he leaves us slowly, extricating himself inch by inch from the tissues of legs, arms and eventually torso. I imagine roving, cotton candy strands fraying apart as if the air between the strands is growing wider, exposing the fact that their binding was temporary.

"He hasn't actively started dying yet," the visiting hospice nurse says to my sister Laurel and me as she passes us in the doorway where we're unproductively hovering. When she arrived we left his bedside to let her move about freely to take vital signs and adjust his position in bed, trying to make sure he's comfortable. We don't go far away because we can't take our attention away from the sphere surrounding his bed. The nurse offers us time to ask questions but neither of us can pull together a question to ask. What we want her to tell us is unanswerable – when?

Another reason I don't ask anything is because I'm a bit confused. The nurse's words don't match what I've been feeling under my hands: a departure that seems methodical, ordered, even ordained. Four days ago when I arrived I placed my hands on his arms and legs. I wasn't trying to change anything, or call forth healing. I only wanted to bear witness to his internal journey. I sensed pulsations of fluids, slow like tidal pools, cut off from the ocean by patches of dry sand. The beginning of separation yet each part still resonating with the whole.

Dudley and I had been here to say goodbye to Dad just ten days ago. On the day we left, Mom said aloud, "Candace needs to go pack now. They're leaving in an hour." His head bobbed slightly seeming to signal he understood. And then, in a motion I didn't think he was capable of, one we hadn't seen anything like in the whole last year, he reached out with his left arm, took hold of my hand, and drew it hard across his tray to his solar plexus. I felt impossible strength. It wasn't the power of muscles. It was something more elemental, as if alignment were snapping objects gone too far afield back into right relationship. The word "sinew," with its connotations of enduring binding, comes to mind as I write this. In that instant, however, I wasn't aware of any distinct body system. For that minute we were out of normal time and space. All the hours that he had seemed to not hear me or participate in my world disappeared. Although my tears were near the surface I didn't cry. Instead I inhaled the sweetness of belonging, of knowing we had loved one another the best we could.

That instant that Dad took my hand made it easier to receive the phone call from Mom. "Come back. Dad is going." He no longer speaks, yet, the hospice nurse reminds us that it matters that we're here because he most likely can hear us and can feel our presence with him.

Before the nurse's proclamation that he isn't "active" yet I know he is already leaving. Two days ago the pulsation of aliveness was gone from his legs. I returned from a break, touched his leg to hear him. His legs felt like the air in an abandoned building, empty of sound, slightly stale because no life stirred it.

To you the reader it must seem natural that I listen with my hands to the sounds of my father's death. But for me to hear him and support him through touch was not part of our relationship. He would have considered it "wacko," teasing me in an Archie Bunker voice. He might not have understood that he would maintain his valued privacy while simultaneously allowing such deep knowing. Physical affection in our family was formulaic, a brief hug and kiss on the cheek with arrivals and departures.

Because of that I am very slow and careful about touching him during the week he dies. I make sure I leave my hand lightly resting on his arm when he is semi-awake so that it becomes familiar to him. With each new placement of my hand I begin with the intention of waiting at the door and more consciously internally vocalize, "it's me," pause, "how are you now?" As he readies himself to die the slick surface over his muscles softens. The doorways in his skin remain permanently open.

A transformation in presence is happening for each of us in the family as well. I vow to hold nothing back in shyness. It feels too crucial to present all of myself, including "wacko" gifts, regardless of anyone else's opinion. Each member of the family more assertively assumes roles that aid us in working as a team to support his passage and build continuity. Later when I reflect on this time I see that we were silently communicating to Dad that we would pick up fragments of his place in the family. He would forever be missed, yet his keystone qualities live on.

Late yesterday I had my hands on his right arm. Throughout the day the pulsing tidal pool had become fainter and fainter. An image spontaneously appeared in my mind. The two of us were traveling in pitch blackness down a long dark corridor, closed windows and doors on each side. The corridor seemed literally imbedded in the center of his forearm. I was only halfway down the corridor when I felt stopped, sensed him moving away quickly, continuing down the dark space ahead of me. I heard his message that I couldn't go any further with him, then a snippet of angel song, distinct in the moment yet indescribable later. I stood glued to my spot in the darkness, perceiving the walls of the corridor ahead widening, dissolving. I wished I could go further, yet thought to myself, "the journey now is between him and God."

I know from the nurse's perspective his body tissue death process has not begun. But regarding the word "active," she and I are talking different languages, measuring a different substance. I have been witnessing the departure of life force and she is speaking organic metabolism. Under normal conditions the two substances are seamlessly interspersed or glued. As he dies they become differentiated.

My oldest brother, Gary, assumes the role of soldier, a profession he and Dad shared. Gary has spent years helping Dad manage his decline of function. Now, he doesn't join the vigil sessions at Dad's bedside. He stays on the periphery, as if he is sentry for the sacred space. He comes to Dad's room only once during the final week. A few hours after the nurse tells us Dad isn't "actively dying" yet, Gary, heeding some sixth sense, arrives. He leans over Dad, places his hands on his shoulders and positions his face inches from Dad's eyes. He says commandingly, "It's time to go." My eyes are frozen as I watch, suddenly flashing back to a few years ago sitting on the couch with Dad watching a WW II special on storming the beaches of Normandy. "How do you run like that into bullets flying?" I asked. He just gave me an I-don't- know shrug. "It's what you're trained to do, to go when they say so." Witnessing this moment I'm seeing soldier-to-soldier, not father and son. I can't see Gary's eyes because he still has his sunglasses on but I know from his constricted swallow that they're filled with tears. I don't breathe again until Gary pats Dad's left shoulder hard and leaves the room.

Later that evening I sit beside Dad, not speaking, not even touching him. I get the sensation of another presence in the room and looking up to the right I see, as if through a picture window, a different realm of space where a gathering of figures stand. All are shadow to me. Despite the feeling of nearness it's also like they're too far away to see. When I turn back to Dad he has his eyes open and he's looking at the same spot I was, as if he stares straight at them. I can't look, as if it would be a breach of privacy, and cast my eyes down to the bedsheets. I keep my head down too because I don't want to know what I know.

Two days later Mom, my sister, two younger brothers and I spend the day in Dad's room. We're almost lighthearted. There's teasing and bantering between us as we sprawl in chairs and even across Dad's bed. In a childhood replay we watch Sunday afternoon sports on his TV. Maybe the fatigue has made us punch crazy. We're less mesmerized by the seriousness of death and taking up the celebration of a life well lived. When it's time to leave we each kiss Dad, thinking it was a good family day to go out on, a party he wouldn't have wanted to miss. No one cries.

A little after 3 AM we receive the call from the nursing home that Dad has died. I don't remember us waking one another up. It's more like we each have an ear listening and, without even registering that we hear a sound, we rise and meet in the kitchen. We hug Mom. Within minutes we're dressed and in the car. No words are spoken on the twenty-minute drive to the nursing home. Dad is alone in his room. I place my hand on his head, in the manner Aunt Florence's death taught me. A counter-clockwise spiral is already arcing beyond the placement of my left hand. Laurel places her hand on his shoulder and says an extemporaneous prayer. Jamie picks up the Bible and reads the 23rd Psalm. Mom leans in to kiss Dad, says she loves him, and turns crying into Bill's waiting arms. In the next split second the velocity of the spiral increases and shoots out of the room as if propelled by a booster rocket into space. Dad's presence is wholly gone. Even though he lived in this room for a year it's now devoid of him. Bill orchestrates loading the last few possessions into the car. We drive off in search of an all night Dunkin' Donuts to "toast" Dad with a sunrise beach picnic of coffee and his favorite donuts. Gary meets us there just before sunrise. We watch the sun come up and imagine Dad headed toward that same place in the sky.

Rippling Out

2010-2012

> *So divinely is the world organized that every one of us, in our place and time, is in balance with everything else.*
>
> Johann Wolfgang von Goethe

Candace

It's early afternoon when Dudley and I climb up the short hill near Fishing Bridge, overlooking the place where Yellowstone Lake becomes the Yellowstone River. The slant of September sunshine makes the water sparkle and shimmer, so bright we need sunglasses. Despite the cloudless sky, sun and mid-70's temperature, we've donned sweatshirts to keep us warm in a strong wind funneling into this channel.

We come to this spot after a week of camping and hiking in the Wind River and Teton mountains. We have slowed down thanks to the simplicities of all day trail hikes, following meandering creeks, switchbacking up to passes, and crossing meadows of tall grasses. We've patiently made morning coffee and evening soup over a single burner stove, and aimlessly gazed into campfires. A few nights ago, under a new moon, we stood holding each other's mittened hands on the shore of Worthen Meadow Reservoir. We counted stars winking open in its still surface. My intellect told me the lake's stars were reflections. But my heart told me they were diamonds from underground, showing themselves in this one magic moment to their twin sisters in the sky above.

A new moon is a time of renewing beginnings, of planting seeds for that which we hope to grow in the month ahead. But standing at the shoreline we weren't planting yet. We're survivors who finally reach safety with no enthusiasm for celebration, just a deep need to stop striving. For now we need to just stand in a dark-earthed empty garden. In the past two years we've weathered an economic recession that rocked our business nearly to the breaking point. Then Dudley had a horrific mountain bike wreck that broke his neck, miraculously sparing injury to his spinal cord. Still, recovery, for both the business and his neck, took nearly a full year.

On this trip we've spent a lot of time being quiet, savoring the deepest rhythmic place where we belong to one another. We've been lying on the ground and drinking intensely cold water running down from mountaintops. We haven't needed a clock except to warn of hours till nightfall and the need to make our way back to camp, yielding the forest to bears and owls. I think we're falling inward, resting down into our bones. Replenishing our reserves will take months, not days. Yet I know if we go slowly enough we'll feel again the place inside where we too shine back the light of the stars.

I've had a hungry ache to come to this north edge of Yellowstone Lake to steep myself in the moment where lake becomes river. This is the spot where the water has finished its ten-year journey from where it entered far on the SE shore. From our spot on the overlook I can see how at the edge of the outlet the surface lake water determinedly races sideways in waves across the opening toward the western shoreline. There is no intention of going into the river. Rather the waves bounce off the shoreline back toward the lake's center. Beneath the visible surface another pull must be taking place because water, as if rising groundwater, is filling the start of the river. Here the water is slow, imperceptible current barely seeming to move it. The water is unhurried, as if lazily basking beneath the rays of sunshine. When I turn north, past the bridge, I see the river has become certain of itself. It's narrowing and beginning to pick up speed as it begins a new journey differentiated from its years in the lake. There is no looking back. Everything now dedicated to forward momentum and the surprises ahead.

Years ago I wrote after my meditation retreat with Eugene that sometimes you need to lay your head back and let the current take you. I know the time is coming for the Yellowstone to teach me more about that. I know it is coming for Christi and Sue. But we are not yet at that time. Looking back out at the lake I imagine the Forests in a rowboat, not too far off shore lest the waves pick up, making steady, deliberate progress. I think they're somewhere on the lake's northeastern edge, perhaps by now passing the hot springs.

Although I'm eager for the next stage of my life I know I'm not yet even in the lazy water. I am still in the waves careening off the shoreline. I remain on the verge, sensing the underneath current, but I haven't entered.

Christi and Sue

After nearly two years using the ERGYS bikes Christi's legs and arms have grown much stronger and her coordination in keeping up the rhythmic motion is smoother. In the beginning a stuttering lag sometimes interrupted the extension of her arm or leg and the push of the opposite limb. Now she sustains the flow of pedaling more continuously.

During the years Christi was using the ERGYS bikes she was also walking with the extensive support of an over-land gait trainer. This equipment is a larger, sturdier, and slightly more complex version of walkers most commonly seen in the elderly population. Christi's version has a seat harness that helps lift and stabilize her pelvis. The arm rests are rib cage high. An extension up the back allows her head to be lifted with a supportive chin or head strap.

When Christi began using the walker, years ago in her own basement therapy room, the goal was to facilitate stepping and weight bearing, a moving version of the standing frame she used from the very beginning of rehab at Craig. Taking a dozen steps was a fifteen-minute process as the aides helped her carefully weight shift to one side, adjust her hip, balance on her straightened supporting leg and then signal her with hand cues to bend her opposite knee. Then they assisted her in drawing her foot forward, often Christi only lifting high enough to scrape the ball of her foot ahead in a six- inch step. Sue reminded, "Heel down, rebalance in the middle." Then the whole process was repeated. In the very beginning they often had to backtrack and remind Christi to hold herself with her standing leg because when she attempted to bend the moving knee her weight supporting one would start to go instead. Christi was re-weaving incoming sensation with the neuro-muscular motor circuits for each limb. She had to become specific, not any knee moving but the intended one.

Watching Christi now it's almost hard to remember back to where she started. In the last two years her coordination has been exponentially increasing. Christi initiates the movement herself. The aides who assist her on each side act like guidewires, ensuring her foot landing is straight and her hips rotate forward and back. They tap behind her leg to amplify the signal of which leg is moving. Christi holds her head up with minimal assistance. In the fifteen minutes it once took her to go a dozen steps she now walks down and back the length of two hallways in the classroom basement of the New Directions gym.

For the last two years Christi has also been walking on a treadmill with the use of a body weight suspension system. This treatment is called body weight support treadmill training (BWSTT). Most of us associate it with the pioneering efforts of Christopher Reeve to regain movement after his horseback riding accident caused a spinal cord injury resulting in paralysis. Basically, it's like the over-land gait trainer but the patient walks on a treadmill instead of over ground.

When Christi began using this equipment, on a treadmill located in a downstairs room from the main New Directions gym, her walking pace was super slow, probably close to the pace of fifty-five minutes per mile. Similar to when she started on the Bioness and ERGYS systems, the stimulation of all the sensory input was so great that they had to reduce all extraneous noise and activity. The four-person team working with Christi all had their set roles, assisting leg motion, torso control, head control. If a substitute team member was required it made the whole process slower and awkward as Christi adjusted to the difference in that person's hands on touch.

As Christi became comfortable with the BWSTT her coordination improved. The unweighting system supported about 40% of her weight so she could concentrate on the motion of walking without having to overcome as much gravity pull. She gained control over her torso and head. The rhythm of her steps picked up speed. Current theories in locomotion attribute her stepping to neural circuits in the spine, particularly in the lumbar region. These circuits, called central pattern generators (CPG), exist in multiple locations in our bodies. Chewing, breathing and digesting are all rhythmic activities governed by CPGs. They operate without our conscious thought, yet are also responsive to sensory input and mental command. Different CPGs resonate with one another in ways not yet understood to create increasingly complex and responsive movement patterns.

As Christi gained in her capacity to integrate sensory data, her rhythmic patterns of walking got stronger. Sue began turning up the treadmill pace. Christi walked faster and then practiced varying her speeds. And on one surprising day, when her forward strike foot kept mistiming, Sue realized Christi wanted to go faster still. Always willing to follow her intuition and reading of subtle signals,

Sue turned the treadmill all the way up to running speed. Christi loved it. From that day forward running on the treadmill became a weekly reward for Christi. A fun day after the more laborious and precise work of walking practice that required focus on integrating smoother pelvic rotations and rolling through her foot in each step. As time went on Christi released the tension in her arms so that her forearm was waist high, in the classic runners bent arm position, as she strode forward. Eventually she became so adept at her BWSTT sessions that they went smoothly even when a replacement team member assisted. Even when music played in the background, just as it would in any gym a twenty-something works out in.

The benefits of all the walking are most evident when Sue and the caregivers help Christi move from her wheelchair to the mat, the bike or shower. Instead of Christi balancing on the balls of her feet while she is pivoted into position she is stepping into the ground and holding up a major portion of her own weight. She even sometimes begins the sideways step on her own. And on one exciting day for everyone, in April of 2011, Christi spontaneously takes 24 walking steps when she is transferring between her wheelchair and mat.

I'm not a part of Christi's treatment team anymore so I hear about these milestones rather than participate. Every month or so, Sue and I have coffee and she brings me up to date on how things are progressing. And every four or five months I drop in on one of Christi's therapy sessions to see for myself the remarkable skill progression.

On one of these visits I go to see her at the New Directions gym. Christi is there five days a week, alternating treadmill sessions with ERGYS sessions. After her treadmill workouts she also walks in the over land gait trainer. I had heard from Sue that they sometimes used the upstairs main gym instead of being in a private room. When I see this in person I am amazed.

I visit on a warm day when the door to the main gym is open to the outside. As I approach I can see them in the far corner of the gym, Christi already standing on the treadmill. She is facing the mirror. For a moment I think I see her eye flutter in recognition when she sees me, via the mirror, as I enter. Maybe it wasn't personal, just awareness of motion headed in her direction. Either way, this startles me because I haven't been around her enough lately to know how her vision has improved. Or how her sensory processing speed has increased so that she is taking in peripheral information.

I disbelieve my own experience at the same time I hold on to the memory of that moment. I approach the treadmill and say my hellos just as Christi begins walking. A substitute physical therapy student helps her with her hips because the usual aide hasn't arrived yet. And when he does join a few minutes later Christi doesn't even miss a stride as he takes over that position. Myriah and another PT student aide are guiding Christi's legs. Sue is perched in the small space beside the front console and frame. Christi is walking an eighteen-minute mile pace. Dr. Ostertag drops by and says something to Christi I can't hear, yet watching the rhythm of words, pause, words I recognize the pattern of conversation despite Christi's side of the exchange being silent. Sue and Dr. Ostertag talk over some detail about equipment and follow up on an adjustment made after the last session. As Dr. Ostertag walks away, Myriah says, "I think she's ready to run." Sue reaches in to up the pace to a fifteen-minute mile jogging pace.

All of this is taking place in a loud room. Probably a dozen other program participants and PTs are talking, doing weight machines, walking across the space. Especially with the mirror reflecting everything there is constant sound and motion in Christi's perceptual space. And still she focuses on her own running. When Myriah gives her a cue to lift her knee more Christi responds with the correction on the very next step.

Of course I'm wowed by Christi's ability to run. But I'm even more awed by the speed at which she processes the commotion around her. The healing taking place in Christi goes far beyond the ability to take a step. Later, I ask Dr. Ostertag about her communication with Christi. She tells me that in the beginning she only understood Christi through feedback from Sue, Myriah and the other aides familiar with Christi. She took the risk of them utilizing the Bioness and Ergyss equipment because she trusted that those close to Christi could give accurate feedback on the impact, especially any discomfort. She can't say when it changed for her, but now she perceives "something else" from Christi that kinesthetically feels like she gets her. As a scientist, Dr. Ostertag says this is hard to quantify. It's impossible to objectively measure even though she knows and trusts it. She thinks it's related to that intangible other that they look for in a physical therapy student who naturally relates to patients with attunement. Dr. Ostertag says, "You can see it in how they help a patient transition from wheelchair to exercise equipment." I know she's talking about intuitive caregiving skills, an underpinning so essential yet not quantified.

Myriah has this intuitive gift in spades. She is a fulltime part of Christi's caregiving team, participating in everything from reading a book to yoga to all the mobility training. Her initial work was just helping with range of motion exercises but her ability to read Christi quickly made her a go-to team member. Myriah is both patient and perceptive of little details. If Christi is struggling with movement on a given day she doesn't just assume it's "just brain injury high tone." She says, "I keep in mind that just because someone doesn't have control over their body doesn't mean something doesn't have meaning." She looks closely at the situation and helps make adjustments, for instance, maybe the issue isn't tone but a support belt is too tight and inhibiting Christi from accurately reading muscle signals.

On the day I watch Christi on the treadmill I can see the importance of Myriah on the team. Sue has her attention focused on Christi's upper body and elapsed time and pace. She asks for Myriah's input on leg motions instead of trying to read all things at once solo. If an adjustment were needed Myriah would problem solve, not just wait for Sue to know the answer. The trust Sue has in Myriah is palpable, the equivalent of being able to relax one's shoulders. Trust is another one of those invisible other qualities that supports Christi's rehab efforts to flourish.

One of the most frequent conversations Sue and I have when we get together is the growing importance of setting Christi up for a future independent of their caregiving. Terry is nearing retirement age. Sue is increasingly experiencing tweaks and pains from the logistics of physically assisting Christi. She also perceives the developmental importance of Christi continuing to take ownership of her own life even with high assistance needs. If Sue's schedule requires her to miss some of Christi's therapies, including treadmill walking, Christi still performs at her current skill level. This wasn't always true. If Sue was gone the rehab aides often reported that the session was mediocre because Christi "wasn't into it." There has been a subtle shift occurring that Christi is allied with her PT team, not just with Sue.

Sue and I share the same vision of the next step: a residential home providing a high stimulation environment so Christi, and others in a similar healing journey, will be able to continue their accumulated miracle of recovery even without parental assistance. Everything we know about a staff steeped in intuitive caregiving would be in place. It could become a research center on best practices, counting both stabilization of symptoms as well as progress over time spans long enough to capture change. We know it'll need to be economically self-sustaining so nobody will lose a home because of funding fluctuations in the nonprofit world. I love brainstorming this idea with Sue because I imagine it as a way to continue utilizing the gift Christi's journey gives us.

But I'm busy writing the book and Sue manages Christi's full time schedule. Neither of us can do the necessary legwork to find the resources to make the dream real.

Candace

My writing life is going well. I've found a just right balance with my other work responsibilities. Most days I'm aware of how happy I am. Yet, memories of myself as a little girl keep popping into my head. I write in my journal, "There is some pebble in the five/six period trying to get smoothed by current events." I remember a picture of myself just before a dance recital. My mother is applying lipstick as I sit queen like on a chair, my tutu jutting out twice the width of my body. And then the contrast comes, the memory of being rushed along the edge of the park after dance class, confused by why I must give wide berth to the old man giving away candy to little girls. I remember running through the woods with my brother and cousins on the day I broke my arm. Before I slipped I was proud to be swift enough to take the short cut route with the big kids.

Despite my overall state of well-being, chronic nausea and fatigue, problems from several years ago, return. I decide this time to see what acupuncture can offer me as a treatment. Unlike Western medicine, this treatment approach looks at the body as a system, including the way chi (life force) is and isn't flowing. For the first few sessions, dropping into the language of the body, I get lots of sensations and images throughout the half hour treatment. The images are dreamlike, representations of states without any story line. In one, just below my right elbow, an ancient Chinese army takes position on a battlefield. A couple of weeks into my treatments I begin having tingling sensations into my nose and wrist, along the hairline seams of the bones I broke.

In the next session a surprising dream like scene pops into my mind. I am in a medical room alone. I'm extremely angry. Even while I perceive myself in current time lying still on the massage table with needles in my forelegs, arm and forehead, I am simultaneously in the dream scene. Two perceptions are overlapping. In the altered realm I begin screaming in rage. With big swipes of my arm I'm knocking everything off the countertops. I hear and see sounds of shattering glass and pings of metal hitting the floor. I have no literal memory of anger when I broke my arm at age 6 but this feels like rage that's been trapped somewhere in my arm. I am on the verge of hyper-ventilating when the internal sound of my screaming finally subsides. The vision disappears and I am lying still beneath the warm blanket, ethereal music playing on the CD machine. It's hard to reconcile the two states stitched together in a single whole.

In the next acupuncture session I have no imagery, but my right arm begins to ache so badly I want to call the acupuncturist back into the room to take the needles out. But I can't find the bell he usually leaves for me to signal that I need something and my voice is blocked. I begin to cry, hiccup like breaths punctuate words in my head. "I'm hurt," I repeat over and over. I feel young and alone, wanting someone to hear my silent cry. In real time I'm afraid to move lest the pain intensify. Just when I think I can't stand it another second the pain peters out and I'm aware of deep exhaustion. When the acupuncturist comes back into the room, his eyes inquisitive when he sees the lines of tears that ran down my face, I can't generate words beyond, "I couldn't find the bell."

That night when I go to bed I still feel residual ache in my forearm, just above where the bones broke. Although it's never my position of choice, tonight I sleep on my back, just as I had to when my arm was casted. I hold my right arm across my solar plexus and lay my left hand across the bone as if it's the compression of a heating pad. My left hand acts as caress for the hurt girl, a softly murmured touch speaking, "I heard you." When I wake in the morning my arm is lighter. The sensation is like a tiny channel of liquid jet stream has opened and runs through my wrist and into my hand.

A few weeks later I remember a flash of my father's eyes. A memory comes of just his eyes, pained and fierce. I think he must be angry with me or deeply disappointed. I remember the day he told me, two years before he died, that one of the worst memories of his life was holding me down when they set my broken arm. In an instant a match clicks. I blamed myself for not being fast enough, nimble enough, to avoid the rock slick with fallen leaves. I thought he blamed me for falling. In reality his eyes spoke his anguish of trapping me in my pain.

Logically I don't know what these memories in my arm have to do with the nausea but I'm grateful for the release of the emotional states. I feel as though a corner in my house has been swept clean of dusty cobwebs I didn't even know existed. I reflect on the many years the story of my break has unwound. Way back in 2000 I felt the sparks of release in the nerves of my arm. These new memories are connected but from another channel or layer, one where life force moves through my whole system simultaneously. I am more aware of the entirety of a geodesic puzzle than of a single surface. It's like observing the story of connections across space rather than the earthly elements of water and mineral, blood or bone. I appreciate how long the understanding and release of an event can take in all of us. My injuries are minor compared to Christi's, yet for both of us healing is staying open to a complex layering of information. I'm awed by how important it is to trust that the wisdom of our bodies will transform things in its own timing and sequence. Our task isn't to lead but to support with deep listening.

Working with these memories doesn't darken my spirits. Rather I feel even lighter, happier. My arms swing spontaneously as I run miles of trails in the forest around my house. I run faster, further, more effortlessly than ever before. The eagerness of an explorer builds inside me. I return to studying with Bonnie Bainbridge Cohen, inquiring into the mystery of physical form and flow of life force swirling together. I'm not seeking answers, just guidance throwing lamplight into the expanse of bodymind. I have more pleasure than ever in open-ended discoveries. I don't insist they add up to some useful purpose even while knowing they are markers to someplace too soon to know. Inside my ears and heart, like the sound in a seashell, I hear the current of the river grow louder and know someday soon I'll begin that voyage.

In spring I present a short excerpt of the work with Christi at the University of Arizona's Science and Consciousness conference. Neuro-scientists, cognitive psychologists, philosophers, and physicists are all here to dialogue with one another. The plenary and workshop speakers detail their work trying to understand consciousness. There are vastly more questions than answers. Where is it exactly in the brain and body? How can it be measured? What is the interaction between people and the Universe? What can account for paranormal events?

I am fortunate to be on a panel with a woman from Russia who works in a rehab center. She presents video of her work with a team of physical therapists helping a traumatic brain injured patient move around on the floor. They are relying on the same attuned, non-verbal interactive touch and communication we used with Christi. Another panelist, from London, explains their efforts to record with skin sensors and video footage subtle shifts occurring in coma patients in response to interactions with family and staff. Listening to them I have hope that those of us in small pockets around the world documenting our work, trying to find ways to speak about and work with a presence we feel but can't measure, will have increasing opportunities to share with one another. I realize we may be isolated here in Missoula, yet we're in sync with the times. We're not alone.

A young woman approaches me after the panel. She works as a physical therapy aide in a nursing home. She says she knows the same intuitive engagement with patients I have spoken of and wants her supervisors to read our story so they'll understand what she wants to incorporate. As I nod to her I'm reminded why I wrote the book and the importance of launching it into the world, letting it begin its own journey separate from me. I know the importance of these words becoming someone else's tool. I sense how my once broken arm easily extends this offering to her.

Christi

In spring of 2012 I'm here in Christi's room watching her negotiate computer games utilizing the Brainfingers[xlvii] program. She wears a narrow band, the width of a narrow headband, across her forehead that picks up slight signals of motion and mental attention. These signals convey action commands to the computer. Myriah and Aericka, the speech therapy graduate student working with Christi, encourage her to relax her forehead muscles so the micro-movements of eyebrow lift and eye focus can be registered and control the cursor. In one game a series of ping pong sized colored balls cross the screen and Christi must hit them at the appropriate moment. In another a series of letters appear on the screen in an arc and as each is highlighted by a moving light, Christi signals a letter she wants. Eventually this could lead to spelling words. But for now the purpose is coordinating vision and intention with consistent action and sustaining attention. When Christi first began using the program two years ago she fatigued after five minutes and required a rest break. Now she continues her attention for 45 minutes at a time.

Using the Brainfingers program has been a series of trial and error sessions. One reason is because setting the registry levels for the signals varies widely based on "where her bodymind is on that day." If Christi is experiencing high tone, the controlling signals and strength differ from a day with much lower tone. If one's agenda is doing the game this might be frustrating but for the team it's more an interesting puzzle that they're figuring out with Christi. "With" is the operative word. In today's session when the eyebrow lift isn't consistent Aericka and Myriah both suggest options to Christi. Even though Christi is vocally silent she responds to them with appropriate shifts in facial action. Watching them the feeling is of teamwork. Their interactions are a bit slowed down but not significantly time delayed.

The Brainfingers program is a lot like the ERGYS bike and treadmill. The point is to support Christi in what she can experience now to optimize her life. Sue is not attached to the eventual outcome that may arise. This attitude of expansive realism is one of the things Dr. Ostertag has appreciated so much about working with Sue at New Directions. Dr. Ostertag remarks, "Sue holds a balance between believing in more and being satisfied with what is." It's an attitude that has built the trust necessary to take risks on the unknown.

Sue doesn't have an agenda for Christi to be able to spell as her communication system. She sees that Christi's ability to pay attention and mentally work for sustained bouts of time is strengthening something un-nameable in future outcomes. It's like exercising a muscle you can't individually perceive, yet still know is there. In ways not directly attributable it may even be supporting the fact that more people say they can "read" Christi even though she doesn't speak. Whatever leads to more people being able to communicate with Christi, the more her ease of function will increase.

In 2009 I read a story under the headline "Belgian alert, mute for 23 years." Rom Houben, who had a car accident when he was 20, had been misdiagnosed for 23 years as being in a vegetative state. His mother never gave up hope that the presence she felt in her son would be recognized by others. She kept seeking out tests sensitive enough to convince others. Finally when a PET scan revealed that his brain was almost normal, a treatment team was formed to help find a method of communication. He began with a slight movement of his foot that activated a computer. He eventually regained the ability to use one finger to tap on a screen and spell words. Houben describes his many years of inability to communicate, even to shed tears when he heard about the death of his father, as "Powerlessness. Utter powerlessness. At first I was angry, then I learned to live with it."[xlviii]

Those of us around Christi are like Houben's mother. We won't give up hope that there is a way to bridge the gap to help Christi communicate more fully with others. Sometimes I worry that Christi too has "learned to live with it." Knowing she can't, she doesn't try except in those instances when something big pushes her to forcefully sound a protest or exclamation.

Thankfully, most days I'm not captured by my worries. I know Sue and Terry and the whole team have kept Christi's bodymind network nourished and challenged. Most of us still expect Christi to speak someday. Perhaps she'll be like the young man in the Miles City nursing home who after 19 years of silence says to his parents, "Can I have a coke." I keep in mind Brucker's words that we don't know the timing of internal healing because we can't see exactly what was damaged. When our system completes internal priorities it'll begin to engage more externally. And when that happens more treatment options become possible and growth is exponential.

After watching the Brainfingers session I visit with Sue and Christi before they transition to the next activity. I tell Christi a brainstorm I've had, laying the challenge out as a question of interest. Every March I begin leading a training program for walkers to complete the Missoula Marathon or half marathon in July. This inspires me to throw out the same goal for her. Since I know Christi is running on the treadmill I suggest her marathon will be to run a mile each week and then complete her final steps at the finish line. I question if she'd want something that public, but I toss it out. Christi raises her right eyebrow ever so slightly, nearly imperceptibly tips her head. She seems intrigued by the idea. A few days later Sue sends me an e-mail saying Christi has accepted the goal. What's more, it'll be a fundraiser. Sponsors can support Christi, as well as Myriah and other students from the PT department who will run the half marathon, to donate money to New Directions to purchase a ceiling hanging unweighting system.

Sue

Synergistically assistance comes to Sue in late spring. A professional colleague is taking a leave of absence and in her spare time is eager to help research options for a group living space. Like Sue, she has a background in early intervention services and program management. Philosophically she completely understands the milieu therapy model Sue and I have dreamed of so many times. They begin fleshing out the ideas in planning meetings and reaching out to other stakeholders in the community. Getting a facility up and going is likely a two-year project. For the first time though it's not pipe dream smoke but hard lines of shape begin being sketched in.

Sue is invited to speak as a keynote presenter at the statewide Brain Injury Association conference. As she begins preparing Sue realizes that her Mom/family hat and professional interventionist hat have become one. Personal experience and professional training are inseparable. The past four years she has mentored the students who work with Christi as aides. She's witnessed how it deepens their studies at the University. She encourages them to trust themselves when they see contradictions between a "fact" in the textbook about TBI recovery and what they observe with their own eyes with Christi. She knows they are learning to hold a vision of possibility that will benefit all the patients they work with in the future. Knowing the difference she's making reminds her that her role as a teacher is intact. Myriah, under the shared tutelage of Sue and Dr. Ostertag, begins a journal article about Christi's advancements at the New Directions gym.

Sue is realistic as always. She knows she'll be intimately involved with Christi's rehab journey even in the transition to a group home. But she and Terry can also begin imagining a life where they're both retired.

Christi

July 8, 2012. It's a ridiculously hot day for the marathon. Morning temperatures hold steady the first few hours but by 10:30 begin to climb, headed to the mid-90s. Myriah and her PT friends have just finished the half-marathon. They have only a short time to pass through the runners' food station and head back over the bridge to meet Christi. They are buzzing with their own success and eagerness to share Christi's. I am still on the racecourse, running-walking the marathon with the friends I trained with all spring.

Christi rose to Sue's challenge of finishing her marathon with a public, ten-step walk using the gait trainer. Christi even agreed to a newspaper story about her quest, the first publicity her case ever received. A week ago a reporter and photographer came to watch her final mile on the treadmill. Christi stayed focused on her run while the interviewer asked questions. At first the reporter couldn't see past all the helpers hands guiding Christi along, but then mid-way realized the rhythm and muscle action was all Christi and blurted out, "She really is doing it herself."

The race finishes at the end of a bridge crossing the Clark Fork River. Christi and her parents drive to the far end and unload. Myriah and friends roll the gait trainer while Terry pushes Christi in her wheelchair over the crest of the bridge.

Runners race by on their left. The announcers, perched thirty feet high beneath an arch of balloons, call out names and finish times. Music blares from two-foot high speakers. The sidewalks all across the bridge are lined with spectators hollering for loved ones.

On Christi's side of the finish line she has her own loud cheer squad. Debra Shorrock and Pat Skergan, still working with Christi nearly every week, are here. Serena Early has come dressed in a cheer outfit. Three former rehab aides, one pushing a stroller, join the magic, as do various friends of the treatment team who have heard Christi's story second hand for many years and now want to support her milestone achievement.

They're ten minutes ahead of the planned finish time when Myriah leans in to help Christi stand. Sue is swept along in everyone else's momentum, no need for her to lead. Instead Sue sits down on her rolling stool so she can scoot along in front of Christi, reaching in to tap the back of whichever leg is about to take the step forward. Christi no longer needs the guidewire hands of an aide on her thigh and ankle. Myriah walks tight to Christi's right side, ready to support her neck or chin if necessary.

Christi holds her head high herself. Her steps are deliberate. She lifts each knee and places her foot down the same distance of anyone's walking stride. In everyone's excitement they've started her further away from the finish line than they meant to. Ten steps turn into twenty, into thirty. Terry waits for her at the edge of the finish line with her wheelchair. His pride so palpable it looks as if it'll burst his chest open. The announcers call out Christi's name, praise her "rehab marathon." Strangers whistle, holler, clap wildly.

I cross the finish line ten minutes after Christi, disappointed to not see her cross the line in person, yet eager to still participate in the celebration. Although hot and sweat stained I can't resist taking a picture for my scrapbook. Sue, radiant, stands at the right hand corner of Christi's wheelchair. I crouch down to Christi's level on the left and we look toward the camera, medals hanging around our necks.

November, 2013

"There is another world in addition to the one that we live in. When looking at our world from that world, we can see things that we cannot see now."
                            Masaru Emoto, The Hidden Messages in Water

Sue and I are sitting at a table in Buttercup Café, cappuccinos in front us, winter coats recently dug from our closets slung across the backs of our chairs. We've met here every couple of months for the past two years. We engage in the chit-chat of friends whose lives have intersected over so many years. How is your mother? Terry? Your husband? His business?

The tone between us is slightly different than in times past. Although on the surface all looks the same, we both are settled in different ways. It used to be as if we were catching up and racing out the door all in the same breath. Now there are longer pauses in our conversation, more gliding from topic to topic. Sue tells me a funny story of how satisfying the simple task of cleaning the bathroom is. Concrete, specific, accomplishable. I understand something of this meaning, of the simplicity of being stripped down to just what is in front of me instead of striving toward. Maybe this is the wisdom of our age, accepting the truth of what energy we have, of what we can make happen and what we can't.

We both seem as if we are relishing the relative pause in our lives. We're trekkers, finished a long climb, relaxing in an open meadow before the next phase of the adventure.

The word consolidation fits. Sue tells me, "People say, 'Well, it's been 14 years.' And I say 'Yeah…'" long and drawn out. In that expanse of one word she means, "Of course I know how long it's been, I've walked every step of it" and "I know you think this journey too long, not successful enough. But without all we've done, the same 14 years would have passed with no changes."

Exponential changes do continue in Christi's skill level and in the support team around her. Two months ago I visited one of her sessions at the New Directions gym and was brought to tears by the breadth and strength of her movement repertoire.

On the day I observed, Christi was getting hooked up to a revision of the facilitated walking apparatus. Christi has been using a version of this system for nearly a year. A fifteen-foot track line runs along the ceiling that allows her to walk forward and back supported by the unweighting system she initially utilized on the treadmill. Over the course of the last year Christi gained more and more ability to initiate stepping and posture adjustments on her own. She continued to strengthen her head control, independent almost all of the time she's walking, albeit with an exaggerated lift of her chin which makes her head tilt back.

Four months ago Dr. Ostertag designed a new series of challenging exercises for Christi. Walking forward, turning around and walking back wasn't enough. In the new protocol Christi walks forward for 15 feet, backwards – rolling toe to heel, and repeats. Then she turns sideways and steps the whole distance again, leading first with her right leg and returning with the left. Next she stands on a rocker board, a two-foot long platform with a half moon shaped bottom. She weight shifts to her right foot and then left, strengthening her ability to support her weight on one leg. For part two she turns on the platform and rocks toe to heel. Her range of motion isn't very large, but to see her fine-tune her balance and control like this is amazing.

The next task requires even more coordination. A two-step stair is placed on the ground. Christi initiates lifting her foot and her aides help guide her foot onto the step. She steps down and lifts her other foot all in the same motion, landing two feet together on the first step. Repeat beginning with the other foot. And then she steps backwards down each step. After she does this sequence a couple of times she spontaneously combines her steps so that she sequences up both steps in one continuous motion. Her workout finishes with touching her toe to a rolling board that she has to swing out to the side and back. This requires her to maintain stability by standing on one leg while she initiates movement with the muscles on the outside and inside of her thigh. The whole workout takes nearly one hour.

On the day I visited Christi was wearing a new pair of shorts designed specifically for her. Straps from the unweighting apparatus on the track above hung down and attached to her shorts with clips. This new system gives her more freedom to move unobstructed by the previous straps that impeded lateral motion. Wearing the shorts was made possible because over the past three months Christi gained so much abdominal strength that she can hold herself upright without support around her torso. Another benefit of the new system is that she can practice "sit-stand." Before she began walking steps today she twice initiated standing from her seated position in her wheelchair and then sat back down.

During the session Dr. Ostertag drops by to see the new shorts. She is very pleased to have a new option for patients to practice standing up and sitting down. As I listen to the interaction I appreciate how much Christi is processing all at the same time. She is continuing, without a pause, her tasks at hand even while there is conversation.

Sue was incredibly proud to share this success with me. I was awed. I remembered back to when our sessions were on the mat in Christi's basement and it took a team of four and up to five minutes to help her find the muscle to push forward the distance of one crawl. After the session I said to Sue, "This team of aides takes for granted that Christi can make adjustments within seconds. That she can initiate on her own with just a verbal command. They have no idea what it was like before."

What I saw in the physical therapy aides that day was evidence of the change that Christi has helped catalyze. When she began her rehab at New Directions it was under the terms of allowing her to use the equipment, but not with a shared vision of her success. Dr. Ostertag is now an active believer in the change that's possible and regularly checks in on their progress. She has modified the neuro-rehab curriculum at UM because of it. She even used video clips of Christi as part of a national webinar she taught last summer. The designer of the track unweighting system reports the results he observes with Christi's mobility in his research reports and future grant requests. He's even designing a new custom equipment piece that will support her neck, giving her the opportunity for improved visual coordination. Christi is helping the New Directions team learn and teach others about the needs of severe TBI patients that are different than spinal cord injury patients who use similar equipment.

Myriah, based on her work with Christi, was accepted into the highly competitive physical therapy program and is at work on two significant projects. One is a single case study about Christi that she and Dr. Ostertag will submit for publication. The second is a comparison of the rehab textbook students used when Christi was first injured and the one newly released. In the old model all changes were assumed evident in the first 18 months post injury. Students now will learn a new protocol that includes continued movement exercises to build strength and skill over the period of many years. It even includes yoga as a modality. The ripple effects of Christi's unpredicted journey are just beginning to bear fruit.

I remember back to one of the silent conversations between Christi and I in the first year. She had once dreamed of a career in medicine. Surely this isn't the path she would have chosen in her imagination, but in many ways her dream has come true. Her example has made a difference in changing the field of rehab. She has inspired both students and teachers to believe in unlimited possibilities and to see beyond limitation to the humanity beneath.

The new students who work with Christi cause me to pause in reflection about the importance of telling Christi's history. Those who meet her now are not hampered by previous perceptions of impossibility or memories of when nearly all communication was subterranean. And yet, I can't help think that they miss some of the richness of her story. To understand the magnitude of her recovery it's important to take note of the subtleties and tiny increments that blended together to repair and strengthen the foundation upon which she now builds a greater repertoire of action. Her bodymind needed to release the realities of her trauma before her movement abilities could come to the fore. And to do that she needed the extensive network of emotionally and physically attuned caregivers, most notably her parents, as well as diverse treatment team members and approaches. I see that the qualitative research Sue and I first proposed ten years ago is as necessary and relevant now as it was then. If we create records of the complexity of the healing process we'll benefit the patients, families and treatment professionals of tomorrow.

Sitting with Sue in Buttercup Café I am aware of being part of Christi's history, like someone who took care of her when she was an infant and toddler, but who has little bearing on her life now. Although whenever I see Christi she seems genuinely accommodating that I am there, we don't share any special gaze or thread of energy. For many years, even when I wasn't part of her daily treatment team, I still had intuitions of what could assist her progress or had a sense of a new goal as I did with the marathon challenge. Now my connection to Christi is almost exclusively through

Sue. I follow Christi's progress through Sue's descriptions just as I track the lives of my friends' adult children.

Recently I received a graduation announcement card in the mail from the family of a child I saw in therapy when she was only four-years old. I treated her for three years and then for the next four kept up with her life when I met her and her adopted mother for an annual cup of hot chocolate at the holidays. When they moved away I lost contact until this card came. It wasn't from the girl herself. Likely I am only a vague memory for her. It came from her mother who knew I would want to share the happiness of the girl's success. I feel something similar for Christi. I am sometimes nostalgic about the special bond we shared but not sad. It is the natural order of things that she outgrew me. Going forward, when I drop by to observe the next new thing at New Directions it will be as one does when they go to a recital. I will be an audience member.

The increased confidence and active support from Dr. Ostertag and the New Directions clinic is a big reason Sue is more relaxed. It's not that her daily workload has changed. She is still mother, case manager and rehab aide. But in the early years it was her faith and will that pulled everyone along with her. Now Sue is met halfway and aided by true team members working toward the same vision.

Longevity of the team members, all facilitating their piece of the complex healing puzzle, makes a huge difference. Serena still does yoga with Christi and has brought in and trained two new teachers to continue the work at times she's absent. Interestingly these new teachers have both begun dreaming of Christi. This unconscious channel of communication between Christi and others expresses both the relationship bond and information related to changes and treatment. Debra continues to offer Body Mind Centering inspired treatments integrated with other forms, such as Body Talk. And Myriah maintains a part time work schedule even while she works on a physical therapy degree. Twice Myriah has heard Christi call her name when she's in another room, a verbal expression that may be infrequent and random now but may someday increase in deliberateness. No one who knows Christi discounts that her long held goal to speak for herself, whether literal or through technology, will someday come true.

Myriah helps train new caregivers and physical therapy volunteers so that it's not all on Sue's shoulders. With five years experience Myriah knows a lot of the nuances that help make things run smoothly for Christi. Training others lets Myriah compare old and new. For instance, she says, "It used to take a couple months for Christi to adjust to someone new and now it's a matter of days." Christi's agenda is Myriah's guide for training. Myriah laughs when she tells me an example of how insistent Christi is. She was teaching a new aide how to do transfers and suggested to Christi that they do it the old way until the person is more familiar. But Christi wouldn't oblige. After the third time of taking steps to pivot instead of remaining stationery Myriah asked, "Do you only want her to learn the new?" and Christi raised her brow in assertive reply.

Myriah's dream for Christi isn't so much what specific skills she'll acquire, although of course she hopes her mobility continues to increase. What she desires is that

Christi will always have people in her life who perceive her and can help her achieve whatever goals she chooses. Myriah's words echo the dream and tension in Sue and Terry's vision as well. A new residential therapeutic model is waiting to be created.

During our coffee hour Sue asks about the book. She naturally wants to know the latest in its evolution and anticipated publication. Even though I have been the writer, she has carried the seed of this project in her own heart for an equal number of years. Having it nearly done is part of the mood we share of sitting still after the long upward climb. I tell her about my final round of editing and hopes to be done within the month. Although the frustrations of trying to find an editor and publisher made me sometimes feel alone and unsupported, in retrospect I appreciate how much help I did have. I was fortunate to have a strong writing community surrounding me, helping me grow as a writer. They helped me with my technical skill and increasing my confidence to tell what I know to a wider audience. I even came to believe it most fitting that producing this book about Christi's journey in the new paradigm of self-publishing was the truest match to her rehab journey.

To tell the story of finishing the book as a product or milestone is like naming Christi's recovery as her new skill walking 15 steps. It misses the incremental and multi-faceted changes in my own life that strengthened my capacities. Finding the language to tell Christi's story and my own wasn't just vocabulary or confidence. It required me to live an experience beyond my personal boundaries of understanding.

Bainbridge-Cohen has said, "The paradigm of Western science is to use the nervous system to investigate consciousness. In BMC we're using consciousness to understand the nervous system." To tell this story I had to keep beckoning myself to attune to my own experience of consciousness, something more akin to intuitive knowing, and allow it to inform my words and knowledge.

One of the landmark events in my journey to strengthen my own capacity to experience first and name later was seven years ago. It was on one of my forays to investigate treatment options. I visited Island Dolphin Care, a dolphin assisted therapy program developed by Deena and Peter Hoagland in Key Largo. Since I wanted to know first hand what the dolphins were about and how the interactions with the physically disabled children worked I followed my observation day with my own dolphin swim. I scheduled two sessions, a morning "free" swim and an afternoon "trick" swim, at Dolphins Plus, the original program that started Deena and Joe down their path when their son Joe needed rehabilitation.

On the day I arrived I was surprised that Meghan, the instructor, was waiting for me at the front desk. Since I was only three minutes late I presumed the group would just be getting settled in the orientation area. To my surprise I found there was no group. Uncharacteristically, no one else signed up for "free" swim so it'd just be my instructor and me in the pool. Or so I assumed.

The orientation went smoothly. I learned that bottlenose dolphins live into their 30s in captivity, longer than the 17-25 year life span in the wild. Meghan held up a stuffed dolphin toy to point out the pectoral and dorsal fins and the fluke. She explained how they see and hear monoscopically or stereoscopically, meaning using each eye and internal hearing channel completely independently or together. Echolocation enables the dolphin to gain precise information about what is in its environment. She told me that Dolphins Plus, started in 1979, was the pioneer of natural and structured dolphin swims. Their goal is to help the public learn more about dolphins in the hopes that we'll then become good stewards of the environment and allow them to live healthy lives. As responsible caretakers of wild animals they provide the dolphins with physical exercise and mental stimulation. That makes my swim a two-way deal: while I checked out the dolphins I also served as their curiosity object. I was encouraged to live up to my part of the bargain by being entertaining while in the water.

In my case this meant being a good toy for Cosmo, Bob, Samantha, and Julian in the "party house." Their pool was named that because of their great playfulness that Meghan described as, "They make a frat house ruckus." She told me how to recognize each dolphin as they swam by me in the pool. Samantha, aged 23, has an offset jaw because it was once dislocated in an episode of rough play (fixing it would have been more traumatic than leaving it be). Her four-year old son, Julian, has sharp features and is the smallest. Cosmo, at five years, is the biggest even though he's six years younger than his half-brother Bob. Bob I should recognize by his underbite and easy going nature.

All the descriptions of dolphins were fine, but when Meghan started to tell me swim etiquette my heart began to race. She said I should slide into the pool gently so the dolphins don't feel like someone just crashed through their roof into the living room. Use no hands in swimming; leave them down to my sides or behind my back. Absolutely no touching because it would violate social codes, like if a complete stranger walked up to me and started pawing at me without permission. When she explained that she might call from her position on the dock for me to look left or right to see one of the dolphins swimming close my heart and breath abruptly paused. I'd be in the pool with them by myself. All along I had assumed she would be at my side like the aides were with the children I observed the day before.

As we walked to the equipment area for fitting my fins, mask and snorkel I sensed my shoulders, hips and knees tightening, as if the space in each joint had shrunk, my bones and muscles cinched tighter by some instinct to stay together. I walked like an automaton as I focused on measured breaths that calmed me only a little. I expressed tentativeness about never having snorkeled, but Meghan made light of it, saying if I knew how to breathe I could do it. As soon as I tried on the mask and my first breath sealed it to my face, claustrophobic panic careened through my body. I was still on land and so freaked out I thought for a split second that I couldn't get in the water. Meghan either didn't see my panic or decided to ignore it and walked away to the entry platform.

To get in the water I commanded each breath and mentally instructed my tensed body to overcome the inertia sticking me to land. I took a swimmer's noodle to occupy my hands, not trusting I'd float by just kicking my legs. I followed Meghan's instructions to swim around the edges of the pool. I was half way around before I relaxed my full face into the water. My eyes registered sunlight and blue tinted pool but my perceptions were so preoccupied with the sputtering of anxiety coursing through my arms and legs that I couldn't actually see anything defined. I didn't want to try to see a dolphin. I definitely didn't want to be in a dolphin party house.

I'm not sure how 2,000 pounds of dolphin mass managed to evade me in a 30x30' pool but they did. Maybe their renowned sensitivity perceived that my capacities were taxed just breathing and kicking. It wasn't until my fourth circuit around the pool that I achieved some normalcy. I was breathing with my face in the water. My brain stopped emitting an alarm bell. Maybe I was ready to see a dolphin. Gingerly I moved my head side to side to scan for them.

I guess the dolphins heard the invitation. Bob swam by me first, not too quickly, but not too slowly either. He was an oblong grey shadow getting me used to motion nearby. It took only half way around the pool for my heart surge to settle down. Then Samantha and Julian swam just below me, close enough that I worried about a collision and froze for an instant. Only a quarter-time around before my heart to resumed its normal beat. The first inkling of "this is fun" lightened the joints in my hips and knees. Meghan called to me from the dock to swim along the fence line because the mother and baby pair in the adjoining pool were swimming alongside trying to see what's happening. I swam up and down twice. They swam parallel, slowed their speed to match mine. Samantha came along my other side. Dolphins flanked me. Suddenly I wanted to laugh. I started kicking so fast I barely averted crashing into the wall. Full of excitement I circumnavigated the pool. My senses muted again. This time though it wasn't from anxiety, rather a desire to fully to absorb the wonderment.

When my senses opened again I perceived quiet all around me. Curiosity made me look deeper into the pool. I saw bubbles and wondered where the dolphins were swimming. Even without seeing them I could sense their presence and that I was swimming in tandem instead of being a surface waterbug on the verge of fleeing.

Cosmo came to my side. He drifted to match my speed and turned on his side to examine me with both eyes. He emitted his signature sound, beyond the range of human hearing. I sensed the impact of his echolocation as it penetrated my core. It felt like a dense, yet yielding, stream of wind, making contact and reverberating back all in one motion. I stared at his eyes and felt a channel open from my belly to my eyes, the motion of a rivulet undammed, racing free. I was simultaneously aware of vulnerability and deep peace. When he swam off I was buoyant, lifted by the effervescence of a deeply familiar song. The sound was a vibration from all my cells, similar to how one senses the sound of loud base through the floor. I swam around my now familiar edges of the pool and felt so much joy pulsing in my chest I wondered if the chambers of my heart were big enough to hold it. Giddiness rippled out to my fingers and flippered toes. I silently offered gratitude to Cosmo, Bob, Samantha and Julian. I thanked the people who mysteriously didn't register so that I had this opportunity to go solo.

In the afternoon I went back for a group swim where we each got to be part of the dolphins' tricks. It was fun because the dolphins touched me and I them. Each trick made me laugh more. Floating on my back, two dolphins pressed their snouts against my feet and pushed me through the water. Then on my belly I spread my arms in a T and they swam by, allowing me to grab their dorsal fins and go for a ride. I treaded water and a dolphin "kissed" my cheek. My favorite of all was when the dolphin came alongside my outstretched hand and glided past my palm. His dense, enlivened flesh made me think of blubber, thick and pliable, and how a jellyfish might feel if we could hold it without getting stung. For the final trick each dolphin dove to the bottom and brought each participant a present. Mine was a piece of sea grass, a keepsake pressed into my journal.

In the weeks following my swim it was the side-by-side swimming memory I returned to over and over. I fell asleep re-envisioning Cosmos' eyes turned to me, holding the image to myself like my childhood security blanket. I called it up when I went for a walk in the mountains, bonding nature to nature. When my friend's mother was dying I soothed myself and wished her peaceful passage with the sensations of traveling beside the dolphins.

No one knows precisely what's healing with the dolphins. Given my own experience, I believe one portion of the healing dose is the combination of being sought out and being seen. It's like coming alive from a moonlit lover's gaze, eyes filled with curiosity without expectations or demands. Whatever block obscures us, be it self-imposed anxiety, deep trauma or physical disability, melts and we are perceived as whole. It is this connection to wholeness that's like fuel, moving us even more fully into sensing and expressing our own unique embodiment of spirit into matter, gesture, expression.

Surely this is part of the magic that was healing for Christi as well. The basis of all the different treatment methods and people in her team was a heartfelt desire to find her and offer connection. The pathways of action, like the rivulet that opened in me, come as a natural response. Sometimes I count myself as one of the luckiest on Christi's treatment team because she gave me the gift of experiencing who, what, exists when all is stripped away. To know presence in that pure way opened my perceptions to see and be with Florence and my Dad as their spirits departed. And to hear so precisely what the echolocation of the dolphin bounced off inside of me.

When Christi and I met I was already on a quest to directly perceive consciousness within my tissues. Yet the experience of resonating with her deep within a wellspring of being made explicit the existence of the same core foundation inside me. She gave me the gift of experientially knowing how consciousness arises in the relationship, how it is both emanating from the individual person and being co-created and shared. Perhaps I could've read books that told me that reality, but it would have stayed conceptual for me without the direct experience Christi gave me.

As I sit telling Sue about the completion of the book I am aware of how much calmer I am than the self who joined the treatment team so many years ago. Taking a breath I sense my own bodymind state. I am literally settled deeper into my body, as if each new insight over these years knocked loose and washed away accumulated bits of crud. Cleansed are the grainy, crystallized particles, hardened residue of memories and habits, that had been stuck to muscle fibers and the strands of cytoskeleton shaping each cell. My internal perception of the territory of myself is as denser, wider, and deeper, as if the literal volume of my body has increased. I sense greater continuity throughout all the systems of my body. I am distinct tidal pool yet open to constant flow inward and outward, in dynamic interplay with the world around me. It's obvious when Christi releases tone in her body and gains a new range of motion, a new ability to both express and receive. For the rest of us the same process is available and ongoing, albeit usually in a less consciously visible manner. The range of motion we gain is in the ease with which we lift our arm, feel and express emotions, or experience liberation from self-limiting beliefs.

As our coffee hour nears a close Sue and I speak briefly of the future. We don't lean forward, determination set, as if pushing our way into it as we did so many times in the past.

So early in this journey I wrote about will and intention thinking only of Christi. I understand now as Sue and I sit together that we also bound ourselves with will to persevere against the odds. The successes we've achieved combined with increased help of others who believe in Christi's future, my future, have allowed this overdrive to melt. Softer, more pliable, intention and clarity fill us now.

We lay our ambitions down gently on the table as bits of treasure. Terry is retiring in April and Sue will have greater freedom to travel and speak to other families and professionals about all she's learned. The dream of someday having a group home is held tender despite the dead ends of the previous year. Sue knows its creation will be when other leaders come forward to help manifest it. She has accepted the limitations of time and energy. I know the wisdom I've gained in this journey is already propelling me forward. I sense the drift of this current within me like very slow moving water, the kind that carries us down the stream even while we lazily watch the clouds. Christi deepened my trust that if I stay present, balanced on the border between what I already know and the unknown, discoveries beyond my imagination await.

CANDACE'S ACKNOWLEDGMENTS

Mid-way into writing this book a friend gave me a magnet for my refrigerator that reads, "It takes a village to raise a writer." I'll add to this, "and to create a story." Christi, Sue and Terry gifted me with sharing their intimate journey. I appreciate the trust they placed in me to convey the depth of what we learned. I continue to be inspired by their family's love and dedication to healing. And by Sue's endless attunement and creativity in seeing each emerging possibility and finding a means to fruition for Christi. I am inspired also by Christi's determination and adherence to her own priorities.

In the village of stories are those of Nick, Kyle, Brucker's lab, Dolphins Plus and Nanshan Hospital. I thank all those generous families who shared their experiences in order to widen the breadth of understanding of what's possible in rehabilitation.

Thanks go to all those on Christi's treatment team who shared this recovery journey. Many spent extra hours in interviews with me so that I could include their perspectives in telling the story. I especially want to thank Debra Shorrock and Serena Early for the collegial time they spent with me which helped me in my own work with Christi as well as in telling this story.

My "village" thanks also go to my extended family. And to the members of my writing group who helped me with multiple drafts of this book, as well as to those who read a first edition and offered encouragement and suggestions for improvement. These include Robin Childers, Ann Cook, Vera Orlock, Laurel Burrill, Bill Crosby, Susan Leaphart, Chris Fiore, Sarah Baxter-Cronauer, Dave Rosengren, and Paula Parcheta.

Special gratitude to Nancy Heil, Joyce Hocker, Leslie Burgess and Peggy Christian. Each spent innumerable hours handholding, urging and critiquing, from concept to finished product. Leslie gifted me with patience and expertise in editing line by line, challenging and helping me to refine my words to say exactly what I meant. Peggy assisted me with her abilities to envision the optimum flow of the manuscript as a whole and was brave enough to tell me I was wrong in places even when she knew I didn't want to hear it.

Bonnie Bainbridge-Cohen has been inspiration for me throughout. I've learned from her way more than the facts of embodiment. The spirit of curiosity and inclusion which infuses Body Mind Centering and her invitation that each of us stand – literally and figuratively – in our place in the world has been both essential support and prodding.

Dudley Dana, who's beautiful photograph graces the cover of this book, has offered support for this project throughout, even when it required sacrifices on his part. It's a blessing to have a partner who says, "I don't always understand how you experience things, but I believe in you." His steadfast faith helped make this book possible.

SUE'S ACKNOWLEDGMENTS

I want to take this opportunity to thank all of "The Angels" who have come to provide encouragement, support, care giving, meals, respite, conversation, and/or friendship. First of all I want to thank all family members who have been there for us from the beginning. Your love and encouragement gave us the strength through the bad times and good. Terry, I want to thank you for hanging in there through thick and thin and supporting me through good times and bad. Your love and devotion helped us muster the courage to continue our journey as a family.

I shall never forget the kind highway patrol officer and his wife who came to visit us several hours after the accident to let us know that Christi did nothing wrong and she was wearing her seat belt that retracted in the roll over. To the emergency room doctor and team who saved her life and kept in contact with us by phone as we made the long drive to Idaho. I shall never forget Rita and Patti the weekend ICU nurses who greeted us and proclaimed – "a girl has to look good no matter what, so we washed her hair and put lotion on her". A special thank-you to the powers to be at St. Pat's who gave the "go ahead" to transport Christi from Couer d' Alene to Missoula. I shall never forget Dr. Seagraves who put together an amazing team of specialists to help us through the many months in St. Pat's and the many years of home visits. Dr. Nick Chandler I shall never forget your honesty when asked about the future, you let us know that "we need to take it one day at a time" and there are no hard and fast answers. I want to thank all of the nursing and therapy staff at St. Pat's who cared for our daughter and who allowed her dogs to visit and for us to crank up the music and decorate her room. I am also appreciative of the professionals at Craig Rehabilitation Hospital in Englewood, Colorado who spent hours training me on the many therapy techniques I would use throughout Christi's long slow rehabilitation.

I want to thank each and every caregiver who has come to our house and assisted us in caring for Christi – I do not want to mention names as there are too many and you need to know that you all have a very special place in our hearts. We appreciate all that you did so that we could keep Christi at home and get some respite from the 24 hour care giving. I do want to acknowledge all of the caregivers from the "Chalice of Repose Program" for bringing the harp, songs, and puppetry into our home. I want to thank Leah who brought dance into Christi's life and for bringing Dexter Grove to our house for private concerts. There are two long term care givers, Myriah and Bree, who went above and beyond the call of duty at times so that I could have a break away or so I could go to care for my mother with Alzheimer's – for that I thank-you. It gave me peace of mind to know that Christi was in such capable hands.

I want to take the opportunity to thank all of the therapists who put up with my optimism and drive to continue, no matter what the odds. Mary O'Connell , thank-you for "thinking outside the box" and encouraging me to do the same. A special thank-you to the many PT students who helped us to continue with therapies when formal therapy services ended. We loved to watch you learn and grow into amazing professionals. I want to single out Nikki the PT student who introduced us and encouraged us to try the electrical stimulation. Your idea was the initial step to further opportunities for Christi to regain control over her muscles and gain strength and stamina. I want to thank New Directions Health and Wellness Center and especially Dr. Sue Ostertag for providing us with the opportunity to try new equipment and for providing support, guidance, and direction in Christi's rehabilitation. To Peggy from CDC I want to thank-you for your friendship and giving me the opportunity to practice my profession. You provided me with the opportunity to do what I loved in a flexible way.

Throughout the years there have been and continue to be some very special dedicated angels who enabled our family to be where we are today. These dedicated angels truly helped us throughout the many years of healing and gave our family the strength to continue. They include Dr. Pat Skergan and Dr. Linda Matz who provided care for Christi's back and body as she regained strength and stamina. Deb Shorrock provided inner and outer healing and support. Deb there are not words to describe what a valuable role you play in Christi and our families healing. You are an amazing woman with a "gift". Serena, thank-you for brining yoga into our home and lives. You were the first to help Christi and "the mom" learn how to rest down. You are a very inspiring woman who provided many creative ways to enhance our physical goals so that Christi could gain strength and learn how to produce new movements. Your sense of humor was just what we needed and thank-you for sharing you bountiful garden. Finally, I want to take this opportunity to thank Candace Crosby who came to support Christi, Terry, and I from day one. Your many hours were so valued and appreciated by our family. Thank-you for listening as I processed the experience. Thank-you for getting me in touch with the many resources and supports along the way. And most of all thank you for your dedication and determination to get out Christi's story. We could not have accomplished what we did or endured the journey without you.

Read more about Nick, Kyle, Brucker's Lab, Island Dolphin Care and Nan Shan Hospital stem cell center at bodymindinquiry.com

ENDNOTES

May, 1999

[i] Howard Gardner authored Frames of Mind. The theory of multiple intelligences. In this text he identifies the importance of diverse types of intelligence.

[ii] I began studying in the School for Body Mind Centering in 1990; became certified as a practitioner in 1994 and then for two years assisted in the school's training program.

[iii] Humor is a common coping strategy for people who successfully navigate stressful, life-threatening events. "Laughter stimulates the left prefrontal cortex, an area in the brain that helps us to feel good and to be motivated. That stimulation alleviates anxiety and frustration." P.41, Deep Survival: Who Lives, Who Dies, and Why, Laurence Gonzales, WW Norton & Co, 2003

[iv] One example of research in this area is Amanda Bulette Coakley, RN, PhD and Mary E Duffy, PhD, The Effect of Therapeutic Touch on Postoperative Patients, Journal of Holistic Nursing, 2010, vol 28 (3), 193-200. Patients who received therapeutic touch, compared to controls, had significantly lower level of pain, lower cortisol level and higher natural killer cells.

[v] You can try this rolling up by stacking organs on your own. Many people report that it gives them a sense of relaxation, a personal sense of comfort, and grounding into their own perspective. Infants are a good example of movement from the perspective of the organ system because their muscular-skeleton system is not yet organized into a posture holding configuration.

Summer, 1999

[vi] Amy Mindell published the book, *Coma: A Healing Journey* in 1999 based on work by herself and Arnold Mindell with adults and children in coma. The book contains exercises to help one communicate in non-traditional ways with the person and help their recovery. The Mindell's describe coma as similar to other forms of altered states of consciousness.

[vii] Multiple types of glia are found in the brain. They are part of the lymph system and "knit all the cellular components of the nervous system into a functional network." Glia are actively in control of physical coordination and "muscle memory" in the cerebellum as well as cycles of attention. They are highly active during REM sleep. During in utero development the nerves climb through a trellis of glia, building the network in the brain. A valuable book that explains the research on the many types of glia cells and what is currently known about their function is "The Other Brain: The Scientific and Medical Breakthroughs that Will Heal Our Brains and Revolutionize our Health," R. Douglas Fields, PhD, 2009, Simon and Schuster Paperbacks, New York.

[viii] Hanus and Mechthild Papousek are internationally renowned child development researchers who coined the term "intuitive parenting" to describe how parents and infants interact using subtle signals to communicate. The behaviors they describe are seen in cultures all around the world. Parental responses take place at a speed faster than conscious thought which means that parents are reading signals and responding at lightening quick speed.

Fall, 1999

[ix] This is not her real name or accident story. However, the details witnessed by Sue and Christi are as perceived and described by Sue.

[x] Benjamin Libet's work can be easily found in literature searches regarding consciousness. He wrote a summary of the evolution of his ideas through his career in *Mind Time The Temporal Factor in Consciousness*.

[xi] Bonnie Bainbridge Cohen calls this phenomenon a nerve reversal. An excerpt from the BMC study manual, © 1992: When more sensory information passes into the dorsal horns of the spinal cord than can be processed at the synapses, the incoming impulses than can not be passed on to internuncial neurons in the cord are rejected and sent back out the dorsal roots of the corresponding spinal nerves to their points of origin in both the somatic and autonomic system. The impulses are then recycled from the smaller sensory nerves into the larger and more capable motor nerves and into the anterior horns of the spinal cord. This reaction allows the experience to remain in one's tissues and nervous system until one can accept and process the impulses via the dorsal horn synapses into the nerves of the spinal cord and brain. They can then be processed and sent outward

through the synapses of the anterior horn cells and out the anterior roots of the corresponding spinal nerves. This reversal mechanism imprints the experience in the tissues and allows one as much time as is needed to accept and process the experience and to respond directly to it, thereby resolving it. As the experience is released from the tissues, one is not longer locked into a past experience, through which all present experience is filtered. Greater choice based upon the wisdom gained is then possible. Releasing the nerves facilitates both the de-reversal of nerves and the balancing of muscle and organ tone.

[xii] Dr. Scott Haig, Times Special Edition, Mind-Body Health.

[xiii] p. 71, Deepak Chopra, Quantum Healing Exploring the Frontiers of Mind/body Medicine

[xiv] Bill Moyers and Margaret Kemeny interview, Emotions and The Immune System (195-211), Healing and The Mind, Bill Moyers, Doubleday, 1993.

Year 2000

[xv] Here's a simple experiment to do with a friend. One person lies down on the floor. Without saying anything aloud mentally think either "I'm ready to be moved" or "I don't want to move." The second person places two hands on the friends side, like hip and rib cage, and rolls the friend onto their side. Do it a second time, the friend imagining the second thought. Reverse roles. Then talk about what you discovered.

[xvi] Bainbridge Cohen's Body Mind Centering perspective is that scoliosis is originally an issue of organ tone and alignment which then becomes the pattern for the spine. An infant initially moves with weight shifting of organs which then patterns muscles and bones.

[xvii] Allan Schore presents the cycles of parasympathetic and sympathetic dominance in Affect Regulation and the Origin of the Self: the Neurobiology of Emotional Development, Lawrence Erlbaum & Associates, 1994.

[xviii] Gabrielle Roth has 8 musical cds to inspire and guide movement, including Bones and Waves. She is also the author of Sweat Your Prayers and Maps to Ecstasy.

Year 2001

[xix] Karen Kaufmann, Inclusive Creative Movement and Dance, Human Kinetics, 2005

[xx] Current understandings of trauma recovery indicate that the patient must re-learn or re-connect inner experience with the ability to physically act. One of the exercises used to facilitate this is mirrored partner movements because it provides the experience of being seen by another with movement.

[xxi] Hofer "concludes that a key function of early fetal activity is to aid the process of constructing the brain, so that from the very start, experience can act on the brain's development." P.26 *Rethinking the Brain, New Insights into Early Development*, Rima Shore, Families and Work Institute.

[xxii] Esther Thelen's work has been an integral part of the reconceptualization of motor development, especially in regards to dynamic systems.

[xxiii] Heidelise Als is a developmental psychologist at Harvard Medical School and Children's Hospital. She has pushed for changes in NICU environments that respond to the infant's needs for comfort and movement, emphasizing the unique needs of each infant.

[xxiv] Bainbridge Cohen explains her alphabet of movement analysis, including this example, in *Sensing, Feeling and Action, The Experiential Anatomy of Body-Mind Centering*.

[xxv] Psychologists differentiate these two types of memory as implicit and explicit or narrative. Implicit memory lies outside the normal parameters of time and feels like a singular whole. Narrative memory, which doesn't begin until age 2 or 3, is more linear, events have an ordered sequence that take place across a block of time. See the work of Daniel Siegel for an excellent delineation of these two forms of memory.

Year 2002

[xxvi] New scientific discoveries indicate that numerous metabolic and reproductive hormones, notably serotonin and oxytocin, activate bone tissue at doses much smaller than what's required to stimulate organs. Gerard Karsenty, professor of genetics and development at Columbia University Medical Center, says, "the skeleton is connected functionally to many more organs than we had anticipated." New York Times, 4/28/09

[xxvii] Daniel Stern, M.D. Diary of a Baby What your child sees, feels, and experiences. Basic Books, 1990.

[xxviii] In BMC training we often practiced "cellular rest." This meant lying on the floor much like Debra and Christi do here, awareness tuned to active yield, where the full self is resting onto the contact with the mat. It's not being an undefined puddle on the floor but feeling the distinctness of one's own membrane (skin surface) fully met. Sometimes each practitioner was solo, sometimes we laid down spooned together allowing front or back surface to also feel supported differentiation.

[xxix] The work of A.H. Almass is a helpful guide in understanding how our family object relations scripts become projected onto God. The Pearl Beyond Price Integration of Personality into Being: An Object Relations Approach, Diamond Books, Berkeley, CA.

Year 2003-4

[xxx] Bainbridge Cohen's explorations regarding the "mind" of physiology links the otoliths to relationship and bonding and the semi-circular canals as about going out into the world.
[xxxi] The work of Ayers and DeGangi are valuable resources to examine regarding sensory integration issues.
[xxxii] You can try this exercise at home. Lie on your side, knees bent, head turned toward the ground in the crook of your arms, and eyes closed. Allow your attention to be inward. Allow your curiosity about the external to grow until it fuels your opening, rolling onto your back, eyes open to what's outside you, arms and legs still bent yet falling open. When this phase is enough, slowly let go of outer attention, allowing the desire for inner focus to pull you into completing the roll, resting onto your opposite side. Invite your inner ear on both sides of the body to register where you are, noticing if one ear rests while the other still stays tuned externally. There are many layers of subtlety to this exercise, for instance, specific attention can be paid to the sympathetic (outer focus) and parasympathetic (inner focus) nervous system balance.
[xxxiii] "Doctor credits medicines in firefighter's rehab" Baltimore Sun story as printed in the Missoulian, May 5, 2005
[xxxiv] Candace Pert wrote the groundbreaking work, "Molecules of Emotion" which documented the neuropeptide communication that occurs throughout the body- neurons, lymph system, and digestive system.
[xxxv] Vertosick's book, *The Genius Within Discovering the Intelligence of Every Living Thing*, is an excellent discussion of intelligence from a whole body and ecosystem perspective.
[xxxvi] The work of Pennebaker is notable in identifying changes in T-cells as the result of writing about life events. Personally I think it is interesting to consider that the changes in how the neural network fires once a person has solidified new meaning regarding a portion of their life story may be related to changes in the glial/lymph system and not just the neurons.

Year 2005

[xxxvii] Dan tien, hara- this source point has many names in meditation, yoga, tai chi, etc. What they have in common is a perception that it serves as a reservoir of energy/spirit embodiment. Bainbridge-Cohen's intention was to increase awareness of physical location and tissue sensation of this centerpoint.
[xxxviii] Bainbridge-Cohen likes to cite the example of a startled baby monkey. In the split second of alarm the baby releases her grip and then re-grasps her mother's coat secure enough for quick flight.
[xxxix] Annie Brook, From Conception to Crawling, AnnieBrook.com

[xl] Two excellent articles summarizing research aided me in writing this text. "The First Ache" by Annie Murphy Paul, New York Times, February 10, 2008. "Two Voices from the Womb: Evidence for Physically Transcendent and a Cellular Source of Fetal Consciousness," by Jenny Wade, PhD, Journal of Prenatal and Perinatal Psychology and Health, 13(2), Winter 1998.

[xli] Jill Bolte Taylor writes about her experience of stroke and what it taught her about right and left brain functions in *My Stroke of Insight A Brain Scientist's Personal Journey*. This excerpt is from the chapter, Bare to the Bone, p. 73.

[xlii] An excellent story about Bach-y-Rita's work can be found in Norman Doidge's book, *The Brain that Changes Itself*. Paul Bach-y-Rita went on his career to develop technological devices that fed electrical information to the brain to compensate for a damaged organ, for instance, teaching the tongue to compensate for damaged vestibular function.

[xliii] "Patterning" has adherents and skeptics. Adherents point to individual case studies where dramatic improvements occur in cognitive processing and attention capacities. They cite brain research that demonstrates the lifelong importance of links between the cerebellum and frontal cortex as well as cerebellum deficits in cases of attention deficit disorder and autism. Skeptics often begin with their own anecdotes of "my child never crawled and she reads just fine." They point to the absence of methodologically sound research studies on this treatment modality.

[xliv] *Walking Papers A True Story*, Francesco Clark. New York: Hyperion, 2010.

Year 2007-9

[xlv] "Automatic attention is a low brain function. An animal, for example, is attentive at a very deep level. It could be sleeping, but if something rustles, it wakes up. Short attention span suggests low brain inefficiency." P 5 *Sensing, Feeling, and Action*, Contact Quarterly Reprint, No 1 (Contact Quarterly, Vol. VI No. 2, Winter 1981.)

[xlvi] *Relax and Renew: Restful Yoga for Stressful Times*. Judith Lasater, Ph.D., P.T. Rodmell Press, Berkeley, CA, 1995.

[xlvii] Brainfingers was developed by Andrew Junker, a former researcher for the United States Air Force. The system interfaces with 3rd party software via electrical signals from facial muscles, eye movements and brainwaves.

[xlviii] Raf Casert, Associated Press, Brussels. "Belgian alert, mute for 23 years." Printed in the Missoulian, 1/24/09.